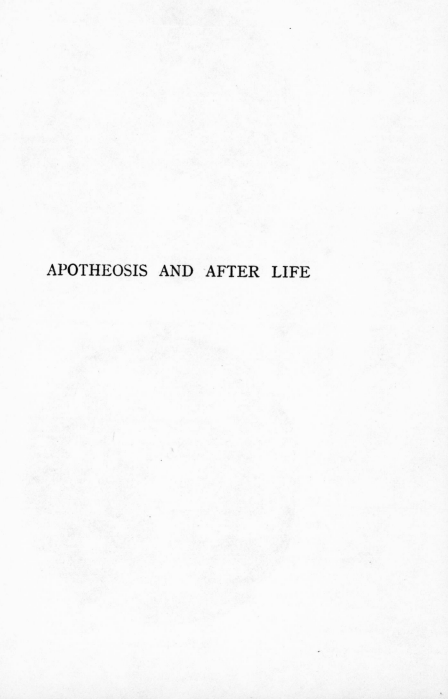

APOTHEOSIS AND AFTER LIFE

PLATE I.

THE EMPEROR JUSTINIAN.
1. Silver Disc in Petrograd.   2. Gold Medallion formerly in Paris.

APOTHEOSIS
AND AFTER LIFE

Three Lectures on Certain Phases of
Art and Religion in the Roman Empire

BY

MRS. ARTHUR STRONG
(EUGENIA SELLERS STRONG)

Select Bibliographies Reprint Series

 BOOKS FOR LIBRARIES PRESS
FREEPORT, NEW YORK

First Published 1915
Reprinted 1969

STANDARD BOOK NUMBER:
8369-5168-9

LIBRARY OF CONGRESS CATALOG CARD NUMBER:
78-103668

PRINTED IN THE UNITED STATES OF AMERICA

ENVOI

À CHRISTIAN MALLET

Maréchal des Logis au XXIIème Régiment de Dragons, IVème Escadron aux Armées, en campagne

MY DEAR CHRISTIAN,—*I always like to remember how we smuggled you, a French subject, into our British School in the guise of honorary assistant secretary. But from the first I preferred to call you my adopted son, as by a premonition that we should be united always in a common love of Rome, and this confidence of mine was never betrayed, for Rome in her every aspect found you responsive. . . . Those were fruitful hours that we spent together in the Villa Giulia, trying to reconstruct some picture of the vanished civilisation of the Latin race; or in the Vatican, where the masterpieces of Greek sculpture revealed to us the spell by which Greece held her grim conqueror captive; or in the Baths of Diocletian, where we traced on the stelae of her Provinces the religious beliefs that helped Rome to establish her Imperial sway, and the soldiers of her legions to live and die faithful to her service. And always, whether among the ruins and relics of classics or of Mediaeval Rome, or in the churches and palaces of the Rome of Sixtus and Bernini, I was glad to balance the impetuous judgments of your youth against the measured conclusions of scholarship.*

Other moods would take us to the Campagna, or to the city's 'enchanted gardens.' Do you remember that Easter Eve on the Via Appia when a great red moon lay in a hollow of the Alban hills? Or that sombre garden on the Esquiline, under whose desolate paths lie the ruins of the Golden House built by the rest-less genius who was Nero? Or the groves of the Villa Mattei and the seat under the old sarcophagus where S. Philip discorreva delle cose dell' anima *with his disciples?*

At times we went further afield—to Arezzo, where the master-piece of Piero della Francesca, transfigured in the evening light, made us forget the humbler Arretine ware we had come to study; to Orvieto, where by a special grace we saw high above the altar, like a vision of the Holy Grail vouchsafed to the Knights of old, the enamelled reliquary that holds the Sanctissimo Corporale.

Do you ever think of the little flat on the Monte Tarpeo, and of the view, perhaps the noblest in the world, which would at times be lifted by music beyond the conditions of time and space? How poignantly these memories and impressions crowded upon us as we left Rome that June morning of last year; yet how swiftly regrets yielded to the magic of the hour, as we were borne through the sunlit Campagna and the hill towns of Latium to the noonday rest at Benedictine Monte Cassino, whence you had written to me a year before ' one could do great things here.' The beauty of the Italian afternoon mellowed as we passed from Latin to Greek lands, and reached the gracious hospitality of the villa embowered in the ilex groves of Posilippo. A few days more and white sails were bearing us over a summer sea from Sicilian to Ionian waters, to your first glimpse of Greece. . . .

It was thus in memory of our Roman friendship that I first wished to dedicate to you this little book, and also because while I was endeavouring to convey to my audiences in America some-thing of what I conceived the spirit of Rome to mean to our modern world, you were putting into practice the Roman virtues of dis-cipline and endurance during the first months of your military service. Little did either of us guess that when I revised the lectures for publication it would be during weeks of alternating hopes and fears, relieved by trust in the alliance of your country

*and of mine in the cause of liberty, lit up by the brave confidence
of your letters which confirmed what we already knew in our
hearts of the valour of yourself and your Dragoons.   On that
fateful night of July* 31st *you had ridden out of Reims with
France's vanguard, a simple* Cavalier (paene miles !); *since then
you have twice won your promotion.   It is with affectionate pride,
therefore, that I inscribe beneath your name the grade you have
just won by an act of great bravery on the battlefield.   Once again
have you proved yourself worthy to serve in one of the proudest
regiments of France,*

Dragons que Rome eût pris pour des légionnaires.

*   *   *   *

*The news of your fresh promotion to the grade of Lieutenant,
and of your decision to pass into the Infantry for the sake of more
continuous work in the trenches, comes as I correct this proof.
But I like to think that you would wish me to retain the original
superscription in remembrance of a sharply defined phase of your
life.*

Feb. 27, 1915.   *E. S.*

PREFACE

DURING the fall of 1913 it was my high privilege, as lecturer on the Charles Eliot Norton foundation of the Archaeological Institute of America, to speak on the subject of the Roman Empire and of Roman art and religion before about twenty-five centres of the Institute, before the Universities of Wisconsin and Princeton, the Colleges of Brynmawr, Wellesley and Vassar, and in the Lecture Hall of the Metropolitan Museum of New York. These Lectures form the basis of the present book. To my audiences I would like to record my thanks for their cordial and encouraging reception, and in a more personal manner I would thank the President of the Archaeological Institute, Professor Shipley of the Washington University, St. Louis, and its indefatigable Secretary, Dr. Mitchell Carroll of Washington. I may add that my choice of subject was determined in the first instance by the belief that any discussion, however modest and restricted in compass, concerned with doctrines of Apotheosis and of the Soul's ultramundane destiny, would be welcomed by audiences, many of whom had listened the previous year to M. Cumont's lectures on Astrology and Religion, now embodied in the brilliant book that we all know.

The lecture on the Apotheosis has developed by

slow degrees out of a lecture on the influence of the Imperial figure on later decorative art, given before the Architectural Society of Oxford as far back as 1908. In the same way, the lectures on the After Life are the expansion of some three pages on the tombstones of the Roman Provinces of Central Europe which appeared in the first number of the *Journal of Roman Studies* in connection with the Exhibition of the art of the Roman Provinces at the Baths of Diocletian in 1911. In both cases the long prelude on the similar problems of Greek art seemed necessary in order to determine more closely than is usually the case in lecture-rooms and handbooks, the precise debt of Rome to Greece and the originality of her own contribution. In their present expanded form the lectures were repeated at Rome in the spring of this year before the students of our British School, which in part accounts for the delay in the publication of the book.

The subjects of the two lectures, though akin, are approached from a somewhat different standpoint. In the first lecture I have tried to account for the centralised formula that appears in late Imperial reliefs by showing the rôle played by the cult of the Emperor in the formation of what appears to be a new type of composition. Primarily, therefore, this is a study of certain phases of antique design. The two lectures on the ' Symbolism of the After Life,' on the other hand, represent the attempt to disentangle the various strains of thought and belief, whether native or foreign, that went to the shaping of the magnificent sepulchral imagery of the Empire. The lectures, which, as the Introductory Address shows, are specially intended for students, are put forward much in the form in which they were delivered, so that I trust that their many deficiencies may be ascribed not to ignorance only, but to the want of space and opportunity for a fuller treatment. In the notes, at least, I hope I have made up for certain unavoidable omissions from the text, and should like to add that the present book is only preparatory to another in which I project to exhibit on a more extended canvas the complicated and intercrossing influences which flowed into the art of Rome.

Of the books dealing with Roman subjects which have appeared since the lectures were delivered in America, I should like to mention with special gratitude Mr. Warde-Fowler's *Roman Ideas of Deity*. To it I owe, with much else, a clearer understanding of that monotheistic current in Roman religion which is, I believe, responsible for certain fundamental characteristics of Roman art which the cult of the Emperor later helped to bring to mature expression.

Without the full complement of illustrations made possible in the lecture-room by the use of the lantern, the lectures may appear inconclusive, but I have done my best, with the liberal help of the publishers, to illustrate the monuments most essential to my theme ; for the rest I have endeavoured to give references to publications easily accessible, such as M. S. Reinach's *Répertoire de Reliefs*, which should be at every student's elbow.

I am only too well aware that I court publication at a moment when all our thoughts are diverted by present anxiety from studies of an academic nature, and not least from everything that touches antiquity. Yet a time of probation which has called forth Roman ideals of national life and personal conduct is, after all, one when an attempt to gauge some of the causes that moulded the aspirations of Rome may not prove useless or out of place.

My thanks are due to His Excellency Don Ramon Piña y Millet, Spanish Ambassador to the Quirinal, for permission to photograph and reproduce here the large sarcophagus in the Palazzo Barberini representing a scene of apotheosis; to Mr. A. H. Smith for leave to illustrate several monuments in his Department, including the fine Flavian medallion-portrait recently acquired by the British Museum and still unpublished; to the Commandant Emile Espérandieu, to Mr. O. M. Dalton and to Dr. E. Krueger for the loan of valuable photographs.

I recall with gratitude the generous help given me by Mrs. Arundell Esdaile in getting the lectures into book shape; by Miss C. Amy Hutton, who, on my departure from England to Rome, relieved me of all anxiety with regard to the illustrations; and by Dr. Ashby, Director of the British School at Rome, in the correction of the proofs.

EUGÉNIE STRONG.

ROME, *March* 1915.

CONTENTS

LIST OF ILLUSTRATIONS

ANALYSIS OF CONTENTS

INTRODUCTORY ADDRESS
ROME AND THE PRESENT STATE OF ROMAN STUDIES

LECTURE I

DIVVS AVGVSTVS: THE INFLUENCE OF THE IMPERIAL APOTHEOSIS ON ANTIQUE DESIGN

b

LECTURE II

THE SYMBOLISM OF THE AFTER LIFE ON
LATE ROMAN TOMBSTONES

LECTURE III

THE AFTER LIFE (continued)

An Imperial Lady and her Children.
Glass Medallion.   Brescia.

INTRODUCTORY ADDRESS TO STUDENTS

ROME AND THE PRESENT STATE OF ROMAN STUDIES

O Roma nobilis
Orbis et domina
Cunctarum urbium
Excellentissima.
Mediaeval Hymn.

I WELCOME the opportunity of offering a few general remarks on the present state of Roman studies all the more gladly that when I come to the special subjects of the lectures I shall be able to unfold them, so to speak, against a prepared background, and you will be able to realise more easily perhaps than might otherwise be the case, the range of phenomena to which they belong.

No modern development of Classical studies is, I think, more striking than the new sympathetic appreciation of the art of the Roman Empire, though the value placed upon this art varies, and its originality has been most violently impugned. This newly awakened interest flows no doubt from a larger Imperialistic movement which turns to Rome once more as to the forerunner of its own aspirations.

A

What has happened is not so much a revival as a quickening of interest in ideals which never entirely died out. Though bereft of political power, Rome, as our mediaeval hymn reminds us, remained *Orbis domina* to the imagination of the Middle Ages. The Renaissance is heralded by Dante's vision of a re-formed Imperialism which should revive the old Roman and Stoic ideal of a city of men, with the Emperor to direct the human race to 'temporal felicity in accordance with the teaching of philosophy,' and Imperialism in one form or other has continued to fire the imagination of mankind and dominates our era with a new prestige. Year by year we see an increase in the number of books and lectures dealing with Roman ideas and their application to the problem of Empire to-day. Archaeology and the history of art have naturally come in for their share of this revival, and while the scholar gains a fresh conception of ancient Rome from the monuments on which her history is hewn in imperishable shapes, the artist feels inspired by those same monuments to seek for new and enduring formulas, wherewith he may clothe the ideals of a modern world.

I. Modern Views and Controversies touching Roman Art. The Pan-Orientalists

To-day I propose first to attempt a brief survey of the stage reached by the burning controversy as to the origins of the art of Imperial Rome, and to follow up these remarks by touching, though perforce more briefly still, on the value which her past bestows upon modern Rome as a centre of study. I must begin by trying to define what is meant by Roman art. The task is not an easy one. In spite of the fact that the importance of the subject is now fully recognised, the difficulties which attend its study seem to increase rather than to lessen with every new discovery and every fresh point of view. Scholars now concede that the art produced under the Roman rule has a place in the long evolution of artistic form ; and that, in the centuries which followed the establishment of the Empire, accepted formulas were revivified by adaptation to new political and religious ideals, and finally quickened into new and vigorous life by the spread of Christianity. Nevertheless deep-rooted superstition dies hard :

> The old dragon underground
> .   .   .   .
> Swinges the scaly horror of his folded tail.

The prejudice against Roman art as inferior still lives, and, lurking even under the latest speculation, rears its head in a new and subtle form. The art of the Roman Empire is no longer dismissed as a last unimportant chapter in the history of the decadent antique ; the endeavour is now to prove that this art was not Roman at all. If, to quote a sentence which has become proverbial, there was not only decadence in the ' three first centuries of the Empire but also progress along an ascending line,' a militant school led by Josef Strzygowski[1] claims this progress as the effect of foreign influences and allows to Rome only the heritage of decadence. These look upon Greece as outworn in the time of the Empire, and upon Rome as sterile ; and trace back the new artistic forms corresponding to new spiritual needs to the Graeco-Oriental cities of Asia Minor or of Egypt, to Syria, to that Asiatic hinterland which looms so large in modern archaeological speculation. Moreover, the controversy has now assumed a double aspect. For the celebrated war-cry, ' Orient or Rome,' with which Strzygowski opened his campaign against the Roman school, he soon instituted that of ' Orient or Byzantium ' in the attack which now extends to Rome's successor, Byzantium, whose position as a long acknowledged centre of artistic inspiration is likewise threatened. The Pan-Orientalists will not admit that any new ideas flowed from the New any more than from the Old Rome, or, as their leader puts it, ' the accession of fresh ideals seems insignificant in comparison with the fund of ideas received.' [2] These views receive the warm support of many important modern writers on the subject of Oriental religions. In the first chapter of his *Religions Orientales dans le Paganisme Romain*, Cumont, whose introductory

remarks I shall venture to paraphrase, asserts that
the Western peoples who have hitherto gloried in
being the direct heirs of Imperial Rome must abandon
their aristocratic pretensions, and learn to bow their
heads before the once despised East, from which they
derive so pre-eminent a share of their intellectual
and artistic patrimony ; and he proceeds to picture
the Orient as penetrating the West, not indeed, as
used to be thought, through the fascination which an
old and corrupt civilisation necessarily exerts over
one less mature, but, on the contrary, in virtue of a
renewed vigour which enabled the East to endow the
failing Graeco-Roman peoples with new technical
resources, with artistic skill and intelligence, and
with the crowning gift of science.

II. CRITICISM OF THE PAN-ORIENTAL THEORY. AT-
   TEMPTED ESTIMATE OF ROME'S RELATION TO
   THE EAST

While a leading part is thus assigned to the East
in the formation of later Classical and early Christian
art, Rome as a contributing factor is thrown back into
the shade and sometimes left altogether out of count.
In addition to this, a small minority—unimportant
perhaps save for their violence—have tried of late to
return to the old point of attack, by representing
Rome as a brutalising influence in the development

of the antique.   Let us try to arrive at some saner view of our own.

Old-fashioned archaeologists have been not unjustly reproached with adopting too easy a solution when they represented the growth of the antique by the direct line—Greek—Roman—Christian, yet it seems an equally artificial formula that represents Greece, with Rome tacked on to her as a negligible aftermath, as a concrete and self-contained episode slowly submerged by the vast wave of Oriental influence.   Such phrases as ' Greece and Rome die smothered in the Orient's embrace ' are admirable catchwords, but they do not represent the infinitely complex factors that went to build up the art which flourished under the Roman Empire.   On the other hand, the claim that an Imperial art originated at Rome under Augustus which spread its influence to the utmost confines of the antique world was equally exaggerated.[3] We now see that the vast culture of the Roman Empire, emanating from nations in the most diverse stages of civilisation and of intellectual development, could not have radiated from one point only.   It is more in keeping with the facts to say that Rome encouraged national development by her Imperial policy and then gathered into her service the diverse phases of art fostered by her régime.   At the same time, in discussing Rome as distinct from the Empire we may still reasonably assert that she ranked from

Augustus onwards as a centre of artistic activity by
the side of Alexandria, of Antioch, of Seleucia herself ;
that it is no more incorrect to speak of Roman than of
Pergamene, Alexandrian, Antiochene or Seleucid art,
though Rome was by no means the only centre of
Roman Imperial art. It is true that when we have
established a legitimate claim to speak of Roman art
we have to acknowledge on historical evidence alone
that the East must have played a major part in its
formation. Artists and architects, craftsmen and
workmen of every description flowed into the great
capital from the Eastern provinces of the Empire,
sometimes attracted by the building operations of
successive Emperors, at others returning in the train
of the conquerors. We hear that after the Mithri-
datic wars and the reduction of Syria, Pompey brought
gangs of Syrian workmen to carry out his building
plans ; Augustus himself wished, it is said, to remodel
Rome upon Alexandria ; Trajan entrusted his vast
engineering and architectural operations to the Syrian
Apollodorus. Long before Trajan's reign, numerous
Syrians must have drifted to Rome in consequence of
the Flavian conquest of Palestine ; it is not yet
known what influence went to shape the profoundly
original genius of Rabirius, the architect of the Flavian
Emperors, but it seems probable that Vespasian
and Titus were inspired by some kingly residence
seen in the East to plan the famous *Domus Flavia* of

the Palatine. This Syrianising process recalls what
happened in Europe at the time of the Crusades.
Richard Coeur de Lion, for instance, found the model
for his great fortress of Château Gaillard in the fortified strongholds of Syria, and the Crusades had an
effect on the marvellous art of the thirteenth century
analogous to that exerted by the East on the art of
the Empire.[4]   Rome assimilated what she borrowed,
and in spite of her debt to both Oriental and Hellenic
models, her art, whether Imperial or Republican,
developed on lines of its own, and is without exact
parallel or counterpart in either Greece or the East.
However mixed the parentage, the offspring grew up
in a way of its own, and even rendered back with
interest the forms taken over from older peoples.
Miss Gertrude Bell, for instance, in the admirable
chapter on the ' Genesis of the Early Mohammedan
Palace ' in her book on *Ukhaidir*, writes as follows of
the origin of vaulted construction :

In the second half of the third century, vaults with
similar characteristics appear under Hellenistic influence
in central Italy, where, after the middle of the second
century, they underwent a development to which the
Hellenistic East can offer no parallel.   At the end of the
second century, while Latin builders threw their stone
vaults securely over a span of 14·50 metres, as in the
Ponte di Cecco on the Via Salaria, and even' of 18·50
metres, as in the Pons Milvius, the Greeks of Asia Minor
did not venture to use a span wider than 7·10 metres, and

confined themselves as a rule to vaults under 4 metres in span. *It was now the part of the East to learn from Imperial Rome.** Western Asia took back its own creation from the hands of Roman builders in the vast proportions which the proficiency of the latter had given to it, and over the whole of the Roman Empire the monumental vault sprang into being. The earliest extant examples on Mesopotamian soil are the great vaults of the palace at Hatra.[5]

This intelligent and lucid statement, contributed, moreover, by one who is an ardent disciple of Strzygowski, should go far to restore the lost equipoise between East and West as contributing factors in the formation of the architecture of the Empire. It is in striking contrast to the violent language in which a recent writer condemns the architectural effort of Rome.[6] Every one is welcome to his own opinion expressed in his own way, even if it lead him to ridicule the daring concrete vaulting of the Empire by comparing it to the 'lid of a saucepan'; but to do this while ignoring the sober and solid vaulting systems of the Republican period, which may still be seen in the arches of the Pons Milvius or the beautiful Ponte di Nona, is at once bad history and bad criticism, much as if we were to take the Pergamene marbles as the supreme and final expression of the Greek genius in art, without so much as a reference to the art of the Parthenon and of the age of Pericles. Again, is it

* The italics are mine.

necessary to exalt the undeniable perfection of Santa
Sophia—as much, be it said in passing, a building
of the Empire and of a Roman Emperor as any
Augustan temple by the Tiber—by decrying the less
mature architecture of the Roman Thermae? Yet
since Rivoira's researches few will deny that the
masterly suspension of the dome of Santa Sophia
above its pendentives was only rendered possible by
the attempts made in this direction by Roman architects in the Baths of Caracalla and of Diocletian.
' Jamais le génie de Rome et celui de l'Orient ne
s'associèrent dans un plus surprenant et plus har-
monieux ensemble,' says the illustrious French architect, Choisy, of Santa Sophia, and at that, I think,
we can leave it (*Histoire de l'Architecture*, ii. 51).

III. CHARACTER OF ROMAN ART

(a) *In Pre-Augustan Times*

In point of fact, Roman Imperial art is neither so
individual nor yet so Graeco-Oriental in character as
the extremists of either party would have us believe ;
nor, again, is it merely Greek of the decadence, as the
archaeologists of a generation now rapidly passing
away were wont to teach ; but different *strata* meet
and mingle in it, and to learn to distinguish between
these is the true task of criticism.   The term ' Antique ' embracing Greece and Rome as the main
factors of one mighty artistic movement, was after all

exact. The old error lay not in linking Rome to Greece, but in representing the Greek or Hellenistic element in Roman art as an accession of the Augustan, or of the late Republican period. On the contrary, Hellenistic art transplanted to Rome flourished anew in a soil long prepared to receive it, a fact which has been overlooked in all our histories, where, until lately, Augustan art followed directly upon Hellenistic, with rarely so much as a glance at that of Republican Rome or ancient Latium which we are only beginning to understand and appreciate.

This early Italic art, as it is convenient to call it, to a great extent derives from Greek, and more especially Ionian art, but it lacks many of the fascinating qualities of its models. At times it clings to tradition with an obstinacy almost Egyptian, at others it adopts Greek ideas with headlong enthusiasm. Beside the more finished and measured achievements of Greece, early art in Rome appears somewhat prosaic and pedestrian. It sinks on occasion to the provincial level ; it has the heavy earnestness, the sturdy conservatism of a community remote from the centres of intellectual activity and production, which the art of the Empire itself did not wholly shake off; but it has also the sterling qualities of the provincial spirit, solidity, and that prudent reliance on tradition which by preserving primitive forms by the side of the innovations introduced from Greece, evolved in time such architectural masterpieces as the round temples—the temple of Vesta in the Forum, the temple of the Sibyl at Tívoli, the Pantheon itself—noble structures which, as has so often been indicated, can be traced back step by step through the centuries to the round huts of the Neolithic peoples of Italy.

The art forms of Latium and Etruria gave way in part to those of Greece, and these in their turn to influences imported from the South or East, which Rome passed on again with her advancing legions to every nation that came within her Empire. But the old was never wholly swallowed up by the new; it was the peculiar quality of Roman art as of Roman religion to be at the same time conservative and hospitable. Primitive customs and the most primitive of magical ceremonies were so strong even in the Rome of Ovid's day that they permeate his Graecised conceptions of religion and literature. We shall therefore not be surprised to find that the conservative Roman, when faced with the necessity of expressing the relation of the deified Emperor to his people— if I may illustrate my meaning from the subject of my first lecture—recurs for the central figure of the State to the primitive 'frontality' which had never been altogether lost to Roman art even at its most Hellenising period.

(b) The Art of the Empire

The fate of Hellenism itself might have been very different had Roman surroundings, like those of Egypt, for instance, been uncongenial to its development. In discussing the relatively trivial achievements of Ptolemaic art, Mr. Hogarth has admirably said : ' Greek art came to Egypt to vivify, and stayed to die.' [7] Precisely the reverse took place in Rome. Here Greek art neither decayed nor died, but stayed to live, and was itself vivified by contact with Roman ideals on the one hand, and on the other with the fresh influences which Rome herself, as we have seen, derived from the East. The chief phases of the new activity were the ages of Augustus and the Flavians, of Trajan and the Antonines. A period of comparative sterility followed, due in great measure to political reasons and the absence of that incentive to production which comes with conquest and military glory. But a reaction for the better set in once more under Aurelian and Diocletian, induced by the victorious campaigns of these Emperors in the East. In this period the East began to play the leading part which in earlier days had been that of Greece ; the result was a first great outburst of activity under Diocletian, and its eventual outcome the splendid massive art of the fourth century, of which I shall have much to say to you in the lectures. From the begin-

ning Rome stood to Greece, to Ionia, and the Nearer
East as these in turn stood to Persia and Meso-
potamia, until Rome became a World-Empire and
could draw her own inspiration direct from the Orient.
But that is no reason for denying that the various
influences were refashioned in the service of Rome
till they emerged, both in the city itself and in the
provinces, as what may still be justly called Roman
Imperial Art.

IV. Proposed Treatment of Subjects chosen to illustrate Roman Imperial Art

In what follows, my endeavour is to show in two
concrete instances how Greek and Oriental influences
combined with certain Roman strains to express new
ideals. One typical example is afforded, I think, by
the slow transformation of the traditional schemes
of antique design brought about by the necessity of
giving prominence to the deified or quasi-deified figure
of the Emperor, who had by slow degrees become the
central theme of the religious art of the Empire.
In the two lectures on the symbolism of the After
Life on Greek and Roman tombstones I shall try to
show how the religious ideas of Greece and Rome,
quickened by the strong current of the Oriental
religions which spread over the Empire, left in the
carved stelae of the Roman provinces the vivid record
of a new Faith. Western artistic formulas that seemed

exhausted were revivified by the magic touch of the East ; and in the Western world a sepulchral imagery developed which in the purity of its ideals and in the strenuous expression of its faith in immortality surpasses everything that the earlier antique had attempted, and comes near to Christian icono-graphy. In both cases I shall devote considerable space to the Greek ideas involved, as inseparable from the later purely Roman phase into which they merged.

My hope as a teacher of the subject of Classical Archaeology is that studies of this character may help to heal that schism between Greece and Rome which is instilled in their school-days even into those brought up in modern methods, and which does more than anything else to retard the progress of Classical studies by weakening and falsifying our scientific outlook on the past. At no time do we show ourselves less Greek in spirit than when we repudiate as un-wholesome that intellectual curiosity which was among the rarest and most distinctive qualities of the Greek mind, and shut ourselves up in satisfied contemplation of the formulas which we have erected into shibboleths. Greek studies have suffered no less than Roman from this attitude of mind. By setting up artificial barriers between what we imagine to be Greek on the one side and Roman on the other, we debar ourselves from observation of the infinitely complex processes of development which unite the two.

If I may permit myself a direct personal allusion, it is to beg of you, should you ever think of me or these lectures again, not to bring it up against me that I pleaded for Roman at the expense of Greek art. On the contrary, I have tried everywhere and always, in what teaching I have been privileged to give, to substitute for barren rhetorical contrasts between Greece and Rome, evidence—based on facts arranged as well as I knew how—of what Rome owed to Greece, for so far this debt seems to me very imperfectly ascertained or understood. Indeed at the present moment I am compiling a book—small in bulk, but covering a wide historical area—in which the debt of Rome to Greece is traced step by step. Do you suppose, that after long years spent in study among the incomparable collection of Greek masterpieces in our British Museum, I am blind to Rome's and the world's debt to Greece? Above all, I realise Greece's infinitely clearer vision of beauty, though I cannot help thinking that this vision was attained by the sacrifice of certain things pertaining to the spiritual world, which the Romans, in spite of their more mediocre endowment as artists, as poets, as thinkers, yet came to realise and to express, partly in forms inherited from the Hellenic Orient, partly also in others surviving from a primitive

stratum of religious art and religious belief. I likewise claim that in the process the Romans touched
at times the great heights of inspiration and achievement, though they left it to Christianity to bring to
a victorious issue in its mediaeval sculpture much for
which Rome could only pave the way.

V. NECESSITY FOR KEEPING IN VIEW THE 'CONTRI-BUTING FACTORS' OF ROMAN ART

One more point. From what I have said it might
be thought that I propose to consider Rome as the
unique centre of the artistic impulse of the Empire.
Far from it ; I merely claim the right to call Roman
any art form which seems to have been inspired or
transformed or invested with new meaning by the
ideas imposed by Rome—whether the subjects under
discussion be the superb type of the *Defensor Fidei*,
or of the Christian *Maiestas*—both of which are, I
admit, of Egyptian origin [8]—or the Apotheosis with
its mixed Oriental and Hellenistic character. We
can see clearly in art as elsewhere how much Rome
gained by substituting for a narrow national ideal the
higher ideal of Empire. Let me repeat here a little
more fully what I have already indicated, namely,
that Rome never showed a greater or more intelligent
sense of her Imperial mission than in her encourage-
ment of the national characteristics of the conquered
races. It is here that the opponents of Roman art

B

come unwittingly to our assistance with theories that are mutually destructive, for it is evident that if, as one school asserts, the art of Rome is entirely non-Roman, then Rome cannot have stamped out all artistic impulse in the people she governed in order brutally to impose her own formulas, as writers of another school would have us believe. Instead of crushing the different nationalities that came within the pale of her Empire by the artificial imposition of a Roman super-nationality, Rome encouraged and developed their national life, and thus bestowed upon them more permanent prosperity than could have otherwise been theirs.[9]   Her Imperial reward, as I hope I may be able to show you in the lectures, was that the artistic formulas of diverse peoples became devoted to the expression of the new Imperial idea.   More than six years ago, I said of the much discussed Barberini ivory, that if this beautiful object really was of Egyptian origin, ' it only illustrated once more the compelling force of the Roman genius that could gather up into its service the art-forms of the different countries under its sway ' (*Roman Sculpture*, p. 346).   I am more than ever convinced that this is the right point of view for looking at the artistic achievement of the Roman Empire, and that in this way the envenomed question ' Orient or Rome,' instead of running to acrid controversy, may lead to illuminating results.

VI. Spirit in which our Studies should be approached. Some Pitfalls

Students of Rome certainly have nothing to gain by obscuring the truth as to the origins of her art or of the manifold forms which it could command. At this point you will perhaps allow me to say a few words as to the spirit in which I conceive our studies should be approached, and to warn you of certain pitfalls against which young students, especially, should ever be on their guard. First a word as to the fashion still prevalent in our Classical teaching of using the Romans as a foil to the Greeks. Perhaps in America you have never fallen a prey to this bad habit : it is certainly on the decrease on the Continent, but we English cling to it stoutly. Let me take an example from a book of great literary beauty which has done a great deal towards restoring to us a saner and juster appreciation of the Greek Genius. The author cannot rid himself of the habit of heightening the value of Greek endeavour by depreciating Roman effort in parallel directions ; his estimate of Greek literature is as admirable as everything which he says of the Greeks, but listen to what, by way of comparing the two literatures, he has to tell us of Rome's poetic achievements :

The Romans took kindly to the literary pastoral and the literary epic, and the sham ·didactic poem ; they revelled in the undigested mythology of another race. They are imitative and second-hand, content to dispense with a direct experience of life and transmit into their own language the emotions and thoughts of others ; for the most part their fingers do not touch the pulse of life. Vergil's *Pastorals* and *Georgics* are charming ; his shepherds are sham ones and keep no sheep, nor are any genuine labourers at work in his fields. Only Lucretius among Latin poets will show us the hard struggle of man with the earth. And if we only keep Vergil in selections, we shall have some difficulty in keeping Ovid at all.[10]

I confess that this airy way of treating Vergil pierces me to the heart, for though I have little time in which to improve classical attainments which were always meagre, I yet try to read through Vergil once every year, not only for the pure beauty of his poetry, best appreciated if we read it in his own country face to face with the landscapes that he loved, but because it is the poetry of one who also understood certain things of the spirit as none had quite done before, and only one or two have done since.[11]   I also know all that Vergil means for the true understanding of Augustan art and of the whole Latin civilisation ; [12] and as it is not often that archaeology comes to us in poetic garb,[13] the idea of keeping Vergil only in selections does not commend itself to me.   You will see in the sequel that I am myself not over tender towards the ' undigested Greek mythology ' which went to spoil so much of the artistic endeavour of

Rome, whether plastic or literary, by diverting it into paths alien to its spirit. But however much we may deplore the sinister effect which wholesale and uncritical imitation of Greece and adoption of Greek standards had upon the development of Roman art, and I admit more especially upon Latin poetry, at certain periods, that is again no reason for hurling an indiscriminating thunderbolt at all her poets, and including them in one catastrophic condemnation. The futility of contrasts was long ago brought out by Mr. J. W. Mackail in a fine sentence on the poetry of Homer and Vergil, which I often like to quote to students, it is so good a text to keep in view :

No great work of art can be usefully judged by comparison with any other great work of art. It may indeed be interesting and fertile to compare one with another, in order to seize more sharply and appreciate more vividly the special beauty of each. But to press comparison further, and to depreciate one because it has not what is a special quality of the other, is to lose sight of the function of criticism.[14]

In spite of all efforts to combat it, the determination to praise the Greek at the expense of the Roman persists. At the close of one of his American lectures, a distinguished Oxford scholar drew a comparison of the civilisation and character of Greece and Rome in which not only were the Greeks endowed with all the amiable virtues, but what is more important

in the bid for popularity, with the endearing and
sympathetic faults as well, while the Romans were
presented as 'severe, strong, well-disciplined, trust-
worthy, self-confident, self-righteous, unimaginative
and harsh,'[15] not all of them agreeable qualities making
for pleasant intercourse, or again such as we fancied
specially characteristic of the Scipios, or of Cicero,
or of Augustus and Vergil and Catullus, but fairly
true perhaps of the race as a whole. So far so good,
but lest we should be left with one shred of sympathy
for the poor Roman, we are further told that he was
a ' heavy feeder.' At what Roman is this shaft of
ridicule levelled ? If the feasts of Lucullus have
remained proverbial, what shall we say of Marcus
Aurelius' praise of abstinence ? Or not to trespass
beyond my own subject, do the harsh spare features
of the portraits of Republican date or the intellectual
and ascetic face of the Augustus from the Via Labi-
cana suggest 'heavy feeding ' ? The Roman Emperors are fairly well charged by now with every
vice of which humanity is capable, but even with
the help of the illuminating *elogia* affixed to their
busts in our British Museum, I have failed to find
the unromantic sin of gluttony attributed to any
Emperor save Claudius, that perpetual butt of
the irony of the historian, whether ancient or
modern.

' They knew,' we are further told of the Greeks by

the same authority, ' what Rome as a whole did not know, the inward meaning and the reverse side of glory. They knew the bitterness of lost battles, the sting of the master's lash ; they knew self-judgment and self-contempt, amazement and despair.' I speak always with diffidence as a mere student of the monuments, but what of the Roman conception of defeat, as we see it depicted on the column of Trajan ? Where in earlier art do we find the pathos of failure and the psychology of despair drawn with such unerring mastery, or the tenderness of the conqueror towards the conquered more nobly delineated ? I need only remind you of the incomparable scene where Trajan, courteous and merciful like the great commander that he was, receives the submission of the Dacians at the close of the first war ; or that other scene where he turns away with a noble gesture of aversion from the soldiers who present to him the heads of enemies as spoils ; or again, of the episode within the walls of Sarmizegetusa, when the conquered chiefs prefer poison to surrender. These ' harsh ' Romans understood the quality of mercy, and remembered the precept of their own poet whom a new generation can only tolerate in selections :

haec tibi erunt artes . . . parcere subiectis.

Indeed it always seems to me that the artists who carved the Trajanic reliefs were inspired by that same sense of pity which Mr. J. W. Mackail justly observes is the ' central charm of Vergil,' and that, like the Augustan poet, they too could ' sound the depths of beauty and sorrow, of patience and magnanimity, of honour in life and hope beyond death.' As further examples let me also recall to you the old Dacian chief who turns away to hide his tears as he receives the body of his dead son, and those many scenes towards the close of the second war in which the prowess and the endurance of Decebalus are held up to admiration and respect. As much and sometimes more imaginative sympathy is needed to realise another's woe as to express one's own.

Remember also the pathos of the later Roman portraiture, with its psychological insight, its tender handling of moral or physical defects. Look at certain Flavian and Antonine portraits ; at the ' Aesop ' of the Villa Albani, or at the bust of the young Marcus Aurelius in the Capitol ; at the por- traits of the women of the Emesene dynasty ; at the wonderful head of an old and wrinkled woman in the Louvre, surmised to be the aged Helena, ' mother and grandmother of Emperors,' and then tell me if our hard and practical Romans had no sense of the *lacrimae rerum*.

One more warning as to the habit of trotting out certain conventional epithets, resembling set *leit Motivs*, whenever the Romans or their achievements are discussed. Roman art and architecture, for instance, invariably call forth the adjectives ' practical ' or ' unimaginative ' even from writers who otherwise are ardent apologists of Rome.[16] Yet I maintain that no people whose formative instinct failed to rise beyond the ' practical ' could have created Roman architecture or imparted even to works of utility such as aqueducts, viaducts, bridges—the Pont du Gard and the bridge of Alcantara—the inspired character which brings them within the region of great art. We are told that ' in the works of their hands and their brains they were not an imaginative people.' But the Pantheon with its astonishing dome, the Thermae of Caracalla and of Diocletian where vast halls are spanned in a manner that has moved to admiration every architect who knows his business from Michael Angelo to our own times, the Basilica Nova with its harmony of spaces and its aerial cofferings reflected as it were in the patterned marble of the pavement—are any of these, I ask you, conceivable as the work of a people who lacked the imaginative quality? In archaeological studies as elsewhere, traditional tricks of thought and speech may result in warping the sanest judgment ; as students you should ever bear in mind the words of the Wisdom of Solomon, that *crooked thoughts separate from God.*

VII. The Present and the Future of Roman Studies

I am well aware that the views I have ventured to criticise survive only as traditional formulas bereft of all driving force, and are therefore bound to pass away. Already our histories of art give every year a larger share to Rome's contribution to the world, and our periodicals welcome articles on Roman subjects as eagerly as on Greek. The great publications on the art of the Roman provinces now undertaken by almost every modern country settled by the Roman legions; the archaeological expeditions to various Roman sites such as the Romanised cities of Asia and the Syrian cities of the Antonine period; the now recognised importance of the art of the Empire and its bearing on Christian art—all are signs of a great revival of interest in the Roman Empire and in Roman studies. Nor should we forget that for many years the nations of modern Europe, all of whom were more or less affected by the civilisation diffused by Rome and her armies, have been represented in Rome as in a mother-city by Institutes of art and archaeology. After a period when their activity was for a time eclipsed by the attraction of archaeological discovery in Greek lands, these Institutes have been strengthened and reorganised and, best omen of all, have attracted a fresh influx of students, whose presence shows that Rome is once more looked upon as the natural centre of these studies. If we are no longer to be allowed to call ourselves solely the heirs of Rome, it is, after all, because history and archaeology have shown us to be something greater still—the heirs, namely, of all the civilisations, whether Western or Eastern, that once came under her sway. And as a proof of the acknowledged vitality of the conceptions that emanated from Imperial Rome as factors in modern art, we should rejoice that two of the Institutes, the American and the British, have decided to amalgamate with the bodies either existing or in process of formation, of practising members of the living arts. In this new alliance of art and archaeology, under the auspices of our British School and of the American Academy, I see the happiest presage for the future of the constructive and the plastic arts. You in America, with architectural triumphs such as the Pennsylvania and the Grand Central Railway Stations of New York, the Station of Chicago, the exquisitely planned 'Hall of all the Americas' at Washington, the mighty 'sky-scrapers' which have restored to modern cities the soaring dignity of the vertical line, do not need to be reminded of what the modern world can learn, and learn, too, in the way of application to modern life, from Roman architecture. Your architects have learnt to build round a central space,

to construct piers that support aerial systems of
roofing, to clothe walls in multi-coloured marble
revetments, in a manner that would astonish Domitian's Rabirius and Trajan's Apollodorus, and that
excellent architect, the Emperor Hadrian himself,
and which would delight the unknown genius who
planned the Basilica Nova. I am not here to speak
to you of the ' Mistress Art,' nor, indeed, am I competent to do so, though I ask you to bear in mind
what I have said of the imaginative quality of Roman
architecture. There emanates from it that vital
impulse of which Americans have not been slow to
avail themselves. In this respect we English lag far
behind, but if anything can help us to shake off the
parochial character which is apt to mar our best
modern efforts, we shall owe it, I think, to a renewed
belief in the efficacy of study in Rome. The very
fact that the art of the Roman Empire has a com-
posite character, and that in order to understand it
we must first grapple with the far-reaching problem
of its origins, redoubles its interest and value, since
we can learn from the manifold forms that went to its
making as well as from the finished product. Our
aesthetic outlook broadens with the archaeological.
The long neglected art of the centuries which preceded the great period of Justinian is slowly coming
to its own. Already we do justice not to its
architecture only but to the grand originality of its

portraiture. The Tetrarchy of San Marco and the Valentinian of Barletta ; the Constantine of the Basilica Nova and the 'Theodora' of Milan; the Imperial group on a glass medallion at Brescia (plate ii.) * and the 'Serena' of Monza, are only a few of the masterpieces which have been rescued from oblivion or the handbooks of specialists for the delight of all lovers of art.

You will not, I know, take it amiss if in conclusion I urge those of you who are artists to shake off once and for all the perverse notion that knowledge of the conditions under which works of art were produced in the past is harmful to the production of works of art in the present, or if I implore the archaeologists among you to abandon the methods of antiquarianism and to let their studies flow once more with the stream of life. Only so can artist and archaeologist alike draw from the past strength and inspiration for present effort and future achievement, and by their combined efforts raise art to greater heights than those attained even in Imperial Rome.

* See note on p. 284.

LECTURE I

DIVVS AVGVSTVS

THE INFLUENCE OF THE IMPERIAL APOTHEOSIS
ON ANTIQUE DESIGN

Human art does not impose problems of form through
caprice or excess of virtuosity, it imposes them only when
they are questions of life and death for the subjects to be
treated : here also in the centre of all progress in art is the
force of religious inspiration.—DELLA SETA.

I. THE PROBLEM

IT is my purpose in this lecture to treat of the Imperial Apotheosis as a factor in those highly centralised compositions which differentiate the art of
the Roman Empire in the fourth and succeeding
centuries from anything that precedes it. None of
the current formulas of Greek or Hellenistic art
proved adequate to express the ideas attaching to
the Apotheosis. The doctrine accordingly called
forth a new artistic scheme in which the central
motive of the deified Emperor was combined with the
narrative element supplied by the representation of
the Imperial deeds, the *res gestae*. The formula
adopted for this central figure was simply a return
to the old frontal principles of primitive art which

30

had been discarded in the great age of Greece; the narrative element was that which, developed originally by Greece, had become the common property of the Graeco-Roman world.

Of recent years there has been much use and also much abuse of the terms ' frontal ' and ' frontality.'[1] In the present instance I shall restrict the words to their simplest meaning, and leave out of consideration, as foreign to my present purpose, any discussion of the aesthetic laws which attach to the frontal position. Thus I shall say of an image or statue that it is *frontal*, when it is placed squarely to the front, face to face with the spectator.[2] This full-face pose, for which we have no entirely adequate English word, expresses the simplest relation that can be established between the image of the god and the suppliant, since this inaction effectually isolates the image for contemplation. In a stimulating essay on the effect of religious belief upon plastic form, Alessandro Della Seta has recently shown that races content to consider the deity under the magical aspect of a power from whom they ask protection only, are apt to retain the primitive full-face, the frontal pose, as I shall call it, for their gods; while the reflective and intellectual Greeks soon abandoned this isolated pose in order to link figures together in a common action and so created the mythological and narrative art which enabled them to illustrate the nature of the gods by representing their dealings with one another and with men, thus at the same time setting their cultus images free from the hieratic stiffness of the primitive frontality.[3] Della Seta's book is at last before the English-speaking public, and it is needless further to summarise his views. In both this lecture and the next I shall have ample opportunity of indicating the greatness of my debt to what is certainly the most important work on the evolution and the function of art that has appeared of recent years. At the same time I continue to differ from Della Seta as to the barren destinies of later Imperial art. He admits that ' Rome had put the Emperor in the place of the gods, and near the image of the Emperor were reliefs commemorating his deeds ' (*Religion and Art*, p. 286), but he does not link this phenomenon with any subsequent progress or with the art of early Christianity. I hold, on the contrary, that as the *Maiestas* of the deified Emperor gathered force it brought with it a centralisation of design that paved the way for the *Maiestas* of Christian art, and that the representation of the Imperial *res gestae* lead up to those of Christ and His Saints and the deeds of the chosen people. Frontality, the full-face pose, reintroduced into art that monolatric element which brings all the parts of a composition into the service of a central idea, and without which there can, I conceive, be no great religious compositions. Thus the subject of the

Imperial Apotheosis can throw light not only on the later art of the Empire, but also on the perplexing period of the transition from Pagan to Christian art. The Emperor, *the man exalted to the rank of god*, comes by degrees to claim for himself the central place in design, to the exclusion of the gods who had been the constant theme of Graeco-Roman art. Then in his turn the Emperor is called upon to abdicate in favour of one greater than himself, and by the same slow degrees that he himself obtained it, he yields his place to the *God made man*.

II. CENTRALISED COMPOSITION IN ROMAN, MEDI-AEVAL AND CHRISTIAN ART CONTRASTED

The problem which we have to examine will at once be clear if we illustrate it by concrete examples. First I would draw your attention to certain reliefs of early fourth century date on the arch of Constantine at Rome. According to investigations lately undertaken by Professor Frothingham, the arch may date as far back as the period of Domitian, after whose death it was doubtless desecrated and fell into neglect.[4] It seems to have been taken in hand by a succession of Emperors, and to have been repeatedly altered and redecorated, till under Constantine it assumed the shape under which we know it and was dedicated afresh. Owing to its association with the name of the first Christian Emperor, it has always

C

exerted a special fascination, and its architecture and sculptures are very familiar.[5]

In the centre of the attic is the proud inscription which records that Constantine liberated the State from its tyrant *instinctu divinitatis*, two words generally accepted as containing a covert allusion to the introduction of Christianity. To either side are arranged eight oblong panels taken from an arch set up to commemorate the campaigns of Marcus Aurelius against the Germans and the Sarmatians (*R.R.*, i. 241-8). Beneath again are eight medallions with hunting scenes, which, from their Flavian character, may have belonged to the original decoration of the arch (*R.R.*, i. 250-1). Below runs a little frieze which, from the style of the carving, cannot well be earlier than the beginning of the fourth century (*R.R.*, i. 254-7). It commemorates on all four sides the *res gestae* of an Emperor, and probably refers to the Persian campaigns of Diocletian of the year 303, and the procession and other ceremonies of the Triumph.[6] On the west side are depicted the siege of a city and a great battle scene, once supposed to be that of the Milvian Bridge ; on either side are scenes from the triumphal pomp ; while on the Eastern face, looking towards the Coliseum, run the two friezes that form the text of this lecture. On the one the Emperor is making to the assembled people a proclamation from the Rostra ; on the other he is

PLATE III.

1. AN IMPERIAL PROCLAMATION AND AN IMPERIAL LARGESSE.
Arch of Constantine.
2. PORTRAIT OF DIOCLETIAN. Spalato.

seen enthroned while officials distribute to eager
crowds the *congiarium* or largesse customary after a
triumph (plate iii., 1 and 2).

In almost every handbook and history of art these
friezes, when mentioned at all, are dismissed as late
and decadent work showing the complete debasement
of art in the fourth century. This judgment has
been repeated in one book after another, since, like
Anatole France's shrewd professor, we all find it
notoriously easier and more popular to repeat old
ideas than to search for new ones. Yet I can imagine
an unprejudiced observer looking at these reliefs, and
failing to see why they should be dismissed as decadent
antique. Surely the first thing that would strike him
would be that their spirit is not antique at all. Where,
in Greek or in Graeco-Roman art, do we find so highly
centralised a composition, figures so consistently
placed in a frontal position, or a similar principle of
lighting, or flat planes thus combined with deep
undercutting ? The deliberate optic effects aimed
at by the Constantinian sculptor have been fully
discussed by others, and I do not propose to touch
upon the question here.[7] I want rather to draw your
attention to the accent laid on the central figure of
the Emperor, to the manner in which all the lines of
the composition flow towards him, so concentrating
the interest upon him that he becomes the centre of
homage to the figures on each side, and is also offered

in full frontal view to the homage of the spectator from without. It is this union of centrality or convergence, with frontality which distinguishes Roman from Greek composition in relief.

The same principle makes itself felt, alongside of the older methods, in early Christian and mediaeval ivories, and finds supreme expression in the sculptures of our cathedrals—in the tympanum of Saint Trophime at Arles, for instance, or in the magnificent Royal porch at Chartres, to take two examples from the Romanesque and Gothic sculptures of the twelfth century.[8] Let us examine for a moment the construction of the design in the Chartres tympanum (plate iv.). The subject, Christ worshipped by the symbols of the four Evangelists, is one familiarly employed in thirteenth century sculpture : within the almond-shaped nimbus or *mandorla* sits the Christ according to the scheme known as the *Maiestas*.[9] On His left knee He holds the book of the Evangels, and He raises His right hand in the act of benediction. The figure faces the spectator in the hieratic frontal attitude, with no inclination to either side. The Evangelists adore Him, but the central figure is unconscious of the act which heightens and emphasises His own majesty ; for the Christ is thought of not in relation to the other figures within the tympanum, but is presented as God to the worshipper who looks up at the image. Consider for one moment what

PLATE IV.

MAIESTAS CHRISTI.
Chartres.

would happen were the Christ drawn into the action of the surrounding scene. He would at once become an historical personage participating in a definite action ; whereas the artist's intention has been to remove Him, by means of the frontal pose, outside all conditions of time and space, and to present Him to us as the pre-existent Christ, the Son of God and of Man.[10]

This method of emphasising the central by the frontal principle was not unknown, as we shall see, to the earliest periods of Greek art ; but from the first the Greeks exhibit a tendency to work away from the frontal pose, so that centralisation with them becomes rather a matter of arrangement of lines, untouched by higher spiritual considerations. Take, for instance, the masterly design of the ' Nativity of Aphrodite ' represented on the principal face of the so-called Ludovisi Throne (Terme Museum · R.R., iii. 326, 1-4=Helbig, 1286). Here, too, you have a strongly centralised composition : the straight slim young figure occupies the exact centre of the panel, and is raised by the two stooping attendant nymphs, who, for all their bending grace and tenderness of movement, hold up the young goddess with the precision of heraldic supporters. So far as the body is concerned, the Aphrodite is placed in a purely frontal pose, which enhances the central note; but look at the head. This is shown in profile, to a certain extent perhaps for technical reasons, since it is easier to draw the head in profile than *en face*, but the technical reasons are assuredly influenced by the Greek desire of arranging figures into self-contained and closely-knit groups. Observe the result; instead of the central figure being, like the Christ on the tympanum of Chartres, removed by the frontal position beyond the conditions of time and space that govern the rest of the design, the profile turn of the head and its upward tilt in the direction of the nymph on the right connect the Aphrodite directly with the ministering figures on either side, and make her, from the passive object of their ministrations, into the active participant of their action and their emotion. There could be no greater contrast to the effect obtained by the frontal formula of late Roman and early Christian art, with its definite withdrawal of the central figure from the surrounding action.

One more comparison, and this time between two objects of Greek art. One is the lovely cylix of early fifth century date in Berlin, representing Selene sinking with her horses into the ocean; the other the bronze phalera from Elis in the British Museum, representing the rising Helios (plate v.). On the first of these the interlacing of the horses, the turn of their heads towards each other, the head of the goddess seen in profile above her body which is placed frontally, all set this work in the class of narrative art,

PLATE V.

1. SELENE. Greek Vase in Berlin.
2. SOL. Greek Phalera in the British Museum.

in spite of the fact that the design as a whole is seen from the front by the spectator. The phalera, on the other hand, with its great Helios facing straight to the spectator, the horses galloping to either side that nothing may stand between the god and his worshipper, exhibits a purely frontal centralised design. The prophylactic virtue of the phalera doubtless kept the figure of the god in this primitive position, while the cylix, being purely decorative, retained the accidents, but not the essentials of primitive religious art.

III. CENTRALISATION OF DESIGN IN GREEK ART

(a) *From the Earliest Period to the Pediments of Olympia*

But in order to seize the different principles that govern composition in Greek and in later Roman art, it is not sufficient to compare monuments which might appear specially selected to support my own personal theory. To make the point clear it will be necessary further to prelude our subject by considering a representative range of examples from archaic times down to the period when Greek artistic activity passed into the service of Rome. I shall draw my illustrations as far as possible from pedimental sculptures, since the triangular shape of the pediment calls for a highly centralised composition as clearly as does the tympanum of a church door. By the degree

of the Greek sculptor's obedience to this demand
shall we be able to gauge his sense of the problem
involved. In the very earliest period the Greek
obeys the frontal law as closely as other primitive
peoples. You can at once appreciate this fact from
the earliest Greek pedimental sculptures known, those,
namely, which were discovered at Corfu in 1910
(plate vi.).[11] They belong to a very archaic temple of
which certain architectural fragments have likewise
been recovered. The centre of the pediment is occupied by the powerful group of the Gorgon, flanked
by her monstrous offspring, Pegasus and Chrysaor.
All three are placed in full frontal view in their double
capacity as protectors of the temple and averters of
evil. This apotropaic function is heightened by the
flanking lions whose heads are likewise turned vigo-
rously to the front.[12] There could be no more direct
illustration of the magical function of early art ; the
power of the divinity is made visible, and through its
concrete form becomes permanently effective. It is
interesting to note that wherever a figure or group
has a prophylactic function—is conceived, that is, as
powerful to avert evil influences—it will be placed
in a frontal pose even if in relief. It is thus that
we can explain the strange and awe-inspiring frontal
figures of the oldest temple at Selinos in Sicily,[13] or
the awkward combination of frontal head and torso
with running legs placed in profile in the Nike of

PLATE VI.

1. SUGGESTED RECONSTRUCTION OF PEDIMENT OF TEMPLE IN CORFU.
2. GORGON FROM TEMPLE IN CORFU.

Archermos ; [14] again, when it is desired to mark the divinity of one figure within a group, it will be emphasised by means of the frontal pose, as is the deified ancestor on the famous Laconian stele from Chrysapha in Berlin, which we shall have much to say about in another lecture. Let me point out that the design of the group from Corfu is centripetal, that is to say, the figures of the sides contribute to the support of the central image. This monolatric quality, which, under the influence of Athens and Athenian thought, was lost in what we call the great period of Greek art, is at the base of all centralised design. When the Greeks abandoned the centripetal construction as on the pediments of Aegina and Olympia, we get that barrenness of design for which the most ardent admirers of Greek art have not been able to find an entirely satisfactory apology, and we shall see that the gradual disappearance of a monolatric principle deprived Greek sculpture of the factor essential to religious art, where everything should minister to a figure of supreme and central importance.

We have so far only spoken of the central part of the pediment at Corfu. The figures of the wings, however, illustrate the tendency, prevalent from the first in Greek art, to throw off the tyranny of frontality. The subject is the struggle of the gods against the giants, and here an attempt is made to get rid of frontal poses and parallel lines so as to obtain groups in which the figures are interrelated in a common action.

Frontality was never entirely abandoned at any period, but it was thrown into the background as a secondary motive in Greek art from the end of the sixth century onward, when the whole attention was directed to expressing relation in terms of mythology. But the principle was always there, as the minor arts attest. The frontal figure and pose were beloved not only in gold-work and in embroideries and textiles, but in much minor sculpture, a fact of which we can easily convince ourselves by looking through Reinach's *Répertoire de Reliefs.* In the major sculpture, however, it was suppressed ; but it was beginning to emerge again in Hellenistic days, and it reasserted itself in the art of the Empire, strengthened and purified by its obstinate though often obscure resistance to more fashionable methods. In this persistence and re-emergence lay the proof of its vital significance as a principle of artistic expression.

A long interval separates the pedimental sculptures found at Corfu from those which come next in date.[15] In the early poros pediments from the archaic temples on the Acropolis of Athens there is little attempt at centralisation (*R.R.,* i. 42, 1-4). In the ' Heracles and the Hydra ' or ' Heracles struggling with Triton,' while other serpent-bodied monsters are introduced as spectators of the conflict,[16] the artist, in order to satisfy the exigencies of the central space, is content to make the monster rear his head and fore-parts at this point, or else places here the attacking figure of Heracles. In these instances, at least, the centralised composition is abandoned in favour of the narrative method, and there is no such harmonious subordination of the figures of the sides to a central motive as in the Corfu pediment. Equally unsatisfactory as meeting the requirements of a centralised composition is the design from the small pediment of the Cnidians at Delphi (*R.R.*, i. 135, 1).[17] The subject selected is appropriately enough the contest of Apollo and Heracles for the sacred tripod. Apollo, on the left, assisted by a goddess (Leto or Artemis ?) who stands immediately behind him, pulls at one of the legs of the tripod to which Heracles, on the right, clings stoutly, while Athena, in the centre, is present to aid her favourite hero. The scene is conceived as a pursuit rather than a contest, the movement running in a straight line from left to right. Furtwängler, in commenting upon the composition, rightly remarked that it resembled a piece cut out of a frieze rather than a pedimental group. The backward turn of the head of Heracles towards his pursuing enemy, and the heightening of the figure of Athena to fill the pediment at the apex, are the sole concessions to the demand for a central note. The pose of Athena tends to be frontal, without providing a true centre ;

for the sculptor, with a more genuine feeling for narrative than for decorative art, avoids giving to the figure the definite aspect which should tend to isolate it from the rest of the personages of the action.

These early sculptors were satisfied with making the figures increase in size towards the middle, but as time went on the childish device was abandoned for a definite central figure, as on our next example from the pediments of the temple of Aphaia at Aegina. Let us consider their composition as revealed by the recent examination of the figures and of the traces for their attachment on the floor of the pediments.[18] The subject of both pediments is a combat between Greeks and Trojans, the combatants being arranged in two groups of three at either side, with the solitary figure of Athena in the centre. In the western pediment her attitude is rigid, almost frontal, her feet alone being placed in profile to the right, but the movement of her body does not follow that of the action within the pediment ; on the contrary, she appears to move forward towards the spectator. At first sight one might think, ' If this is not centralisation, what is ? ' But if you look closely at the structure of the design you will find that it breaks up on each side into isolated groups which, in spite of the balanced symmetry of their parts, are without organic relation either to one another or to the figure of the goddess. The old idea, based on our modern point of view, that Athena is controlling the action, that she is present to favour the Greeks as against the Trojans, and that the battle is waged, so to speak, in her honour, was well enough so long as archaeologists could shuffle the Munich figures about to suit their preconceived notions of the composition, but it must be abandoned in the light of recent investigations which have definitely shown that the action moves away from the centre and has no relation to the goddess. Athena here is not present as god of hosts, she is at most an impassive symbol of battle, and her image, while marking the central architectonic space, is so little required by the meaning of the composition that it might be left out and replaced by some other figure or object without injury to the sense of the groups as a whole. Although Athena has the frontal pose of a cultus image, the fact that the actors are unaffected by her presence leaves the spectator in doubt as to the meaning she is intended to convey, and the centrifugal design of the wings effectively neutralises the monolatric formula which the central image seems to claim. On the east pediment, the sculptor, whether the same or another, dissatisfied with the cold mechanical effect of the central western group, attempts to make the goddess participate in the general movement of the fray by stretching out her aegis ; but as her gesture is without effect on the action, it remains unconvincing and a little trivial.

Although Greek sculptors for a time recognised that the centre of the pediment required a dominant motive, they were powerless, in spite of their mastery of line, to invest this central figure with an emotional idea, a spiritual meaning, that should flow from it through the whole composition, knitting the various groups and figures to one another and to itself; and so it is that in spite of the great beauty and the noble movement of figures and groups, the composition as a whole is not only poor and ineffective, but violates the main laws of pedimental decoration. The same defects and the same attempts at compromise which we note at Aegina recur in the pedimental sculpture from a temple of Apollo at Eretria (in the Museum of Chalcis), where Theseus, as he ravishes his Amazon, runs rapidly away from the centre and from his protectress Athena.[19]   In both pediments of the temple of Zeus at Olympia, the central figures, Zeus on the eastern, Apollo on the western pediment, are no integral part of the composition; they neither join in the action with the other personages of the scene, nor are they isolated as objects of reverence and worship. There is, however, a marked difference in the two pediments at Olympia. The Eastern, with its dull mechanical arrangement of the figures on the principle of a clock on the mantlepiece between two candlesticks, falls short even of the Aeginetan compositions; on the other hand, the solidly con-

structed groups so splendidly massed on either side
of the Apollo, in spite of their centrifugal movement,
bring the Western pediment, to my mind, nearer to
the great compositions of early Christian art than
anything else accomplished by Greek sculpture.[20]

(b) The Pediments of the Parthenon. Pedimental Composition in the Fourth Century

So slight was the intellectual hold of the central
figure upon the artistic imagination of the Greeks
that the scheme was abandoned by the sculptors of
the great period.   When we come to the pediments of
the Parthenon, we find that the supreme genius who
carved their figures, whether Pheidias or another,
when brought face to face with the pedimental
problem, solved it, at any rate on the west side, of
which alone we can speak with certainty, by abandon-
ing the central scheme altogether, and by imparting
to the composition a centrifugal rather than a centripetal principle.   No figure marks the dividing vertical
line ; its place is taken by the group of the two combatants, each of whom starts back from the centre in
a diagonal line.   The subject is the contest of Athena
and Poseidon for the land of Attica, and we know
that Athena was destined to be the victor ; but there
is nothing to indicate this in the design, in which the
artist accepts the scene of the contest as a whole,
and substitutes for a dominant central motive the

moment when the divinities move asunder to disclose their gifts. In other words, we might say that Pheidias took as basis of his composition the same centrifugal scheme that appears at Aegina or Olympia, but omitted the disturbing central figure, for which he substitutes, in order to fill up the space, the minor motive of the olive tree. By what we may call the principle of the divided centre the Pheidian school attains to that unity of composition which preceding artists, in their effort to combine opposite motives, had altogether missed.   Carrey's drawing has preserved for us the main lines of the Western pedimental scheme, and since the torsos of Athena and Poseidon have been placed in position in the British Museum we can form a very good idea of the effect of the design. On the Eastern side, where the Nativity of Athena was represented, the attempt was also made, to judge from the marks on the floor of the pediment, to establish the principle of the divided centre.   But the nature of the subject, which imposed an inert or inactive position for the Zeus, must have resulted in a less pleasing and well-balanced arrangement.[21]

After the Parthenon, and in the hands of lesser men than Pheidias, pedimental composition, which his genius had momentarily raised to a higher power, seems again to have declined. The statement must, however, be made with caution, since the pediments attributed to Scopas, Praxiteles, and other great masters of the fourth century are unknown. But there are a sufficient number of lesser pedimental sculptures preserved from stelae and sarcophagi to show that the demand for a dominant central motive was once more satisfied by devices akin to those of archaic art. This appears from the pediments of later sepulchral stelae or from those of the ' sarcophagus of Alexander ' at Constantinople, where in the battle episode of the one side a Greek is made to tower high above his fallen foe in order to fill the space, while on the other side the figure of a horseman on his rearing horse fills the pediment up to its apex. In this case again we might say, as of the Cnidian group, that this is a piece cut out of a frieze rather than a pedimental composition.

(c) *Character of Greek Religion responsible for the Character of Greek Art. Influence of a Pantheon*

If we stop for a moment to consider this lack of true centralisation in Greek design, remembering at the same time that Pheidias gave the problem a solution which was quite the opposite of what the space of a pediment seems to demand, we shall, I think, find the reason in the character of Greek religion. The highest ideals of every national art have always gathered round the national conception of the Deity ; if Greek art never discovered a strong central formula, it was because such a formula was

D

not called forth by some dominating conception such as that which inspired the strongly centralised compositions of Christian art. The feeling had been there in the magical art of primitive Greece in the pediment at Corfu, the metope of Selinus, but instead of being purified and developed by some central religious ideal, it was stifled by the claims of the Olympian religion. Had any one of the Olympian gods made a supreme claim to the adoration and devotion of man, his figure would have imposed upon art a type expressive of that claim, and all art, even when not directly in the service of religion, would have been inspired by that type. But Greek art was without a central theme to unify and concentrate the artistic impulse ; it was in the service of many masters, dedicated to a religion with many gods, with an anthropomorphic Pantheon where none reigned supreme, and it therefore lacks the theurgic quality that is so vital an element both in Mediaeval Art and in the art of the early Renaissance.

Much has been said of late years in scorn of the Olympians, and concerning the spiritual aridity of a system represented as already decadent and outworn when it makes its appearance in Homer. Yet the enduring strength of the system is nowhere so manifest as in the successful resistance which the Olympians offered to any serious or sustained expression of the monotheism which was after all latent in Greek

religion. Monotheism was the central doctrine of
the powerful Orphic sects, and was proclaimed by
one school of philosophy after the other ; in the sixth
and fifth centuries, as Professor Gilbert Murray has
reminded us, it nearly gained the day ; [22] it was
inherent in Zeus himself as supreme lord of the skies ;
yet Zeus, for all his leadership of the other Olympians,
was never strong enough to impose himself upon art
as a dominant religious type. The Olympians held
their ground triumphantly and penetrated with
Hellenism into Rome, where they nearly suffocated
the monotheistic tendencies of Roman religion. But
the figure of the Emperor arose in good time to expel
these foreign gods from the scene ; and in art at
least brought to fruition much that they had sought
to destroy.

It may be that once, in the Zeus of Olympia—and
unfortunately we only have literary criticisms and
indifferent copies or distant imitations to guide us
in our judgment—Greek art attained through the
genius of Pheidias to the expression of a great monotheistic ideal, and made visible the Divine Fatherhood.
But as a rule, and judging not only from extant
copies, but from a certain number of originals, the
Hermes of Olympia, the Demeter of Cnidus, etc.,[23]
Greek artists, I venture to assert, failed to create
religious figures that make the same direct appeal to
the devotional sense as the Beau Dieu of Rheims or

the Holy Face of Albert Dürer's Sudarium, or Raphael's 'Madonna di San Sisto,' that unsurpassed example of a composition in which a central group is enframed within a monolatric design. I do not say that Greek art was inferior on this account ; I, at any rate, believe that, where the rendering of the human figure is concerned, its sculpture is the greatest in the world; but its aim was not primarily religious.

In the end, and in spite of much that has been said to the contrary, it is the subject that informs the art, not directly perhaps, but by creating in connection with itself a spiritual temper, an atmosphere which emanates from the subject and reacts upon it, and which colours, directly or indirectly, the whole art of the period. In simpler language it might simply be called the way of looking at things. Now, because in Greece this way of looking at things tended to distribute the interest through the parts of a composition rather than to concentrate it on one central figure, Greek artists enjoyed a freedom of action and of discovery which could never have been theirs had they been fettered by hieratic formulas requiring the interest to be focused on one point. They were able to apply themselves to the rendering of every aspect of the human form, which they interpreted in a manner probably destined to remain unsurpassed, though their compositions lack the depth of emotion which turns the decoration of Gothic Cathedrals into what has been so well defined as ' one great act of adoration in stone.'

Professor Gardner in his *Principles of Greek Art* has doubtless made out a better case for Greek pedimental construction than I am able to do, but even he can only say of the principles which govern it they are ' defined and rigid,' [24] two qualities which scarcely suggest the glow and play of artistic inspiration.

(d) Weakness and Strength of Greek Design further illustrated from Panel Compositions and Friezes

In panel composition and in those parts of a frieze that demand a central note, Greek composition betrays the same weakness as in the temple pediment. The more I think of the suave lines of Greek sculpture, its voluptuous modelling and fluid contours, its studied avoidance of all angularity and harshness, the less do I feel that its greatness could ever have lain in the direction of monumental composition. It lacked the necessary solemnity and massiveness that can only be imparted by subordination to a central religious idea. For one moment, towards the close of the archaic period, there was a flash of inspiration which resulted in the uniquely beautiful design—so strong, so tense, so vivid—of the ' Nativity of Aphrodite ' on the Ludovisi Throne ; with this we may compare, as being already one degree less powerful, the exquisite relief

from Eleusis with Triptolemos between his patronesses
Demeter and Persephone (*R.R.*, ii. 339, 3) ; [25] here,
too, as in the Ludovisi relief, we have the dip at the
centre intended to draw towards this point the lines
of the design ; but the aesthetic conception is weakened, to my mind, by placing the figure of Triptolemos
in profile instead of frontally. The motive continues
to lose strength and effectiveness—at least so it seems
to me when I compare with earlier works the ' Medea
and the Daughters of Pelias' of the Lateran (*R.R.*,
iii. 277, 1) ; or the ' Theseus, Heracles and Peirithoos '
of the Torlonia collection (*R. R.*, iii. 340, 4). After
all, the central slab of the Parthenon frieze, with its
humble subordinate motive, is as good an example
as any of the weak spot in much Greek design—its
failure, namely, to discover an arresting motive where
this is most needed. In the same way sepulchral art
in Attica ignored, as we shall see in another lecture,
the definite central note which a cult of the heroised
dead seemed to demand ; nor, as a consequence, did
the deification of the living — a commoner event
even in the pre-Alexandrine period than is generally
supposed—affect, so far as we can tell, the principles
of design. It is true that now and again we catch
in the designs of Greek vases the central note which
was suppressed in the major arts. The beautiful
ritual scene in honour of Dionysus, on a vase in
Naples, exhibits a centralised composition which does

not fall short of a mediaeval altar-piece.[26] Every movement of the ministering Maenads, even when directed
from the centre, is subordinated to the expressive
sweep of the lines that flow towards the frontal image
of the god in the middle of the picture. We perceive
here what masters of this type of religious design the
Greeks might have proved had not the atmosphere
emanating from the gods of the State been hostile to
its development.

Greek artists, accordingly, were weakest in pedimental and other compositions, where, as in the tympanum of a church, an impressive central note is demanded. On the other hand, they showed themselves
incomparable masters of design where the space to
be decorated could be filled, as in their friezes, by
long processional groups in which the interest must be
distributed in order to be sustained, or by a series
of combat or hunting scenes linked in a continuous
chain. In this style of composition, indeed, where
the figures need only to be arranged in relation to
one another, the Greeks produced exquisitely centralised designs of a kind, as on the friezes of the so-
called sarcophagus of Alexander ; the principle which
prevails in these reliefs, however, is not really centralisation so much as harmony or balance of corresponding parts. A figure like the splendid horseman
formerly identified as Alexander, on one long side of
the Sidon sarcophagus (R.R., i. 415), may divide a

group or mark the meeting point of convergent movements ; but the centre itself is not given emphatic
weight and prominence. It is a mere resting-place
in a decorative scheme where in reality all parts have
equal value.[27]

IV. Tendencies of Greek Design in the Hellenistic Period

So little Hellenistic art has survived, and that little
is so imperfectly known, that it is difficult to realise
the stage reached by Greek sculptors in the development of centralised composition when the antique
passed into the service of Rome and was called upon
to represent Roman subjects. Of especial interest
would it be to know what innovations, if any, were
introduced into art by the influence of the cult of the
deified Alexander, whether in life or after death.
Diodorus has left an elaborate if obscure description
of the panel pictures that decorated his funeral
chariot, and we find ourselves speculating as to
whether the scheme of the picture in which Alexander
was shown surrounded, like an Oriental despot, by
his bodyguard,[28] already heralded compositions such
as those of the narrow friezes on the principal face
of the arch of Constantine. In art, as elsewhere,
Alexander is certainly responsible for not a few of
the ideas which used to be fathered upon the Roman
Emperors, but there is little or nothing at present to

throw light on questions which are so vital for the history of the antique. The Pergamene friezes show a number of new elements : close grouping, landscape setting, dramatic gesture, and so on, unknown to earlier art, which will reappear in the art of Rome ; but the action is still unfolded along a surface, with little tendency towards grouping masses about a central point (*R.R.*, i. 207-19).

More striking are the system of grouping and the arrangement of groups and figures on the frieze from the temple of Hecate at Lagina (first century B.C.), now in the Museum of Constantinople (*R.R.*, i. 171-5) : the figures, for instance, are to a great extent shown in full face ; overlapping of either figures or groups is avoided, and there is an obvious attempt to isolate them from one another. Moreover, and this is above all important, there is apparent in various of the groups an effort at concentrating interest on a central motive which is far in excess of what had so far been attempted by the Greek antique. I would specially call your attention to two admirable compositions on the South frieze (*R.R.*, i. 174, 25 and 28). This frieze has been described as ' confused and awkward,' a mere imitation of Pergamene work. When it has been better studied it will be found to contain many traits which seem to have passed straight into the Hellenistic art of Rome. It is certainly in the sculpture of this period that we must

look for many of the innovations which imperfect
knowledge had attributed to Rome. At the same
time, in any Hellenistic sculpture so far known—
there is little enough indeed, and that little has been
neglected—we look in vain for the unifying touch
which can be imparted to composition by a figure
or a motive of commanding interest. This last and
all-important factor was to be contributed, as we
shall now see, by Rome and the ideas embodied in
the figure of her Emperor.

V. HELLENISTIC ART IN ROME

In the last years of the Republic and the first of
the Empire, when the centre of artistic production
was gradually shifting to Rome, design shows certain
innovations which at once distinguish the Graeco-
Roman art of Rome from that of Greek countries.
The composition of the 'Sacrifice to Mars' in the
Louvre (*R.R.*, i. 277), from a basis set up about
B.C. 42 by Gn. Domitius Ahenobarbus in the temple
of Neptune, is an instance in point. It exhibits the
same tendency to a full-face pose of the figures already
noted in the case of certain later Hellenistic sculptures,
but this is combined with a symmetry severer than
any observed in Greek schemes of decoration. The
altar occupies the centre; Domitius, in sacrificial
attire, is on the right; Mars, a stately figure in armour,
balances him on the left. The god is present at the

sacrifice in his own honour, and stands in a prominent
position, with one foot on the altar step, as if in token
of possession ; at the same time the turn of head and
body so draw him into the scene of the relief that the
interest of the central group is about equally divided
between the god and Domitius, who in the spirit of
Greek art turns not towards the centre but towards
the advancing procession of the sacred animals.[29]
With regard to the general composition, I should like
for one instant to compare it with that of the two
groups from the south frieze of Lagina ; you will be
struck, I think, by the contrast which the stiffer,
almost crystallised poses of the figures at the centre
of the Roman relief offer to the fluid lines of the
Hellenistic example. The composition of the sides,
on the other hand, is more frankly Hellenistic, and
if we had time to look at it in detail we should find it
to be closely inspired by Hellenistic prototypes.

Some thirty years later, in B.C. 12-9, the Ara
Pacis Augustae, set up by command of Augustus to
commemorate his successful settlement of Gaul
and Spain, was decorated with scenes intended to
represent the Emperor followed by a long cortège
(*R.R.*, i. 232-7). The difficulty which archaeologists
have experienced in identifying the figure of Augustus
shows how slight an accent was laid upon the
leading personages of the pageant. At one time
the Emperor was seen in the stately aged man, with

veiled head, afterwards variously interpreted as
Agrippa, Caesar, and Lepidus (*R.R.*, i. 235, 3) ; again,
he was thought to be the figure surrounded by lictors
and *flamines* on a slab which is now rejected from
the Ara Pacis (below, p. 79), while Augustus seems
now finally identified with a veiled figure (who has
also been taken for the *Rex Sacrificulus*) on a slab
discovered in 1902 (*R. R.*, i. 236, 3).   We cannot
imagine any such difficulties and uncertainties attend-
ing the identification of Christ on mediaeval or early
Renaissance monuments, or that of the Emperor on
the works of the late Empire.   It is true that the
tendency to place figures in a full-face position makes
itself felt here as on the basis of Ahenobarbus, with
this difference, that in the earlier work the figures
are isolated in space, and in the later they are isolated
against a crowded background by means of the frontal
turn imparted to them.[30]   But without a dominant
central motive and without any monolatric scheme
of the attendant figures the invention is ineffective.
The main spirit of the composition of the Ara Pacis
remains Hellenic, still aiming at diffusion rather than
at concentration of interest.

VI. The Imperial Apotheosis and Deification as a Theme of Art

This Hellenistic art transplanted to Roman soil
contained, it is true, many new and vital traits, such

as the crowding of the figures; the introduction of children; the vivacity of the glance introduced by hollowing the pupil of the eye, which imparted to it a new vitality.[31] Yet it might easily have degenerated into meaningless imitation of Greek formulas and become purely academic, had it not been for the intrusion of a fresh idea destined slowly to transform all the laws of antique design. This was the doctrine of the Imperial Apotheosis, of the deification of the Emperor after death, upon the art-type of which Cumont's researches have thrown so vivid a light.[32] The doctrine is so familiar that I need hardly remind you of the manner of its introduction by Augustus in honour of his adopted father, the great Julius Caesar, whose star, the *Julium sidus* of Horace, the *Caesaris astrum* of Vergil, had been seen in the sky heralding the new god.[33] Caesar is said to have received an altar and a column twenty feet high at the spot where his body was burnt, and where afterwards rose the temple of Divus Julius, the core of which stands to this day.[34] We may note incidentally that column and altar should be borne in mind by students of Roman art for the light which they throw upon the later columns of Nero at Mayence, and of Trajan and of Marcus Aurelius in Rome. The deification of Augustus, already acknowledged in his lifetime as *Divi filius*, followed as a matter of course, and the Apotheosis of the Roman Emperor

soon became the rule.[35]   It was based largely on that
cult of the ruler which was so prominent a religious
and political feature under the Ptolemies of Egypt
and the Graeco-Syrian Seleucids : [36] the very wreath
worn by the Caesars was imitated from that of the
Hellenistic rulers ; their eagle was borrowed from
Oriental solar symbols ; yet from the first the art
form of the Imperial Apotheosis acquired a distinctly
Western and Roman character, and this because the
primary inspiring factors were already an integral
part of religious belief.

The religious conscience was better prepared for
the doctrine of the Imperial Deification than is often
supposed. Apotheosis, admission of the great dead
among the gods, was a not unfamiliar idea in pre-
Imperial Rome.   Ennius (239-170 B.C.) had already
sung of the admission of the elder Scipio into the
courts of heaven.[37]   Not only had Cicero desired
Apotheosis for his daughter,[38] but he has left us in the
wonderful myth of the ' Dream of Scipio,' [39] a noble
vision as to the ultimate fate of those who had deserved well of the State. The picture he presents
of the elder Scipio appearing to his illustrious descen-
dant and pointing to Carthage *de excelso et pleno
stellarum inlustri et claro quodam loco*—implying the
ascent of the Soul to the Stars—must have belonged
to a widely current range of ideas. On a relief from
Amiternum, for instance, which we shall consider in

detail in the next lecture (p. 175), representing the funeral procession of a military official of the close of the late Republican or early Augustan period, the idea of astral Apotheosis is conveyed by the star-spangled canopy above the bier. Such conceptions, as we shall see, were largely the fruit of the teaching of Posidonius of Apamea and of the Orphic beliefs which had filtered into Rome from Southern Italy. The Stoic philosophy which attained to its fullest expression in Rome from the end of the Republic onwards, laid special stress on the reabsorption of the soul into the fiery aether after its separation from the body. All these ideas were part of a new religious movement that set in before the Empire, though, as we shall see in the lecture on the ' After Life,' the belief in the immortality of the soul and in the soul's return to the heavenly seats, was to gain fresh lustre from the Apotheosis of the ruler.

It must also be remembered that the divine honours so frequently rendered to Roman generals and governors in Greece and the East, must have early familiarised Romans with the idea of the deification of a living man. According to Plutarch, Flamininus, the ' Liberator' of Greece (B.C. 196), had been associated at Chalcis with the worship of both Heracles and Apollo ; [40] Pompey, it seems, had received several temples ; [41] Cicero records with pride that he refused similar honours—among them shrines (*fana*)

—offered to him in B.C. 50 during his governorship of Cilicia ; [42] and it is probably present to all your minds that Cicero twits Verres more than once in the famous second Verrine Oration, for allowing games (*praeclara illa Verria*) to be celebrated in his honour.[43] As to Julius Caesar, whatever his own personal beliefs and attitude of mind, there is no doubt that he received and accepted unmistakable offers of deification alike from the Greek cities and in Rome.[44]

Above all, this deification of the ruler could not come as a new conception to a people who, like the Romans, had from a period of high antiquity been accustomed to see victorious generals, to whom the honours of a triumph were accorded, arrayed in the insignia of the chief god of the state, Jupiter Optimus Maximus himself. It is not sufficient to say with the classical dictionaries that the general wore for the time being the attributes of Jupiter : during the pageant the general *was* Jupiter,[45] in token of which his face, in early times at least, was painted blood-red like the god's ; he carried the thunderbolt and ivory sceptre ; he wore the *toga picta*—the great embroidered mantle—as talisman of dominion and of victory ; and he rode in the four-horse chariot, the *quadriga*, which is no other than the chariot of the Sun god—of Sol,[46] who, long before he figured as Apollo in the Graeco-Roman Pantheon, was identified with the great Jupiter of the Capitol. I venture to assert

PLATE VII.

APOTHEOSIS OF JULIUS CAESAR.

Altar in the Vatican.

that the growing belief in an after life of blessedness
reserved for those who had deserved well of the
State, combined with the temporary deification of
the *Triumphator*, were more powerful factors in Imperial Deification and Imperial Apotheosis than any
attempt on the part of the ruler to model an astute
piece of religious policy on that of Alexander and his
successors. Religious ideas, it has been well said,
' are easily assimilated only when there already
exists an indigenous system of thought into which
they readily fit.' [47] Had not the soil been ready,
neither Imperial Apotheosis nor Imperial Deification
would have struck root so quickly and so firmly.
We now have to examine their influence upon art.
Here, too, I hope to show you that the way had been
prepared—that Etrusco-Roman art had a predilection
for certain centralised formulas, the reflection perhaps
of monotheistic religious tendencies, which were to
mature in the service of the Imperial idea.

VII. The Monuments of the Apotheosis and Kin-
    dred Works from Augustus to the End of
    the Julio-Claudian Dynasty

(a) *The Imperial Idea in Augustan Art*

In the age of Augustus we are a long way still from
the adoption of the old frontal pose into the official
art of the Empire. The earliest instance of Imperial
Apotheosis, except on coins, occurs on an altar which

E

stands in the Cortile del Belvedere of the Vatican (Helbig, 155 ;=*R. R.*, iii. 398).* The purely Augustan style of the reliefs is of singular beauty (plates vii., viii.), yet the monument has attracted little attention. The Victory on the principal face carries a shield inscribed with the dedication of the altar to Augustus by the Senate and the People. As the Emperor is given the title of Pontifex Maximus, the date of the dedication must be subsequent to B.C. 12, in which year Augustus assumed the high priesthood left vacant by the death of Lepidus. The relief on the left evidently commemorates the restoration of the cult of the Lares by Augustus between 14 and 7 B.C. ; this composition is centralised round the altar somewhat after the manner of the scene of sacrifice on the back of the basis of Domitius Ahenobarbus from the temple of Neptune. On the one side, Augustus himself, accompanied by two attendants ; facing him on the other side is the priest *capite velato*, who stretches both hands to the Emperor over the altar to receive from him the statuettes of the two Lares. The relief of the opposite face bears a direct relation to the ceremony we have just witnessed ; it represents the ' Prodigy of the Laurentine Sow,' likewise depicted on the Ara Pacis,

---

* A vast literature has gathered round the Imperial Apotheosis and Deification, but the numerous monuments have so far never been grouped together or exhaustively discussed. The theme is one that should prove attractive to students, and I heartily recommend it to any one who is looking round for the subject of a thesis.

PLATE VIII.

Two Reliefs from Altar in the Vatican.

by which Father Aeneas was to know that he had reached the spiritual metropolis of Latium. And on the rear of the altar occurs what is probably the earliest representation of the Imperial Apotheosis : the first *Divus*, the great Caesar himself, is seen borne heavenward in the flaming chariot drawn by winged horses in the presence of Augustus, here figuring as the *Divi filius* of the inscription, and the princes of his house. Above the *Divus* hovers the Eagle of the Apotheosis, now much effaced ; the Sun in his chariot, and Coelus personified as Jupiter within the arching folds of the cosmic mantle, come down to meet him from the left and from the right respectively. Cumont has aptly remarked that the intended correspondence between the chariot that comes down from heaven and the one which rises upward from the earth shows without a doubt that in this first manifestation of the Imperial cult in plastic art, a relation is already clearly established between the deified personage and the Sun.[48]

The subject of the Apotheosis is common on gems. We have no actual example showing the Apotheosis of Augustus, but two cameos with the deification of princes of his house will serve to recall the familiar scheme to your minds. One, a fine cameo in the Cabinet des Médailles, shows a young Julio-Claudian Prince, possibly Germanicus, borne aloft by the eagle, and bearing in his left hand the cornucopiae ; in his right is the lituus or augur's staff, while Victory hovers over him with the crown (*R.R.*, ii. 236, 4). The second cameo is in the Library of Nancy; it reproduces the same scheme, but this time the Imperial personage is Nero, and in his right hand he carries in place of the augural staff the actual image of Victory holding a crown as if to place it on his head.[49] We shall see when we come to discuss ancient beliefs as to the After Life and the Apotheosis of the soul that the eagle, messenger of the sun, was from a period of high antiquity a favourite vehicle of the soul in its ascent to the celestial sphere. The first example quoted shows that deification was early extended to other members of the Imperial family besides the Emperor. The doctrine soon affected the religious status of the living ruler also. Since he was *Divi filius* he was exalted spiritually above the rest of mankind. The most splendid of all antique cameos, the Grand Camée de France of the Cabinet des Médailles in Paris, shows us in pictorial form the ideas that attached as early as the time of Tiberius to the Emperor and the Imperial family (plate ix. 1).[50] Here in the centre is Tiberius, enthroned, wearing the aegis and other attributes of Jupiter, and though as *Triumphator* the Emperor had a traditional right to these insignia, yet the fixing of the Imperial image in art, with all the attributes of the chief deity of the State, must have gone far towards building up the con-

ception of a deified living ruler. Let me put this
rather more emphatically—my point is that as
Triumphator, the Emperor, like all generals to whom
triumph was accorded (see above, p. 64), was for the
time being the god, was in very truth Jupiter Optimus
Maximus, and that art contributes to give permanence and fixity to the otherwise ephemeral notion of a
deified prince. By the side of Tiberius sits his mother
Livia, represented as Ceres, with ears of corn and
poppy flowers, since the security brought about by
the Imperial victories encourages the divinities of
fertility and increase to put forth their powers ;
around the Imperial pair are grouped the younger
princes and princesses of their house. Such an image
as this central group seems conjured up by the description in ancient authors of the *Triumphator* surrounded during the pageant by his sons and other
members of his family, and even by friends of high
standing. In the upper zone appears the majestic
figure of Augustus, partly supported on a figure which
from its Phrygian costume must be one of the mythic
ancestors of the Julian race—Anchises or Iulus. On
the left is a deified prince, thought to be the elder
Drusus ; on the right, springing towards Augustus
on a magnificent winged steed, is another deified
prince, possibly Marcellus. The winged horse, like
the winged chariot on the Augustan altar in the
Vatican, is the vehicle of the soul's ascent,[51] and

belongs to the same cycle of ideas as the winged chariot in which the dead are rapt to the other world on archaic Greek and Etruscan monuments, a subject about which I shall have much to say in the next lecture. As we look at this wonderful pictorial allegory of Augustus and the deified princes of his house we are reminded of the lines :

> quos inter Augustus recumbens
> purpureo bibit ore nectar.
>
> Hor., *Od*. iii. 3, 12.[52]

May not indeed the Horatian verses have been directly inspired by some picture similar to the one before us ? The figures and groups both of the Vienna cameo and of the Grand Camée represent, I surmise, actual triumphal pictures or triumphal statuary groups taken from real life.

The cult of the living Emperor, of the *divi filius*, was the natural sequel to the deification of his predecessor. We already hear of divine honours being offered to Augustus, and, it is commonly alleged, refused by him. Like Caesar he may have feared lest the simple-minded Romans should look askance at any attempt on his part to invest himself with the religious attributes associated in their mind with the idea of an Oriental despot. In Rome, it is generally said, he was content to be worshipped in the guise of his own *Genius*, a conception beautifully expressed in the statue of the Vatican (Helbig, 304), though a

PLATE IX.

1. THE GRAND CAMÉE DE FRANCE.
2. COINS WITH APOTHEOSIS OF SABINA AND OF FAUSTINA.

host of statues show that he willingly allowed the images of the gods to bear his features.[53] At any rate Augustus soon represented himself as compelled to accept divine honours in the eastern provinces of the Empire, where he wisely recognised that the figure of the Roman military leader would not carry with it the necessary prestige unless invested with a supernatural character. But in order to soothe Roman susceptibilities he made it a condition that his cult should be associated with that of the goddess Roma, as in the lovely temple at Ancyra, erected to Roma and Augustus as early as 25 B.C. by the grateful Galatians, who had that year received autonomy from the Emperor. Other well-known instances of the double cult are the temples at Pergamon and at Nicomedia, while the great altars at Lugdunum and Tarraco show that the cult soon spread to the West.[54] Tiberius, a man of stiffer morality, perhaps, than Augustus, but with less imagination, declined, according to Tacitus (*Annals*, iv. 38), the divine honours offered him in Spain,[55] though the Grand Camée shows him as not averse to being represented with all the insignia of a god.

Augustus and Roma appear enthroned side by side on a magnificent cameo of the Imperial Library of Vienna (*R.R.*, ii. 144).[56] The cameo is specially important for our purpose, owing to its strongly centralised composition ; Roma and Augustus form a compact group, as the *Dea* looks round at her *paredros*, who, wearing the insignia of Jupiter as *Triumphator*, receives the crown of victory or of empire from a figure symbolising the *Oikoumene*, the inhabited earth. Below the throne is the Eagle, the bird of Jupiter, symbol at once of Empire and of Apotheosis ; between Roma and Augustus appears the natal sign of the Emperor, the constellation of Capricorn.[57] The other figures of the allegorical group on the right of Augustus are, besides the Oikoumene already mentioned, Neptune, the watery element well placed here with the figures of the inhabited world and of Terra Mater, the Nature Mother, who is seen reclining below holding the horn of plenty, and with children about her. In all these Roman monuments which commemorate victory and triumph we find incessant insistence on the fact that the fertility of the earth, encouraged and protected by the *Pax Augusta*, is the grand result of the Emperor's victorious campaigns. On the left is the young victorious prince himself alighting from his chariot ; and to make his identity doubly sure the natal constellation of Tiberius, the Scorpion, is depicted on the shield that hangs from the tree which Roman legionaries are setting up as a trophy of victory in the lower frieze. These two cameos, worthy to be placed in the Imperial collection, the *dactyliotheca* of which Pliny has left us an account, are almost certainly copies or adaptations of large pictures set up in temples or public buildings, where they would largely influence the popular conception of the Imperial power.

The spiritual atmosphere now beginning to envelop the Imperial person is everywhere manifest in the new prominence given to his image in art. On one of the cups from Boscoreale, in the Edmond de Rothschild collection in Paris, the attitude of Augustus is already made more emphatic than on the Ara Pacis.[58] On the one side Augustus receives the submission of conquered barbarians. The noble pose and gesture of the Emperor at once command attention. The tendency, already apparent on the Ara Pacis, of isolating the figure against a crowded background is worked up here to a higher effectiveness. A new pathetic quality, characteristic of Imperial art, is introduced, and that the central scene should be one of a father recommending his little child to the Imperial mercy inclines me to think that Vergil had some real picture in his mind when he wrote the celebrated

These be thine arts, thy glories, the way of peace to proclaim,
Mercy to show to the fallen, . . .

                    (Dryden's transl.)

On the other side we see Augustus surrounded by allegorical figures and divinities. In both scenes he is placed not in profile but in three-quarter view, in a first attempt to relate him not only to the attendant personages in the picture, but also to the spectator. Especially is this the case in the scene where the Emperor, enthroned in solitary majesty, is approached on the one side by figures allegorical of Empire, on the other by a group of the conquered provinces, who are brought into the Imperial presence by Mars ; the first instance, I believe, of his appearance in the direct service of the Princeps. The old Latin war-god was not merely killed, as has lately been said, by literary convention,[59] but, like the other gods, including Jupiter Optimus Maximus, his godhead paled and eventually disappeared before the rising *numen Augusti*. Not Vergil, nor any Augustan poet, but the Emperor himself, or, more correctly, the Imperial idea, is responsible for ' taking the life out of Jupiter, Mars and Apollo.' The gods had perforce to efface themselves before the Imperial power emanating from the Emperor, though the Emperor might for a time encourage their worship and reinstate their cults with a new splendour.

The Emperor's majestic pose on the Rothschild cup is in complete harmony with the spirit of the epoch which witnessed the birth of the Imperial cult and of the religion of Augustus and Roma. To a great extent these cults were evolved out of ideas familiar to the Orient from the period of Alexander the Great onwards ; yet the Emperor as you see him here is essentially a Western conception, and his image will retain this character even when in time, by the constant admixture of Oriental ideas, he himself can be described as more of an Oriental despot than of a military leader of the West.

(b) Influence of Augustan Art upon Popular Imagination

The compositions before us help us to grasp mankind's belief that the Emperor was the promised redeemer and saviour (σωτὴρ καὶ εὐεργέτης) who, according to the prophecies of the Sibyl, was to close the cycle of the ages and open a new era of salvation and peace, who was to bid the gates of war be shut, and the golden age of Saturn return.[60]

To students of the Augustan period, it is clear that Augustus called in the service of art to help his religious schemes to an extent as great, or even greater than that of poetry. The assistance he received from poetry has been fully recognised,[61] but art with its greater because more concrete influence is often dismissed as almost irrelevant to the question. English scholars especially have a tendency to underrate the rôle played in the formation of religious ideas by the visible form given to deities and abstractions.[62] Yet the works we have just considered—whether representing the actual deification, or merely showing the Emperor in the majestic pose which his exalted state demanded—seen in every public place, at every street corner, repeated, we may add, in miniature for the sideboard and the dining-table, must have gone far to fill the popular imagination with the Imperial idea. We are apt to forget that art in antiquity has the same didactic mission as in the Middle Ages before the invention of printing. Its function was largely utilitarian : one of its purposes was to impress upon the people a definite attitude towards religion or politics. For one man who had access to Vergil or Horace, thousands would see on their daily rounds the great monuments on which, to borrow Whistler's phrase, ' the nation had learnt to hew its history in marble.' The opening of the First Georgic, the Sixth Aeneid, the Imperial lyrics of Horace were possibly less potent factors in the establishment of the Empire than the pictures of the Imperial ' might, majesty and dominion,' of which cameos and coins and silver cups have preserved for us the copies ; the lovely composition of the young Tiberius, who descends with modest grace from the triumphal chariot to do homage to Roma and Imperator in the Vienna Cameo, or the group of the deified young heroes of the Grand Camée, would serve the same high purpose as the famous Horatian odes (Book iv. 4 and 14) which celebrate the military valour of the stepsons of Augustus. Poet and artist alike contrived to endear the Imperial dynasty to the people by fostering admiration for the prowess of individual princes. Not the Emperor alone but his house is exalted in these scenes as

> tutela praesens
> Italiae dominaeque Romae.

(c) Characteristics of Roman Art favourable to Expression of the Imperial Idea

Before resuming our examination of the monuments which commemorate the Emperor, I should like to point out that outside the official art of Hellenised Rome factors survived which were to gain in importance as suiting the growing Imperial idea. Beside the new Hellenic manner the intrusion or persistence of principles long rejected by classic art, such as frontality and the isolation of the figure, may be observed. Both principles make themselves distinctly felt in the stiff portraiture of Roman sepulchral monuments,[63] and seem to govern such temple decoration as survives. In pedimental composition the Greeks had often been content with a frieze-like arrangement of the figures, though the shape of the space demanded a dominant central figure ; but the Romans seem to have sought from the first to place a well-centralised group or a frontal figure beneath the apex of the triangle. This principle is already obvious in the terra-cotta decorations of the ancient Latin temples.[64] The pediments from the temple of Apollo at Civita Castellana (Faleri Veteres), to which belonged a fine torso of the god, must have been centralised in composition, to judge from the pose of the torso, which is turned nearly full to the front and moves, so to speak, out of its architectural setting (Helbig, 1784).[65] The same remark applies to the two pediments from Luni at Florence, where in the one a triad of divinities with Apollo in the centre is placed facing the spectator, while in the other, which represents the slaughter of the Niobids, the desire to get a frontal figure as central note is carried so far that a Niobid on horseback is shown riding straight out of the frame.[66] Even the curiously involved battle scene on the pediment from the temple of Telamon shows a tendency towards frontal composition. The same laws of design make themselves felt in the temple sculptures of Augustan Rome. The pediment of the temple of Mars Ultor, preserved on a monument of Julio-Claudian date walled into the Villa Medici, shows a god in the centre (*R.R.*, iii. 313, 1). The pediment of the temple of the Magna Mater from the same series has the black stone from Pessinus placed right in the centre of the pediment, with recumbent figures at either side (*R.R.*, iii. 313, 2),[67] while the pediment of the temple of Jupiter Optimus Maximus in the Capitol, though known to us only in an Antonine version, must always have exhibited a strongly centralised composition, with the emphatic accent laid upon the figure of Jupiter in the centre (*R.R.*, iii. 203).

The monotheistic element in Roman religion, so eloquently brought forward by Mr Warde Fowler in his latest book, seems to confront us in these compositions. As we look at them we reflect that had it not been for the stifling influences of Greek Olympianism the old Capitoline Jupiter, who came so near embodying a monotheistic religion, might have called forth a centralised art type to set beside the Imperial and the Christian *Maiestates*. As it was the Emperor and not Jupiter Optimus Maximus was responsible for bringing out the specifically Roman element in antique art.

We shall now see that the growing necessity for giving prominence to the figure of the deified Emperor brought back by degrees the old frontal method of composition, never, as we see, entirely discarded by Italic art, even at the period when Greek influence was at its height.

(d) *Principles of Roman Design in the Service of the Imperial Idea*

On a series of five reliefs, once allotted to the Ara Pacis and now thought to belong to an altar erected by a Julio-Claudian Emperor, perhaps Claudius himself, we have a processional scene and sacrificial episode in the style of the Ara Pacis, but the figure of the Emperor or leading Imperial personage is emphatically distinguished by its pose from his escort.

On the Ara Pacis all the figures, not excepting the one now usually identified as Augustus,[68] are either placed in profile or else, as in the case of the so-called Livia or Julia, though the body is given a frontal pose, the profile idea is suggested or recaptured by the turn of the head or the glance of the eye. On the later slab of Julio-Claudian date the Princeps is placed in an attitude which is almost frontal, the outward direction of which is emphasised by the searching outward gaze (*R.R.*, i. 235, 2).

On a charming altar to Augustus and the Lares in the Uffizi, we see Augustus, flanked by Livia and one of his grandsons, in a pose so far tending to the frontal as to suggest that the Imperial figure is already presented to the homage both of the personages at either side of him and of the spectator (*R.R.*, iii. 32).[69] Augustus, who is represented as officiating augur, clad in sacerdotal vestments, with the curved augural rod in his right hand, the patera in his left, and at his feet a bird picking at the sacred grain, is here in the service of the gods; but the isolation of the figure and its self-involved character, combined with the monolatric element contributed by the two attendant personages, impart to the composition the same grave dignity that we shall discover at a much later date in the group of Septimius Servius and Iulia Domna sacrificing.

The great storied column found on the site of the

ancient Celtic Moguntiacum, and now in the Museum
at Mayence (*R.R.*, i. 186, 187), shows even more
directly than any monument of Rome or Italy the
force of the religious beliefs that were beginning to
centre about the person of the Emperor by the middle
of the first century. It was dedicated about 66 A.D.
to Jupiter Optimus Maximus, for the safety of the
Emperor Nero. I have recently offered a new interpretation of certain of the figures of this column and
of its general intention, which was the glorification
of the Empire as represented by the Emperor ; and
it is unnecessary to resume the subject here.[70] I will
only draw your attention to the position occupied by
the Emperor on the top drum but one, immediately
below the protecting figure of Juno Coelestis, who, in
her character of Queen of the Sky, is flanked by the
chariots of the Sun and Moon to show that the *Orbis
Romanus* is conterminous with the world. The
Emperor attended by the Imperial Lares stands in
simple frontal attitude, offering libation at an altar ;
his escort is formed by the ancient gods of Latium
and the allegorical figures of the Empire, who look
down at the sacrifice accomplished in their honour
at the altar in front of the column. The Emperor
is shown sacrificing to the gods, and is therefore not
as yet of their number ; but his emphatic position,
in line with Pax, Tellus and Victory, and surrounded
by ancient Latin divinities of fertility and increase

F

marks him as dispenser of the blessings of peace.[71]
Nero—the Emperor—is represented here, in accordance with the legend on one of his coins, as
σωτὴρ τῆς οἰκουμένης—Saviour of Mankind [72]—and the
Empire as the source whence flow the blessings which
he guards and dispenses. The column is dedicated
to Jupiter, Best and Highest, the builder-up of the
Roman Empire, protector and arbiter of the destinies of the Roman world (see below, p. 85). But
even the *numen* of Jupiter had in time to make way
for the *numen* of the Augustus. On the column of
Mayence we look at the prologue, so to speak, of a
great drama, the last scene of which is carved on the
attic of the front face of the arch of Trajan at Benevento, where the gods abdicate in favour of the
Emperor, to whom the old Jupiter of the Capitol
hands over the thunderbolt as time-honoured symbol
of his power (p. 85). Similarly, on the columns
which symbolised in the provinces the might of
Rome, a group representing the *numen Augusti*
trampling over the foes of the Empire supplanted in
time the statue of Jupiter Optimus Maximus.

Subjects akin in spirit to the reliefs of the column
of Mayence are very frequent at this period. I may
recall to you the beautiful silver dish from Aquileia
at Vienna (*R.R.*, ii. 146, 1), showing an Emperor
(Claudius ?) sacrificing ; Terra Mater reclines below
him ; above is Jupiter, and all around are divinities

of fertility and increase. The evidence of the monuments goes far to show that the Augustan age which
saw the gradual degradation of the divinities of the
old Graeco-Roman Pantheon first definitely sought for
some visible expression of the monotheistic principle
which is at the root of the highest religions as of the
greatest art. The central formula by which Roman
art gradually sought to isolate the Emperor viewed
almost as a monotheistic source of life and prosperity,
acquired in time so exalted a character that it could
afterwards clothe the God-man of Christianity.

VIII. Centralisation of Design from the Flavians
      to the Close of the Dynasty of the Severi

The reliefs of the arch of Titus, which date from
the latter end of the first century A.D., partake of
two distinct methods. The famous procession on
the panels of the archway reproduces a scheme
familiar to Greek art, but with the same emphasis
laid on the figure of the Emperor in the chariot that
we have already noticed in the figure of Augustus on
the cup from Boscoreale. The chariot with the
Imperial group is placed somewhere between a three-
quarter and a full view, and moves at a different
angle from the horses and from the rest of the procession (R.R., i. 274). Wickhoff, who first drew
attention to the artistic value of these reliefs, saw in
the position of the chariot a mere miscalculation of

perspective ; I believe that we are here in presence of
an attempt to emphásise the Imperial personage by
bringing him full to the front. The relief on the
keystone of the vault, with the apotheosis of Titus,
leaves no doubt as to the artistic intention : here
the Emperor is no longer shown in profile, but is
twisted round somewhat uncomfortably on the eagle
that bears him upward to the heavenly spheres so
that both may be presented in full frontal aspect
(R.R., i. 276, 1).

As a proof of the strength and vitality of the more
purely Greek tradition, I should like to show you
immediately after these massive compositions from
the arch of Titus, a relief, likewise of the Flavian
period, which is in the Louvre ; it represents the procession of the Suovetaurilia—of the sacred pig, bull
and ram—led by a personage who has lately been
recognised as Domitian.[73] The sustained rhythm,
the evenly balanced composition and the studied
avoidance of over-emphasis at any point are obvious
Greek traits.   Technically the work has considerable
merits : the relief is pleasing ; the modelling clear ;
the feeling for the tactile qualities of surface true.
The two laurel trees, which by the way are possibly
those that stood on each side of the Domus Augustana
on the Palatine, betray a close observation of nature
in the rendering of the shimmering leaves, of their
stiff texture, and crinkled edges.   For all its quiet

beauty this type of composition was doomed, though it died slowly and now and again flared up in a work of real inspiration.

The whole interest of Roman sculpture or of sculpture in Rome, whichever way you may prefer to put it, now gathers increasingly about the deeds of the Roman people and the person of the Roman Emperor. We have only to think of the emphatic reiteration of the Imperial figure on the reliefs of the Trajan Column and of the Trajanic battle scenes removed to the arch of Constantine (*R.R.*, i. 252, 253). It is, however, at Benevento, on the arch erected in 115 to glorify Trajan's home and foreign policy, that we become definitely aware of certain changes of political temper and religious thought which were to invest representations of the Emperor with a predominating majesty. In each of the twelve episodes represented on the arch the main stress is always on the figure of Trajan ; concentration, not diffusion of interest, is the order of the day. On the reliefs of the attic the great Olympians receive Trajan, and the old Jupiter of the Capitol, with his *paredroi* Juno and Minerva on either side of him, hands over to Trajan the thunderbolt, no longer to be the ephemeral attribute of the *Triumphator*, but to hold as his own.[74] An eminent scholar has pointed out that Jupiter marks by his act the intrusion of a new material and spiritual order into the Empire.[75] Let us dwell for a

moment longer on the extraordinary significance
of the scene. Mr. Warde-Fowler has recently ex-
pounded afresh the meaning of the great Roman
Jupiter, the *numen praestantissimae mentis* of Cicero
' protecting and controlling the destinies of the
Roman world '—the god who rose above the Graeco-
Roman Pantheon to an exalted position comparable
to that accorded to the god of monotheistic peoples.

This deity was not for small things and small people
but for great ones ; there is a breadth and range about
his action which exceeds that of any Graeco-Roman god,
for he is indeed the reflection of the greatness of his
people, the religious interpretation of their amazing
strength.—*Roman Ideas of Deity*, p. 53.

Yet the great Jupiter, with something about him
of the Hebrew Jehovah, ruler, as Horace says (*Odes*,
i. 12, 17), of heaven and earth

> unde nil maius generatur ipso
> nec viget quidquam simile aut secundum,

had to yield before the *numen Augusti*. The reliefs of
the Benevento arch, like the allegorical group of the
Numen trampling over the foes of the Empire, symbolised as a giant or other monster, which supplants
the image of Jupiter on the later ' Jupiter and Giant
columns,' tell us in the direct and lucid language
of art of the god's abdication before the Emperor.
But the capitulation of Jupiter entailed that of all
the Olympians whom the old god brings in his

PLATE **X.**

THE ABDICATION OF JUPITER.
Benevento.

train, though he had never shown himself quite
capable of overruling them.   The influence on design
was immediate.   The Pantheon of gods, each claiming his place in the scheme of representation, so long
the leading theme of sculpture, definitely vanishes from
the scene, and from henceforth a single figure bestows
on plastic composition a clear and dominant motive.

For these Beneventan scenes Oriental influences
might also be claimed ; something of the same idea
inspired the sculptor of those strange slabs that so
impressively crown the Nemrud Dagh between
Samosata and the Euphrates, and mark the sepulchre
of Antiochus I. of Commagene (*R.R.*, i. 193-6).   The
ruler and his ancestors are each grouped with a god :
in one instance the Oriental despot grasps the hand
of Zeus ; on another that of Heracles ; while a third
relief shows Antiochus and Apollo-Mithras standing
face to face on terms of equality (*R.R.*, i. 195, 2, 3, 4).
It is the dawn of the idea, the fulfilment of which we
see on the Benevento arch.   On the Syrian monument, erected about 40 B.C., the gods consent to admit
the monarch to equality with themselves ; on the
Roman monument, some hundred and fifty years
later, they yield their place to him as their successor
before they vanish for ever from the scene (plate x.).

So true is it that the hybrid character which makes
much Roman art distasteful comes from the attempt
to ' adapt its indigenous inheritance of ideas to the

different conception of the civilisation which came
from Greece,' that we are not sorry to see the Graeco-
Roman gods become subordinate and disappear.   And
Della Seta, from whom I quote, goes on to say
appositely :

Hence the peculiar characteristics of its literature and
its art, hence the diversity of its constituting elements,
a literature and an art non-original when they present
Greek myths, but original in form and content when they
give life to Roman ideas.—*Religion and Art*, p. 290.

It is doubtful whether Greece the perennial en-
chantress has not wrought as much harm as good
upon those who fall under her spell.

IX. THE PRINCIPATE OF HADRIAN TO THE SEVERI

From the Principate of Hadrian and of Marcus
Aurelius respectively we have two important reliefs
representing the Imperial Apotheosis.   The first is a
panel in the Museum of the Capitol with the Apotheosis of the Empress Sabina in presence of the Emperor,
Hadrian.   The *Diva* is borne in her ascension by a
winged female genius personifying *Aeternitas*, holding
in her hand the flaming torch that kindled the fire,
or else, as seems to me more likely, introduced here
as symbol of the eternal light (*R.R.*, i. 375, 2=Helbig,
990).[76]   The character of the composition, however,
is historic rather than religious, the interest is focused
on the ceremony of the deification and not as yet on

the deified personage. The second, the principal relief of the basis of the column of Antoninus and Faustina, now in the Vatican (*R.R.*, i. 291, 1=Helbig, 123),[77] offers the most grandiose representation of the Imperial Apotheosis so far known. On the right side appears Roma—note the shifting of the interest from the goddess to the *divi*. She is now spectator, and they protagonists. In order further to localise the scene, the Campus Martius in person, holding his own obelisk on his knees, reclines on the left. Above them the Imperial pair, deified as Jupiter and Juno, are borne to heaven on the soaring wings of the Aion or Spirit of Eternity,[78] who here, like *Aeternitas* on the former relief, usurps the function of the eagle as vehicle of the Imperial transit, though an eagle with outspread wings appears on either side to guard the Imperial ascension. The composition as a whole is not as yet entirely unified round a central theme. The Emperor and Empress turn towards one another, but even so the pose tends to be more frontal and rigid than on earlier monuments, so that a more direct relation is established between the deified pair and the spectator. You will, I think, appreciate this point if you turn back for a moment to the *Augustus recumbens* of the Grand Camée de France.

The sculpture of the period of the Antonines shows an increasingly strong centralisation. On a slab of the Aurelian column, for instance,[79] we find a com-

position which might at first sight pass for a New
Testament scene by a mediaeval artist, the more so
that the Emperor raises his right hand in a gesture
afterwards borrowed for that of Christian benediction.
The highly centralised design flows from the group
of Marcus between two officers. They are standing
on an eminence or platform in the middle of a circular
camp, the walls of which frame and isolate the Imperial group. Through a gate in the foreground a
scout rushes into the camp to warn Marcus of approaching danger. Who, looking without prejudice
at this noble central group, resembling Christ between
two apostles in a fresco by Duccio, can fail to recognise that new beliefs have invested art with a serious
emotion unknown to earlier periods, which marks
off this relief from the many weak contemporary
imitations of Greek models ?

But the Greek manner was by no means dead. It,
too, could receive fresh life by being brought into the
service of the Emperor. We have an example of its
superb vitality in the reliefs found in recent years
in the Roman Library at Ephesus, and now at Vienna
(*R.R.*, i. 142-5), which represent the Apotheosis of
Marcus Aurelius, and are well worth studying as a
Greek rendering of the theme. The scene spreads over
two slabs. On the first, Selene, the moon, appears
in her stag-drawn chariot accompanied by the evening star and heralded by the figure of Night, and drives

PLATE XI.

APOTHEOSIS OF MARCUS AURELIUS.
Vienna (from Ephesus).

into the stream of Ocean, typified by a youth holding a rudder. On the second (plate xi.), the chariot of the Sun springs heavenward over the familiar figure of Terra Mater, who reclines with the children at her side. The composition is purely Greek, and moves swiftly and equably from end to end without any tendency to centralisation. But the new religious beliefs attaching to the Emperor pervade the scene. He who rides in the solar chariot is not Sol Sanctissimus but the Imperator, and Sol acting as groom guides his own steeds in their course to the starry spheres.[80] Like Jupiter Optimus Maximus on the arch of Benevento, the Sun has capitulated to the Divus Augustus, and passed into his service. Ideas are moving swiftly, and we have already got beyond the conception of the Apotheosis revealed on a papyrus at Giessen,[81] where Apollo announces that after taking Trajan up to Heaven in his chariot, he now reappears to present Hadrian to the world as Trajan's successor. But now the fiery chariot is vacated by its own master and filled with the radiancy of the new Monarch God. Somehow this visible subordination of the Sun to the Emperor, at a period when the solar cult was invading the Empire, is more striking even than that of Jupiter. That the Imperial idea should prove stronger than the moribund cults of Graeco-Roman paganism was natural, but that it should resist and dominate, as on these reliefs, the victorious march of the Oriental creeds is a proof of strength, the effects of which we shall again have occasion to observe.

The portrait reliefs of the Imperial family on the little Gate of the Silversmiths in the Velabrum, from the principate of Septimius Severus (193-211), show the new manner of presenting the Imperial personages which was becoming current in Rome (*R.R.*, i. 271-2). Emperor and Empress no longer turn towards one another as on the Antonine basis, here Septimius and Julia Domna look straight out of the frame. Placed side by side, almost like husband and wife in Egyptian art, they seem unaware of each other's presence, and are thereby brought into direct relation to the spectator. It must not be supposed, however, that this new method of treatment at once took the place of the old. In a little known relief of the Palazzo Sacchetti, which has been interpreted as the presentation of Caracalla to the Senate in 197, we see a curious combination of the old methods with the new (*R.R.*, iii. 319, 1). Septimius Severus, accompanied by his two sons, Caracalla and Geta, and attended by two of the great officers of State, receives a deputation of senators. The processional scheme is still Greek, but the massive group of the Emperor and his companions has the monumental quality of a fresco by Masaccio and superbly expresses the religious majesty with which the Emperor was by now invested.

The period between Septimius Severus and Diocletian is comparatively barren of great sculptured compositions, owing, doubtless, to political unrest, to the frequent changes of emperors and the depression caused by repeated military failures. Nor did religion just then prove a stimulating factor. The great Oriental religions which were predominant in Rome during this period found little expression in art, partly because of their aniconic principle, partly also because artistic effort had been exhausted in creating the type of the Emperor. A notable exception occurs, however, in a relief in the Forum relating to the cult of the black stone of Emesa, which throws a curious light on what has already been said of the effacement of Jupiter. On the arch of Benevento we saw the Capitoline Jupiter despoil himself of his insignia in favour of the Emperor ; soon his *paredroi* Juno and Minerva desert the old god who from the Capitoline heights had so long protected Rome, and on the relief in question we actually see them guarding the recently imported black stone *Elagabal* brought from Syria by the young Emperor Varius Avitus Bassianus, better known to history under the name which he took from the object of his devotion.[82] The composition is a good instance of the monolatric scheme of design which so often corresponds to the monotheistic idea in religion.

X. The Period of Diocletian and Constantine.
The Christ gradually usurps the place
of the Emperor as the Central Theme of
Design

We are once more struck by the powerlessness of the
new Oriental cults to mould or inspire new or striking
art schemes by a carved basis of the period of Diocletian that lies in the Roman Forum not far from
the arch of Septimius Severus. It was one of a pair,
which once stood on either side of the Curia or Senate
House, and supported columns that respectively bore
portrait statues of the two *Augusti*, Diocletian and
Maxentius, and the two *Caesares*, Constantine and
Galerius, each pair grouped perhaps somewhat after
the fashion of the celebrated porphyry 'Tetrarchy'
on St. Mark's at Venice. The columns were presumably set up in the year 303, to commemorate, as
the inscription tells us, the anniversaries of the accession of Diocletian and his colleagues.[83] One of the
bases has now disappeared. The second, in honour
of the Caesars, is now well-known. It was first published by Riegl, who was interested in the technique
and the curious ' black and white ' effect of the relief.
The subject represented has lately been acutely recognised by Professor Frothingham—to whom the debt
of all students of Rome and Roman art increases
daily—as a sacrifice performed by Diocletian in

honour of Mithras who had been recently proclaimed supreme god of the Empire. But see how little even the emotion of a new cult could do for art at this time. On the sides, priests and officials are deployed in profile according to the time-honoured Hellenic method, excepting that the movements are becoming crystallised ; on the front face the Emperor, who pours a libation at an altar, is surrounded by various high officials and faces Mars, no longer the proud god who stood in domineering fashion with one foot on the step of the altar receiving a sacrifice in his own honour, on the basis of Ahenobarbus, but a Mars degraded to the position of a mere spectator. For the sacrifice is no longer to do honour to one of the old Latin or Greek gods. On the right sits the goddess Roma, and within the arch of her veil as within his own cave nestles the bust of the new god who wears the rayed solar nimbus. But instead of facing towards him, as we might expect, all the principal personages turn their back upon Mithras—and no clumsier arrangement could have been devised for his introduction into the scene than this of thrusting his bust into the angle above the right shoulder of the goddess ; it is a direct and naïve way of expressing the fact that Mithras is now the chief divinity of the Empire, and therefore under the direct protection of the State personified by Roma, but there the merits of the design begin and end. We know, now that

Mr. Frothingham has told us so, that the sacrifice is for Mithras, but there is nothing in the composition to indicate it.   In fact, this Diocletianic basis is an interesting instance of the failure of the new religious conceptions to manifest themselves by means of the old traditional forms.   It is true that the actual scene of the Mithraic sacrifice of the bull was still finding grandiose expression in certain of the Mithraic altar-pieces, but the type had been created as far back as in the Pergamene school;[84] moreover it was a scene, an episode depicted by the means of narrative art. To my mind, the solar cults, whether of Mithras or of Sol Sanctissimus himself, failed to impress upon art a new religious type because, as I have already indicated, the creative effort was absorbed in giving expression to the Imperial figure and his acts.   When we revert, in fact, to scenes where the Emperor is the centre of interest, we are at once aware of a keener grasp of the situations to be depicted, and a consequent greater fulness of inspiration.   Conflicting schemes of decoration long subsisted side by side, though narrative art was gradually subordinated to central motives of design.

The scene on a lead medallion of the Cabinet des Médailles, dating from the Principate of Diocletian, shows how matters stood at the beginning of the fourth century.[85]   The images of the two Emperors, Diocletian and his colleague, who, with their solar nimbi, resemble two enthroned apostles rather than any figures familiar from the antique, are seated facing the spectator ; but their heads are turned towards the advancing procession of captives, and by this movement the Emperors are drawn, as on a Greek frieze, within the action of the scene represented. I cannot refrain from describing somewhat more at length the interesting scenes of the medallion. The landscape on the lower half, treated very much as on early illuminated manuscripts, indicates the locality. The scene is laid at Mayence, the old Celtic Moguntiacum ; on the left is the splendid old camp city with her great fortifications, and over the gate is inscribed the city's name ; the gate leads to the famous bridge over the Rhine (inscribed *Fl. Rhenus*) and reaches at the other end the gate of another fortified city, the Castellum, the memory of which survives in the modern Kastell ; across the bridge three Roman Victories escort a tiny captive ; in the background of Mayence rise the hills of the Taunus, whose wooded slopes are somewhat sparsely indicated by a single tree. On the upper tier the captives are brought into the Imperial presence, as on the Boscoreale cup, by the dethroned Latin Mars ; at the foot of the Emperor kneels the conquered province ; on the right is a group of a father with his children. All these are traditional motives long familiar, but a comparison with the designs of the

G

Boscoreale cup or with the groups on the arch of Benevento, shows that the Imperial figure was now invested with a hieratic dignity which tends to isolate it from the other personages of the scene, while these, on the other hand, are brought by the lines of the design into the direct service of the Imperial figure. It is the reappearance of the monolatric principle.

With Diocletian we have got back to the period of the friezes of the arch of Constantine, which I took as the text of this lecture. If we now look at these in detail we shall find more in them than mere material centralisation. The gestures of the officials have been compared to those of the Elders who in early mosaics stand in monotonous rows and cast down their crowns with the same fixed movements before the Lamb of God.[86] The comparison meant to be disparaging is, in fact, admirably accurate ; in the one case as in the other this monotony arises from the deliberate attempt on the part of the artist to avoid any movement or gesture that could distract attention from the central Personage, and in our friezes the very identity of the gestures of the attendants emphasises the importance of the Emperor, and restores to art that monolatric value which had almost disappeared under the influence of the Greek spirit. It is instructive to compare these friezes with the reliefs executed two centuries earlier or more, which adorn the two famous balustrades in the Forum known as the *Anaglypha Traiani*. They date from the period of Trajan or, as I believe, from that of Domitian, and represent various Imperial bene-factions.[87] You at once perceive the different aesthetic effect produced by the one and by the other. On the earlier relief the various scenes are displayed according to the Greek manner with equal distribution of interest ; on the later every detail is so massed and marshalled as to heighten the importance of the central figure.

From the resemblance of these Diocletianic friezes to those on the arch of Galerius at Saloniki, which was put up to commemorate the same Persian vic-tories, it seems probable that Graeco-Oriental models were powerful factors in fixing these centralised types of composition ;[88] but here or there the inspir-ing ideas emanate from the *Imperator* and his *res gestae*.

It is surprising that Riegl, who so clearly understood the significance of the technical and optical laws observed in these reliefs, should barely comment on this new and perfected centralisation ; especially as he had recognised the same phenomena in the archi-tecture of the period. In the course of time archi-tecture had passed from the Hellenic stage, with its feeling for the harmony of outward proportion, to the Imperial phase, with its feeling for the harmonies of internal spaces.[89]   Even as pagan architecture had, in the normal course of its development, evolved forms which, under the stimulus of new Christian ideas, were to enter upon a new phase of life, so sculpture had been transformed into a scheme that could be naturally adapted to the monotheistic beliefs of the religion now triumphing over the Empire. I have already pointed out that Greek religious art had no place for a single figure of supreme interest, claiming to subordinate to itself all the details of the composition. Had Christianity, with much of the old Judaic horror of images clinging to its monotheism, come into direct contact with Greek anthropomorphism, the shock would have been even more violent than it was, and the victory of Christianity might have brought with it the total extinction of the formative arts, or at least of those which represent the human figure. As it was, the Imperial idea smoothed over the transition ; the place was ready and by an almost unconscious change we find the Christ enthroned or standing in the place of the Imperator. On a beautiful sarcophagus at Verona, the noble figures and harmonious composition are arranged according to the same principle of design as the Diocletianic ' Proclamation,' save that the Imperial platform is transformed into the rock whence flow the four rivers of Paradise.[90]   The *Gegenkaiser* conquered and ousted from its throne the central figure of the Imperial cult against which the Christians had waged so fierce a war, and the legend *Christus imperat* imposed itself upon art as forcibly as elsewhere.

I do not suggest for one moment that the art-type of the Christ is derived from that of the Emperor. The evolution I am dwelling on is of place alone, of position, that is, within a decorative scheme.[91] Here again the change was gradual ; the Emperor himself yields his place only by slow degrees, and we can watch the process of his gradual effacement through many centuries. In the grand Barberini ivory with the bust of the young Christ in the frieze above the middle panel, rightly claimed, I think, for the period of Constantine, the Emperor appears in a new scheme. I have been derided for holding up this ivory to admiration in my book on Roman Sculpture,[92] and no doubt our aesthetic sense, trained to the irreproachable contours of Hellenic art, is vexed by the constrained and difficult attitude of the horseman ; yet we are in the presence of a gallant effort to express a new ideal. The world has done with the splendidly silhouetted horsemen of the Parthenon, with conceptions like that embodied in the graceful stele of Dexileos in the Athenian Ceramicus ; the aim of art is now to restore communion between the worshipper and the worshipped, between God and the suppliant —to show the Emperor subordinate to the Christ, but to bring both into direct relation to the spectator by means of the frontal position.

A curious panel in the Kaiser Friedrich Museum at Berlin exhibits on one side of the group Our Lord between the apostles Peter and Paul ; on the other Our Lady crowning the young Emperor Leo VI. (A.D. 886).[93] The latter scene shows how the Imperial figure in its subordinate position long held its own by the side of the God of the new religion and his saints. The beautiful design on the leaf of a diptych in the Cabinet des Médailles (plate xii., 2) represents the central figure of Christian art standing on a high platform between a Byzantine Emperor and Empress of the eleventh century, upon whose head he lays protecting hands.[94] Romanus (1068-71) is a Byzantine Emperor, but his name and the epithet *Basileus Romaion* show how proudly the old connection with the Western Empire was cherished ; his consort, on the other hand, bears the beautiful Greek name of Eudocia, so that they appear almost symbolic of the forces of East and West swept by now into the service of the new religion. The Imperial figures will soon vanish altogether, though the scheme of the protecting figure and the dependent rulers will in time be transformed in the service of new ideas, and become the donors and protecting powers familiar in pictures of the Renaissance.

PLATE XII.

2. The Christ between Romanus and Eudocia.
Paris.

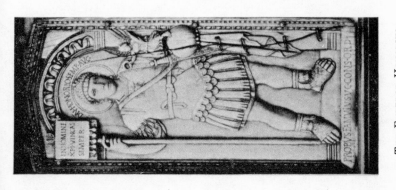

1. The Emperor Honorius.
Aosta.

XI. From Constantine to Justinian. Persistence of Imperial Figure as the Central
Motive of Design. Summary

With the introduction of Christian subjects a new
era had succeeded to the Antique. Art now gradually passes, as we have seen, from the service of the
Emperor and of the *res gestae* into that of the Christ
and of Christian subjects. But by the side of these
new themes the Imperial figure, in the frontal scheme
won for it by the doctrine of the Imperial Deification, long retained its independence, and we must
follow its fortunes to the end.

It is on a monument once more wholly dedicated
to the glorification of the Emperor—the superb gold
medallion of Valentinian I. and his brother Valens
(plate xiii., 1)—that the frontal presentment finds
what seems its most perfect form in Roman Imperial
art.[95] Were it not for the portrait of Valentinian on
the obverse with the inscription Gloria Romanorum,
we might mistake the two majestic figures with the
nimbus and the orb and raised right hand for the
Peter and Paul of a pontifical seal. It is Valentinian
(364-75) again whom we see on the beautiful silver disc
preserved at Geneva (plate xiii., 2=*R.R.*, iii. 524, 2),
with the Emperor standing in a central and frontal
position haranguing his troops.[96] The large solar
aureole that encircles his head and the *labarum* in

his left hand bring the Imperial figure very near to that of the Risen Christ in many works of the Middle Ages and the Renaissance. I shall violate chronology in order to place before you here the fine ivory diptych of Aosta, which shows the Emperor Honorius repeated on each leaf, in a pose very similar to that of the Valentinian on the Geneva disc. This, the earliest consular diptych known, dates from the year 406 (plate xii., 1).[97]

The basis of Theodosius on the Atmeidan at Constantinople shows frontal composition adopted for practically all the personages involved in the principal scenes.[98] On all four sides the Emperor, his family and court, are shown *en face* within the Imperial tribune, while the lower spaces are occupied either by performances of dancers and musicians arranged in animated groups, or else by groups of barbarians bringing offerings (*R.R.*, i. 112-13). The composition of the main groups betrays the weak side of this later Imperial art. The artist by placing all the personages in a full-face position tends to cancel the significance of the frontal figure in the centre, which on the Diocletianic *congiarium*, for instance, was heightened by the monolatric principle of the attendant groups. Della Seta, arguing from his own point of view, puts the matter somewhat differently, and draws attention to the deteriorating quality of the design :

PLATE XIII.

1. VALENS AND VALENTINIAN. Vienna.
2. VALENTINIAN WITH HIS TROOPS. Geneva.

The path of decadence is shown . . . in the reliefs of
the base of the column of Theodosius at Constantinople.
In these last reliefs the action has completely disappeared
and the figures are only present in the scene. They are
of course presented completely facing the spectator, so
that in the scene a sort of inertia and immobility is
established.—*Religion and Art*, p. 279.

On the other hand, the frontal composition of Theodosius and his two sons, shown enthroned like a triad
of gods on the grandiose silver disc at Madrid (*R.R.*,
ii. 195, 1), is superbly effective (plate xiv., 1).[99] Let
us analyse it somewhat in detail. Under an arcuated
pediment Theodosius appears in a purely frontal pose ;
he wears the diadem and his head is illumined by the
solar aureole ; he is flanked by his sons Honorius and
Arcadius, who sit, holding orb and sceptre ; in the
spaces between the columns, to either side the Imperial guards stand on duty with their long spears
and huge shields ; while immediately to the left of
the Emperor, a court prefect, whose inferior rank is
denoted by his small size, advances to do homage.
Classic tradition still triumphs in the subordinate
parts of the design. Within each angle of the pediment flits a love-god, and in the exergue the old
classic Terra Mater, turreted like Cybele the Great
Mother and holding a large cornucopiae, reclines amid
the flowers and plants, while children play around
her or bring her offerings of fruit. She represents

once more the power of the Imperial bounty to bestow the gifts of peace and fruitfulness and wealth upon the earth and her inhabitants. The idea is the same as that which inspired the Augustan cameos or the silver disc of Aquileia ; but while in the earlier scene the Emperor appears as Mediator, so to speak, between Heaven and Earth, the very scheme which now clothes the Imperial Majesty announces that its power is equal to that of the gods whom it has supplanted. The idea of the Imperial beneficence is borne out by the design. By the prominent position given to the Emperor under the arcuated pediment which enframes his head, so to speak, like a second aureole, he dominates the whole scene, for though his sons—partners of their father's majesty—claim homage as Imperial personages, their frontal pose, owing to their subordinate place and lesser stature, in no way detracts from the significance of the central figure. The guards likewise, by their close grouping and by the slight inward turn of the heads, introduce the monolatric quality which enhances the spectator's interest in the central part of the design. Then observe how the solemn stillness of the Imperial figure, removed like the Christ of Chartres (plate iv.) from conditions of time and space, is further enhanced by the somewhat fussy action of the little court prefect as he advances from the left with some petition which leaves the Imperial personage undis-

PLATE XIV.

1. AN IMPERIAL TRIAD. THEODOSIUS AND HIS SONS.
Silver Disc in Madrid.
2. THE MARRIAGE OF DAVID. Nicosia.

turbed. The Madrid disc, like the medal of Valens
and Valentinian, shows Roman art—the art inspired
by the Imperial idea—at a level which it is generally
supposed was only reached by Christian compositions.

A proof of the rapid interchange of ideas that took
place at this time between pagan and Christian art
is afforded by the subjects from the life of David,
embossed on a series of nine silver plates from near
Kyrenia in Cyprus, and partly distributed between
the Pierpont Morgan collection in New York and the
Museum of Nicosia.   In three of these the background
is formed by an arcuated construction similar to that
in the disc of Theodosius, though with the omission
of the line of the gable ; moreover in the ' David
before Saul,' Saul sits enthroned like Theodosius ;
while the composition of the Marriage of David has
been well compared by Mr. Dalton to that of a coin
of Theodosius II., showing this Emperor between
Valentinian III. and Eudocia (plate xiv., 2).[100]

Under the double influence of the Christ and the
Emperor a central composition was becoming the rule.
A striking example is afforded by the group of the
consular chariot on the splendid *opus sectile* at Rome
from the Basilica of Junius Bassus, now in the Palazzo
del Drago.[101] The scheme of the frontal chariot may
be traced through art till it becomes the beautiful
composition of the Ascension of Alexander in his
griffin-drawn car on a relief of the exterior of St. Mark's

at Venice.[102] It is worth comparing with the kindred compositions of the chariot Nyx-Selene on an Attic cup and of the chariot of Helios on the phalera from Elis which we considered earlier in this lecture (p. 38). The design of the Alexander is really the same in spirit and aim as that of the Helios. Just as the Helios, in virtue of his apotropaic function, is placed frontally in the design, so, too, Alexander, because he is represented as deified, is given the fully frontal pose which brings him into direct relation to the spectator; and in each case horses or griffins are arranged to each side in a scheme which not only does not detract interest from the central figure, but actually tends to enhance its importance by imparting to the design a monolatric value. But there is this difference, that what in Greek art from the fifth century B.C. onwards, only made a sporadic appearance with a special purpose in view has now come definitely to the surface and become the rule, while the narrative scheme and self-involved design of the Selene are now the exception, or only survive as traditional motives of decoration.

Another monument of the silversmith's art must close what I have to say about the Emperor as central figure in design. The group engraved on the grand shield or disc found in a tomb in 1891 at Kertsch in the Crimea, and preserved in the Hermitage at Petrograd, shows an emperor of the sixth century—

almost certainly the great Justinian—in the scheme known as the *Adventus Augusti*, the Advent of the victorious Emperor.[103] The Emperor, in splendid panoply,[104] is riding to the right, preceded by Victory holding palm and wreath, and followed by an officer of his bodyguard who carries the great round shield with the monogram of Christ. The movement is deployed in profile, as on a Greek frieze, but see how the Emperor's head and shoulders are turned full to the front towards the spectator, while the figures on either side turn towards him and are interrelated within the composition. There could be no finer example than this exquisite composition of the weaving of two opposite methods into a new and distinguished art scheme (plate i., 1). The artist brings before us an episode, the *adventus*, and yet so contrives to emphasise the Emperor, by giving a frontal turn to his head and bust that Justinian at once draws to himself the attention and homage of the spectator. With this superb conception before us of the great Emperor who is responsible for the *Codex Juris Civilis*, and the Church of the Holy Wisdom, we may pause for one moment to sum up the debt of the antique to the Imperial figure.

In the period of Constantine we saw the antique accomplish under its influence the last stage of a slow artistic evolution. The Imperial figure, by claiming for itself the chief place in design, had imposed upon

art a frontal principle of centralised composition,
which, though not unfamiliar to preceding periods,
was not an integral factor of their decorative schemes.
Centralisation is thus the last gift of the declining
antique to the art that was to take its place, and it is
the peculiar gift of Rome. Only with the prestige
bestowed by Rome upon the central figure could a
mere decorative scheme become imbued with meaning and emotion and take irrevocable hold upon
mankind as that best suited to clothe the Imperial
power, which after unifying the whole civilised world,
had given to it long centuries of peace and prosperity.
We have seen how the Olympian Pantheon checked
the development of a great religious art in Greece.
The same Pantheon when brought over to Rome
effectively stifled, through the conflicting claims of
each Olympian, the formation of a great religious
type that might have corresponded to the monotheism latent in the cult of the Capitoline Jupiter.
The whole weight of the Imperial Majesty, the fer-
vour of enthusiasm inspired by the Imperial Idea, the
belief that the Empire meant both protection and
prosperity, had to come into play before the Olympians
could be banished into the twilight that the Imperial
figure might reign in their stead. Only the image
of the Roman Emperor as the vivid embodiment of
the new centralised authority could have compelled
into his service alike the principle of frontality by

which primitive man sought to assure himself the
direct protection of his gods, and those schemes of
narrative composition by which the Greeks had striven
to illustrate the workings of the divine nature.   Under
the influence of this dual conception, the artists
working for Rome succeeded in fusing into one harmonious whole the *res gestae* of the Roman people
and the *Maiestas* of the Roman Emperor.   The
primitive full-face pose of the god and the monolatric
distribution of the figures attendant upon him,
purified by the genius of Rome of the old magical
intention, passed into the service of Christianity,
and in its wake proved the paramount influence in
the art of both Middle Ages and Renaissance.

Della Seta has lately argued that in the Renaissance
from the time of Dante art was captured anew by
the Greek spirit, and again turned to exemplify the
dealings of God with man by means of the narrative style (*Religion and Art*, p. 364).   But the secret
of centralisation and of the monolatric schemes
which belong to art in the service of a monotheistic
idea was never lost; and if in his *Paradiso* Tintoretto could marshal figures innumerable into the service of a central and dominant motive, this was
because centuries earlier, the necessity of unifying the
Emperor and the Imperial deeds in one comprehensive composition had called forth the centralised
scheme which we have been considering to-day.

LECTURE II

THE SYMBOLISM OF THE AFTER LIFE ON LATE ROMAN TOMBSTONES

Animula vagula blandula
Hospes comesque corporis
Quae nunc abibis in loca
Pallidula rigida nudula
Nec ut soles dabis iocos.

The Emperor Hadrian to his Soul.

I. THE SUBJECT

WERE all other sources of evidence lacking, a study of the monuments which man has set up from time immemorial to mark the resting-place of the dead would alone suffice to give us the measure of his belief in a life beyond the grave. The subject in its entirety has never yet been surveyed, though no branch of archaeology is at once so fascinating and so fertile. To-day it is only a small contribution to the vast subject which I can hope to make. My purpose is to discuss certain late Roman tombs which throw light on the new beliefs in resurrection and immortality which spread over the Empire in the first three centuries of our era, in the wake of the Oriental religions. If I read aright, I believe that Roman

112

1. SARCOPHAGUS OF HAGHIA TRIADA. (Detail.) Museum of Candia
2. TWO SCENES OF APOTHEOSIS. (a) From the Chariot of Monteleone. (b) From the Sarcophag
of Haghia Triada.

tombstones reveal a spiritual conception of death and of the fate of the soul which is far in advance of anything taught by any religious system before the establishment of Christianity. Secondly, and as the necessary corollary of my first proposition, I want to make it clear that the symbolic imagery and decoration taken over from the Greeks and the Graeco-Oriental peoples by the Romans did not sink among them, as is often argued, to the level of mere ornament, but became on the contrary charged with a new significance. Owing to the variety of the phenomena represented, I shall limit myself to those monuments which reveal more particularly the influence of the beliefs underlying the doctrines of the Apotheosis and of Mithraic, Orphic and cognate cults. I take my examples, as a rule, from the provinces rather than from Rome, because the further we get from the sophisticated and cosmopolitan art of the capital, the more spontaneous is the expression of popular belief ; yet even the most elaborate and patrician Roman tombs, as we shall have occasion to see, betray at times the same spirit of faith and hope. In the provinces I shall lay special stress on the monuments of Gallia and the lands bordering on the Rhine and the Danube, not only because the high level of civilisation attained in these regions under the Roman rule results in their stelae being more artistic than those of the other provinces, but because they seem to reveal a keener interest in religious speculation. I have the more material reason for the choice in that the funerary monuments from the Rhine and Danube were admirably represented in the great Exhibition of the Provinces of the Roman Empire held in 1911, where many must have realised for the first time the importance of the civil and religious art of the Empire in the second and third centuries of our era. Again, M. Espérandieu's great volumes on Roman Gaul form a *Corpus* of monuments in which we can read as in an open book the vast strength of the religious movement which inspired the iconography of the Roman Empire. But the movement represented by the imagery of the later Roman gravestones can scarcely be appreciated at its right value unless we first glance back, however briefly, at its origin and history in Greece and in pre-Imperial Rome. I think also that this way of approaching our subject may incidentally help students to appreciate more clearly the points at which the Romans came into contact with the Greek world.

II. THE ORIGIN OF THE GRAVESTONE TRACED TO FEAR OF THE GHOST

To us moderns—as, indeed, to the more cultured races of antiquity—the tombstone has come to have little more than a memorial significance. The dominant motive of decoration or epitaph is regret for the departed life, coloured more or less vividly by the hopes of a life beyond the grave ; and we are apt to consider the sepulchral monuments of the past as expressive of the sentiments that inspire our own. The dolmens of the neolithic period ; the royal pyramids of Egypt ; the delicate carvings of Athenian stelae; Etruscan canopi or Roman tombstones ; the mausoleum that enshrines the grief of Artemisia ; the column that marks the tomb of Trajan, and carries up to the sky the imperishable record of the Imperial campaigns ; the square pillar tombs of the Roman Rhineland ; the sepulchral slabs of our mediaeval cathedrals ; the pseudo-classic tombs of the eighteenth century, with their pompous epitaphs —all the forms that the tombstone has assumed from remotest antiquity to our own times represent to us as we look back from our own point of vantage, the desire to gain, in the face of ineluctable death, some assurance of the life to come, or some consolation in the retrospect of the life that has been. But these ideas are only arrived at by slow degrees ; they presuppose an advanced state of culture of which primitive man is wholly incapable. We think of the tombstone as the last tribute of love and religion ; but fear, rather than any of the nobler emotions, appears to be the motive for which it is set up by primitive man.

In order to understand the primitive purpose of the tombstone, we must bear in mind that every rite of inhumation or incineration has its origin in the desire to banish effectually a dreaded presence by placing it deep under the earth or by reducing it to ashes. In other words, it is inspired by *fear* of the Ghost, of the *revenant*.[1] Even when the corpse is finally disposed of man's fears are not over, for the breath, which he identifies with the principle of life, may work harm to the living if it is allowed to roam at large. A desperate effort must be made to prevent the breath from escaping. The custom of closing the mouth of the dead, of placing the hand over mouth and nostrils,[2] and of closing his eyes—that last pathetic service which it is the privilege of his nearest and dearest to render—all arise from the attempt to prevent the breath from escaping through mouth or nostrils or eyes. Still the mischance might happen ; the breath or *spiritus* might give the survivors the slip ; so it became necessary to catch this detached spirit, and to prevent it from wandering at will. Then, just as the mound above the tomb kept the body safe in the grave where it had been laid to rest, so the rough stone upon the mound was at first intended as a trap for the wandering soul, a place it might be induced to enter ; in other words, primitive man set up his first rough tombstones with a magical intention, in order to provide the ghost of the inhabitant of the tomb with a shrine or dwelling-place. This has been so admirably said by Sir Arthur Evans in the epoch-making paper on Tree and Pillar Cult, that I cannot do better than quote what he says : ' The rites by which the medicine men of primitive races the world over are able to shut up Gods or Spirits in a material object show how easily the idea of attracting or compelling . . . spiritual occupation must have arisen. A proof of this is found in the ideas attaching to the rude stone monuments placed over graves. These have not merely a memorial significance, but are actually a place of indwelling for the ghosts.'[3] The sequel of the passage we shall have occasion to return to.

The fear of the haunting dead, of the *revenant*, which religion, philosophy, and even science have been powerless to eradicate from uncivilised and civilised races alike, is the natural counterpart of the universal and persistent belief that death does not and cannot mean the destruction of existence.[4] It is because mankind is firmly convinced that the dead live somewhere and somehow in a life in which the living have no part, and over which they have no control, that primitive man at once believes in their return and fears it ; hence his idea that if the dead are buried with due rites they will be appeased and give up annoying or disturbing the living.[5] The ghost has been pictured by Pater as ' a dream that lingers a moment . . . a flame in the doorway, a feather in the wind,' but in its primitive phase it wears no halo of romance; it is a grim and oppressive fact that has to be disposed of by fair means or foul. Among highly cultured peoples this fear of the dead is not incompatible with the most passionate sorrow for their loss, or with the most exalted hopes for their welfare in an ultramundane existence. Primitive man, likewise, when once he has made sure that the dead will not disturb his own peace, will do everything in his power to further their interests; he will not only bring them offerings in order to placate and keep them quiet, he will also furnish their tombs with the counterparts of the objects which he conceives to be necessary to their welfare in another life, and as the conception of a world below the earth grows upon him, he will provide the dead with the means of journeying to its furthest ends.

A whimsical pathos attaches to much of the elaborate equipment of the grave, so obviously is it intended to keep the dead quiet and remote from the seats of the living. When we lay aside sentiment and face the truth we realise that the actual return of the dead to this world has never been courted by any religion, and that it is doubtful whether any one ever seriously desired it. Primitive man's fear of the dead becomes civilised man's recognition of the fact that the great experience separates, and must separate, us and them. ' I shall go to him, but he shall not return to me.'

Even when the dead beneath the earth become associated with the divine forces of Nature and are held to exert an influence on the vegetation that springs from the earth, we shall find that, though man welcomes and courts the return of vegetation, and tries to induce the dead man underground to co-operate in the process, he does not court the return of the dead himself. He welcomes in the growth of vegetation the resurrection of a divine spirit ; he trembles before the reappearance on earth of the actual dead whom he has known as human beings like unto himself. This has been expressed with poignant if unconscious irony in the scene of the famous sarcophagus of Haghia Triada,[6] interpreted as the return of the dead in his aspect of spirit of vegetation (plate xv. 1): the dead man—conceived of as something akin to Dionysus or Osiris—stands outside his own tomb wrapped in a sheath-like garment which resembles the swathings of a mummy ; he has come, it seems, in response to a thrilling and elaborate ritual which is represented in great detail ; but lo ! see how afraid they are lest he should be tempted to tarry too long. Three men advance towards him : one brings the boat in which he is to be invited to return whence he came, and two men carry each a calf as provision for the boat, since the journey to the next world is a long one.[7]

In the same way it may be noted that the fulfilment of any hopes of final rebirth and resurrection, however ardent, are ever relegated to a distant and indefinite future.   Once the dead are thought of as living in their own distant world, their return to earth may be admitted, but it must be within certain well-defined limits of time and space, as Boni's discovery of the Palatine *Mundus* has lately reminded us.[8] Whether their return be invited for the benefit of the living, or permitted in order to appease the supposed desire of the dead to revisit their ancient haunts, the times when the spirits were allowed to return were days of fear and warning.   At times, as in cases of prophecy, the dead is officially recalled, so that, from his larger experience, he may give counsel to the living[9]; but here also his coming is a defined and limited act, fraught with fear to the living, who look upon him as an object of awe and wonder and dismiss him gladly to the other world when his mission is accomplished. The return of the dead invariably takes place, as on the Haghia Triada sarcophagus, to the accompaniment of mysterious rites.   Examples present to every one's mind are the calling up of the ghost of Samuel by the witch of Endor at the bidding of Saul ; the apparition of Darius in the *Persae* of Aeschylus in answer to the incantations of Atossa and her

companions ; the tremendous scene of the *Odyssey*
in which Ulysses after accomplishing the prescribed
sacrifices sits by the mouth of Hades awaiting the
spirit of Theban Teiresias.

We moderns have not rid ourselves of fear of the
ghost ; but the modern ghost, unlike his primitive
prototype, neither desires to haunt the living nor seeks
to return among them. In some distant sphere he
dwells beyond recall, or craves for silence and oblivion
within the grave :

> Call me not back, O Love, when I am dead:
> Call me not back with witchcraft of thy will:
> Far beyond thought my spirit will have fled :—
> Call it not back lest it obey thee still.
>
> .   .   .   .   .
>
> And when, at Fate's behest, I wake at last
> To toil on earth, to laugh, to weep again—
> Dense be the darkness that enshrouds the Past,
> Deep be the draught of Lethe that I drain.[10]

III. Origin of Sepulchral Imagery

Like the gravestone or funeral monument itself,
the imagery of the gravestone has a magical function
which manifests itself in a great variety of forms.
Probably the one we first think of is that of the
funerary statue. Once endow a tombstone with
animistic vitality, and it becomes subject to endless
variations and modifications under the influence of
the beliefs that centre round the dead whose soul

the stone is supposed to hold.   At first the boundary-
line between the survivor's conception of the actual
dead, and of the stone which holds his spirit, is thin
and elusive.   The shrine or prison-house of the dead
man's ghost may by a very natural interchange of
ideas be identified with the dead man himself.   The
aniconic grave-stele or pillar, like the aniconic pillar
of the god, may be subject to an anthropomorphising
process, and, since the dead, or his soul, is conceived
as resident within it, the stone may by an easy transition be made to assume the visible form of the inhabitant of the tomb.   At times the transformation
may be only partial, and, owing to the early association of the dead beneath the earth with the fertilising
powers of Nature, it may be limited to expressing
what to the primitive mind were the vital parts of
the human body.   A curious figure in Berlin from
Sardis represents the double process.[11]   On the one
side we see the sepulchral stone transformed into
the image of a man ; on the other the organs of
generation alone are indicated.   A curious group of
pillars at Tamuli in Sardinia is interesting in this
connection.[12]   Each is roughly carved at the top in
the semblance of female breasts, and though it is not
certain that the pillars were placed over graves, they
stood near one of the big Sardinian tombs known as
'Tombs of the Giants.'   Possibly they were magical
stones set up to ensure fertility and increase.

As sculpture developed, the function of the stele might be usurped by a complete statue of the dead, at first of the type commonly known as ' Apollos,' and by the middle of the sixth century these so-called Apollos, now happily renamed κοῦροι, were habitually set up over the graves of men, and the corresponding κόραι over those of women.[13] Even the funerary statue in its classic perfection, whether treated as portrait or as idealised type, may, in a sense, be regarded as preserving, besides its memorial significance, a clear reminiscence of the time when the dead was conceived of as dwelling within his own stele. This, of course, was only one of the many ways which account for the existence of the funerary statue ;[14] it is well not to dwell on this point too insistently, or I might be accused of trying to revive the old theory, now discarded, of the technical evolution of the statue from the pillar or the plank-like stele.[15] One observation, however, occurs to me with regard to the difficulty so many have experienced in admitting that a large proportion of these ' Apollos,' who are invariably young, who are κοῦροι in the fullest sense of the word,[16] were grave statues. Did only the young die ? were there no old men and no gravestones of old men ? The answer is that whether the occupant of the tomb were old or young, he would be figured as young, the state of κοῦρος being that coveted for him and by him in an after life. Eternal youth has ever been one of the postulates of eternal life, and to give to the funeral statue the lineaments of youth was the best way, on the magical principle of primitive peoples, of ensuring the perpetual youth of the occupant of the tomb. To the Greek, moreover, the body of the old was ever a thing of shame, and the sight of it is rather quaintly given by Tyrtaeus as a reason against old men going into battle :

Across the bleeding body lies clenched the wrinkled hand,
A sight to make men sick to see that by the dead shall
    stand
And naked see the honoured forms.   Though every-
    thing in truth
Beseems the valiant man that wears the happy flower
    of youth,
The lover meet for ladies' eyes, the wonder of all men,—
Yet, fallen foremost in the fight, fair is he truly then.*

(*Tyrtaeus*, 8, transl. K. A. Esdaile.)

The gravestone might also assume the shape, or be adorned with, the figure of one of the innumerable objects conceived as the seats of the soul after it had

---

* αἰσχρὸν γὰρ δὴ τοῦτο μετὰ προμάχοισι πεσόντα
    κεῖσθαι πρόσθε νέων ἄνδρα παλαιότερον,
ἤδη λευκὸν ἔχοντα κάρη πολιόν τε γένειον,
    θυμὸν ἀποπνείοντ᾽ ἄλκιμον ἐν κονίῃ,
αἱματόεντ᾽ αἰδοῖα φίλαις ἐν χερσὶν ἔχοντα—
    αἰσχρὰ τάγ᾽ ὀφθαλμοῖς καὶ νεμεσητὸν ἰδεῖν—
καὶ χρόα γυμνωθέντα.   νέοισι δὲ πάντ᾽ ἐπέοικεν,
    ὄφρ᾽ ἐρατῆς ἥβης ἀγλαὸν ἄνθος ἔχῃ·
ἀνδράσι μὲν θνητὸς ἰδεῖν, ἐρατὸς δὲ γυναιξίν,
    ζωὸς ἐών, καλὸς δ᾽ ἐν προμάχοισι πεσών.

departed from its human habitation ; the snake and
the ' soul-bird,' which already appears on the Haghia
Triada sarcophagus,[17] and which develops into the
siren of the Attic grave reliefs, are familiar instances.
Or again, the various apotropaic or prophylactic
figures—we might almost call them by the familiar
name of scarecrows—placed on tombs to ward off
the evil spirits might, as was indeed commonly the
case, be translated into stone in order to ensure their
permanent activity. Sepulchral art early betrays
two distinct points of view with regard to the after
life. The one remains concerned with the material
welfare of the dead in a sub-terrestrial existence ;
the other, with a more exalted conception of the
supreme adventure, seeks to provide the dead with
a vehicle or an escort to an ultramundane abode of
bliss. Man's various conception of this abode,
whether he places the habitation of the dead under
the earth, or beyond its confines, or in some misty
cloud-world above, depends in the first instance upon
his method of disposing of the dead.[18] Where inhumation is prevalent, the dead are thought of as
below the earth ; where incineration, fire is conceived
as purifying and releasing the immortal part, which
is then borne aloft to the rarer air of some region
above the world. The different ways in which it was
conceived the dead might voyage to these distant
regions were productive of an especially rich imagery.

Already on the sarcophagus of Haghia Triada—dating from a pre- or proto-Hellenic civilisation—we beheld the dead borne, like Elijah, on a winged chariot through the flaming aether [19]; chariots winged and unwinged (*ad superos* and *ad inferos*), winged steeds, boats, Harpies, Sirens, eagles, sea monsters of every description, are only a few of the many vehicles of the soul's transit.[20] The conception is refined till it attains to the exalted symbolism of the liberated soul expressed in the group of Ganymede borne aloft by the eagle on the monument of the Secundinii (p. 222).

Again, figures and scenes expressive of beliefs concerning the future state of the dead when they had reached their destination might be carved or painted on the stele. Scenes of ultramundane bliss are of specially frequent occurrence—always with the same magical intention of perpetuating the state desired for the dead by giving it a permanent and visible form. The scenes of hunting, chariot-racing, and revelling are familiar instances—the ' Funeral Banquet' which in one form or other is among the commonest motives of ancient sepulchral imagery, becoming in time the supreme expression of Apotheosis.[21]

The furniture of the tomb, it may be noted in passing, partakes in its origin of the same magic character. In the beginning, at any rate, the tomb is not furnished, as is popularly supposed, with objects known to the dead while yet alive or beloved by them —a late and sentimental notion. The real function of these objects, whether the doll of the child or the armour of the warrior, is rather to obtain for the dead, by a sort of sympathetic magic, the things which may induce them to stay in another world.[22]

Thus while the grave monument—simple slab or elaborate tomb—marks the barrier which separates the dead from the living, its imagery and its furniture have primarily the function of securing for the living immunity from the dead by giving definite and permanent form to advantages and privileges which the survivors conceive of as conducive to well-being in another life. It cannot be too strongly impressed upon students of the antique that this attitude towards the dead lies at the root of much ancient religion and ritual, and consequently inspires ancient art from the earliest times. For the dead, from being objects of terror to be scared away and placated at any cost, passed as we have seen to being objects of awe, and so acquired the character of beings of a superior order endowed with superhuman and magical powers. In fact, they were divine; and this conception of the dead as *daemon* or *hero* governs the formation of all sepulchral art. The idea is presented to us with crude and primitive directness on the early Mycenaean and Spartan reliefs, which we shall now consider. It is modified to vanishing point in the art of the Attic stelae, through the supposed indifference to a future life introduced, it is said, by the Homeric poems.   It persists in the lands least touched by these influences, till in the Roman Empire, purified and modified by the influence of the Oriental religions, it inspires the lofty symbolism of the soul's destiny which appears on the stelae we are more particularly to study here.   The magic intention is gradually suppressed, or relegated to a subordinate rôle ; with the progress of time, the imagery of the tombstone tends to concentrate more and more on the adventures of the soul in the other world and to omit or minimise the relation of the dead to this.   But it was long before thought could be thus focussed on the more spiritual aspects of the After Life.

IV. Conceptions of the After Life on Mycenaean and Peloponnesian Stelae

An example of the desire to secure for the dead joyful pastimes in the life beyond, by carving representations of these on the gravestone, is afforded by the much discussed scenes of hunting and chariot-racing on the famous stelae from the circle of graves on the Acropolis of Mycenae.[23]   These date at latest from the tenth century B.C., and are the earliest figured stelae found on Greek soil ; they are described as follows by Sir Arthur Evans in the passage from which I have already quoted : ' The stelae of the graves at Mycenae must themselves be regarded as baetylic forms of the departed spirits of members of the royal house ; and in the reliefs upon them . . . we may recognise a compromise between the idea of supplying a spirit with an aniconic habitation, and that of pictorially delineating it in human form.' [24] Who that looks at them, with this explanation in mind, can help seeing that because it is the departed spirit which is here delineated, the pastime in which he is engaged refers to his life beyond the tomb ? We have here, in fact, an anticipation of Pindar's picture of the joys of the Blessed, who ' in the space before their city . . . take their delight in horses and games ' (see below, p. 140). More directly than any others found on the soil of Hellas do these stelae enunciate an order of beliefs as to a blessed future life, similar to that which inspires the sepulchral imagery of the later Roman Empire more than a thousand years after.

The scene in which the living bring offerings of drink and food to the dead very early makes its appearance on funerary stelae, with the magical intention of making the scene doubly effective by giving it the permanence of stone. A series of reliefs from the neighbourhood of Sparta, for instance, shows the dead man enthroned with his wife and receiving offerings from the survivors, while he himself holds out the cup for the funerary libation

(*R.R.*, ii. 39 ; 376, etc.).[25]   The idea that the dead
are alive within the tomb, or somewhere in the world
below it, whence they may be recalled, cannot be
more emphatically expressed than it is here.   They
can emerge and meet the living who come to pro-
pitiate or placate them ; they are shown as of heroic
size by comparison with the living who approach
them ; they are majestically enthroned to indicate
the superior power with which they are now endowed.
Moreover, in the more famous and best preserved of
these reliefs (plate xvi. 1, in the museum of Berlin),
a further idea is introduced, inasmuch as the man is
represented not only participating in the scene carved
within the relief, but with head and shoulders facing
outwards in a stiff frontal attitude, as though the
sculptor had wished to establish between the dead
man and his survivors or descendants a relation
equivalent to that between god and suppliant (above,
p. 31).   The stelae are particularly interesting as
offering to the spectator a triple vision of the dead: as
spirits resident in the stele ; as souls dwelling in the
great snake which rears itself up behind the throne ; [26]
and as actual human presences whose more majestic
mien alone differentiates them from ordinary mortals.
The scene is clearly one of Apotheosis.   The fact that
the dead are shown as participants in a solemn revel,
that the very cup they drink from has the shape of
the kantharos of Dionysus, shows that they have

PLATE XVI.

2. Greek Stele.
Grottaferrata.

1. Stele from Crysapha.
Berlin.

been made the equals of the gods and share their special joys. The offerings brought by the survivors are also worthy of attention. The man carries a cock [27] and an egg ; [28] the woman the flower and the fruit of the pomegranate,[29] all of them symbolic of those powers of fertility and rebirth with which, as I have already pointed out, the dead were early associated. Students cannot be too earnestly recommended to master the whole of this series of Spartan reliefs, the type of which persists down to the Pheidian age, as on one of the Chrysapha reliefs, now at Athens (*R.R.*, ii. 366, 2), on which a man, resembling in type the magistrates of the Parthenon frieze, feeds from a deep kantharos the soul-snake that rears itself in front of him.[30] These Peloponnesian reliefs had an influence which the art of the Attic stelae could not entirely suppress.

V. THE ATTIC REACTION. CHARACTER OF ATTIC SEPULCHRAL IMAGERY

The clear and material conception of an ultra-mundane existence of the dead which inspires the Mycenaean stelae and the Spartan hero-reliefs is held to have vanished from the sepulchral art of historic Greece, or more correctly of historic Attica, or to survive only as an underground current of which we see occasional glimpses in the humbler arts that minister to the superstitions of the less educated

classes ; so rarely indeed does it exert any influence
on the major arts that the one or two examples of
its persistence are often neglected in a rapid survey
of the subject. A great deal has been written and
said of late to show that with the Homeric poems a
new conception of the after life was introduced, which
was to influence the funerary art of the Greek and
the Graeco-Roman world until the great reaction
brought about under the Empire by the intrusion
into the West of Oriental religions. In Homer the
dead lead a colourless existence as shadows in a distant Hades where their time is spent in futile regrets
for the past, and he knows of no influence which these
poor shades can exert over the living.[31] Since these
shadows or εἴδωλα are banished to the further confines of the world, whence there is no return, the
living need have no fear of the haunting ghost when
once the dead have been laid to rest, nor do the ghosts
need to be placated with offerings. If the dead are
to live for the living it is in the verse of the poet.
Henceforward, therefore, by the power of art, the
dead cease to be terror-inspiring spirits and become
ideals for the guidance of mankind. In a sense,
therefore, Homer is the creator of the art-type which,
in Attica at least, after the official introduction of
Homer by Pisistratus, is to commemorate the dead.[32]
The sepulchral imagery of classical Athens is likewise
commemorative in character ; the deceased survives

PLATE XVII.

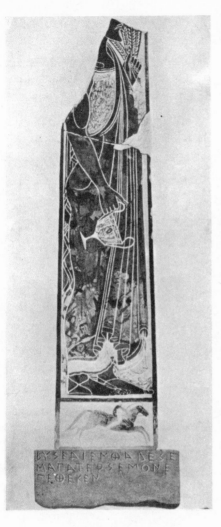

1. STELE OF LYSEAS.
Athens.

2. STELE OF ARCHIPPOS.
Cook Coll., Richmond.

only as a memory in virtue of his past state, or of his past actions.   The long series of Athenian funerary stelae usually exhibits an episode from the past life of the deceased, or some scene illustrative of his condition in this world.   An archaic stele from Velanidezza, signed by Aristocles, represents the dead man in full armour standing quietly in profile, with no suggestion, therefore, of any heroisation (*R.R.*, ii. 373, 2). On another of more recent date, in the Vatican, a young athlete looks down at his little servant (*R.R.*, iii. 408, 4=Helbig, 246).   On a stele at Athens a youth with his pet rabbit in his hand, and his little servant looking up into his master's face, is represented in the attitude which doubtless seemed characteristic to those who survived him (Stele of Telesias, *R.R.*, ii. 387, 3).   Hegeso likewise, who died in the bloom of youth and beauty, is shown seated and receiving from her maid a box of jewels (*R.R.*, ii. 393, 1) ; or a young warrior is commemorated, as on the stele of Dexileos, by the episode in which he lost his life (*R.R.*, ii. 420, 2).   A number of these reliefs likewise refer to the dead man's trade or profession, such as that of the shoemaker Xanthippos (British Museum ;   *R.R.*, ii. 502, 1),[33] or of Sosinos, who appears to have been a worker in bronze (Louvre ; *R.R.*, ii. 290, 2),[34] and those of various actors and poets.[35]   Further, in studying the Attic stelae in their historical sequence, a distinct change as regards the relation of the dead to the living may be observed. In the earlier examples the interest still completely centres round the dead man, who is represented alone ; then we watch the gradual intrusion of the living till in the stelae of the fourth century the interest is about equally balanced between the dead and those who survived him.[36]   We may even go so far as to say that the spectator's sympathy is claimed rather for the sorrow of the survivors than for the fate of the dead. Thus by the influence which the Homeric poems exerted upon the Attic genius the old magical purpose had vanished from the stele and its imagery.

(a) Traces of Beliefs in an After Life in certain Attic Stelae

All this is not so much my own theory as a fair statement, I believe, of the views now currently held of Attic sepulchral art.[37]   They require modifying in not a few important particulars.   Professor Gardner had already pointed out in his Sculptured Tombs of Hellas[38] that Attic stelae retain considerable traces of beliefs identical with those which inspired the Spartan tombstones.   In the archaic period, indeed, the Athenian funerary reliefs are permeated by that primitive faith in an ultramundane existence which continues in force in the sepulchral art of Hellenised Asia Minor and its islands.   Consider, for instance, the beautiful painted stele of Lyseas in Athens (plate

PLATE XVIII.

SCENE AT A TOMB.
Attic Lekythos. Boston.

xvii. 1), where the dead man is seen holding a deep drinking-cup, not in the least as some have supposed because he had been a priest of Dionysus, but because the Dionysiac kantharos is given him, as to the heroised Spartan ancestors, for a sign that he has attained to the status of god. Then again, the galloping horse-man on the socle of this stele seems in the spirit of the Mycenaean stelae, and refers to after-world joys rather than to the man's racing triumphs in this life.[39] Symbols such as we saw in the Spartan stelae, and shall see again in Hellenistic and Roman times, are by no means of rare occurrence on Attic grave imagery. On the stele of a hoplite at Athens, for instance, which must be earlier than 478 B.C., since it was found in the wail of Themistocles, a running Gorgon is carved on the socle with evident prophylactic intention (*R.R.*, ii. 373, 1).[40] On another of the Pheidian period from the Peiraeus, a man lays his hand on the head of a tiny siren on his left, while on the socle Tritons shouldering their oars and blowing their horns are depicted, in clear allusion to the journey to the Isles of the Blessed (*R.R.*, ii. 388, 4). On the stele, inscribed with the name Eutamia, likewise of the fifth century, the dog which appears alone on the ledge above the figures of Eutamia and her daughter or attendant (*R.R.*, ii. 389, 2) is plainly more than a household pet ; the place assigned to it is that given to the horse on one of the Chrysapha reliefs, and the dog here is certainly the underworld guardian.[41]   The same may be said of the dog which not unfrequently appears seated under the chair of the deceased, as in a lovely relief in the museum of the monastery of Grottaferrata (plate xvi. 2).   The bird, very commonly a dove, so frequently interpreted as a mere gift to the dead, is in its origin quite certainly a seat of the departed spirit, and to my mind probably retains to the last an allusion to the soul-bird.[42] The lion which appears as the guardian of tombs in Phrygia from remote antiquity,[43] and the bull who later plays so significant a part in the sepulchral imagery of the Empire, are all known to the art of Attic tomb reliefs, though there is an undeniab¹ᵉ tendency to keep their symbolic value in the background of interest, and to assign to them a value which as time goes on becomes more and more decorative.[44] Finally, we must note a mingling of contradictory ideas in Attic sepulchral imagery : on a stele of the Dipylon (R.R., ii. 392, 3), for instance, Pamphile and Demetria, for all the ' modern ' everyday character of their poses and draperies, are enshrined as solemn presences within a naïskos or chapel, in a manner reminiscent of those archaic stelae where the dead are presented as objects of homage and worship. Again, the stelae where the dead are seen surrounded by survivors, recall that earlier conception of the dead as a god, enthroned and reverently approached by the survivors.   But the magical value of the scene has vanished, leaving us with what represents an episode of daily life, in which, as I have already pointed out, the interest often centres about the anguish of the living rather than about the fate of the dead now passed beyond recall.

(b) After Life Beliefs in Attic Vase Pictures

From the first the humble products of the potter's art are more explicit than the gravestones.   No figured stelae adorned the early graves outside the Dipylon Gate at Athens, but their place appears to have been taken by the vases of geometric style found above the tombs and richly decorated with various scenes pertaining to death and burial.[45] Among them the elaborate picture of a funeral [46] calls for special mention here, for we do not find processions depicted on so extensive a scale or with such a pomp of mourners and display of grief, until we come to Roman times ; and even then they are restricted to few examples (p. 175).   A funeral procession has no necessary reference to belief in an After Life, but the vase shows on the part of the ancient inhabitants of Athens a preoccupation with death which was banished out of sight by their descendants. The funeral is a comparatively rare subject on later vases ; but we find the laying out of the corpse, the lowering of the coffin, the passage in Charon's boat, and, above all, the offerings by survivors at the tomb. The subjects are specially common on the class of vases with paintings on white ground, known as lekythi, exclusively made for the service of the tomb, and justly ranking among the most exquisite pictures that Greek art has left us. One in the splendid vase collection of the museum of Boston displays a scene of appealing beauty : on the left a mourner half kneels on the steps of the grave ; the fully draped figure of a man on the other side is probably intended for the dead himself ; from the figures of athletes which decorate the stele, it has been thought that the grave was that of a young athlete. It seems to me quite as probable that the figures carry the usual allusion to the joys and pastimes of an After Life [47] (plate xviii.).

(c) General Trend of Attic Thought with regard to Death

The sepulchral art of Attica was not, as we have just seen, so devoid of all reference to a future exist-ence as many archaeologists have represented. At the same time it has to be admitted that when we survey the gravestones of Athens as a whole and mark the overwhelming number that contain no reference whatsoever save only to the past life of the dead, we may say of Attic grave reliefs as a whole, with Ales-sandro della Seta, that they *do not represent death*,

but immortalise life. A human melancholy not un-
naturally pervades them, a tender regret for what
has been and is no more, but we look in vain for any
indication of the recompense that may await the dead
beyond the grave. So, too, the funeral speech over
those who fell in the first year of the Peloponnesian
War, put into the mouth of Pericles by Thucydides,
has no word about the reward in after life for bravery,
nor does the speaker attempt to console the survivors
by the suggestion of future reunion.[48]

In this art of the Attic stelae we find everywhere
the frank acceptance of the impenetrable mystery of
death ; no effort is made to lift the veil that separates
the now from the hereafter. It seems worth calling
attention to the fact, not, I think, observed so far,
that the Platonic doctrine of the immortality of the
soul, promulgated in Athens in the fourth century,
has left no traces in the grave reliefs of the period.
It is stranger still that the Orphic doctrines, with
their theory of a future life, which had come into
vogue two centuries earlier, and which now, in its
purer Pythagorean form, gave a new turn to the
mysticism of Plato,[49] practically found no expression on sepulchral reliefs before the days of the
Roman Empire.[50] Yet the influence attributed to
the Homeric poems, if paramount in Athens, was not
universal, and Pindar—a mere Boeotian to be sure—
was possessed of a definite vision of the After Life

and its joys which he takes more than one occasion to dwell upon. One remarkable passage—the noble fragment already referred to, beginning τοῖσι λάμπει μὲν σθένος ἀελίου [51]—I cannot resist quoting here, in Andrew Lang's beautiful translation :

> Now the light of the Sun, in the night of the Earth, on the souls of the True,
> Shines, and their city is girt with the meadow where reigneth the rose ;
> And deep is the shade of the woods, and the wind that flits o'er them and through
> Sings of the sea, and is sweet from the isles where the frankincense blows :
> Green is their garden and orchard, with rare fruits golden it glows,
> And the souls of the Blessed are glad in the pleasures on Earth that they knew,
> And in chariots these have delight, and in dice and in minstrelsy those,
> And the savour of sacrifice clings to the altars and rises anew.*

> (*Rhymes à la Mode*, ed. 2, p. 119.)

---

* τοῖσι λάμπει
  μὲν σθένος ἀελίου τὰν
  ἐνθάδε νύκτα κάτω, φοι-
  νικορόδοις δ' ἐνὶ λειμώ-
  νεσσι προάστιον αὐτῶν
  καὶ λιβάνῳ σκιαρὸν καὶ
  χρυσέοις καρποῖς βεβριθός.
    .   .   .
  καὶ τοὶ μὲν ἱπποισί <τε> γυ-
  μνασίαις <τε>, τοὶ δὲ πεσσοῖς,
  τοὶ δὲ φορμίγγεσσι τέρπον-
  ται, παρὰ δέ σφισιν εὐαν—
  θὴς ἅπας τέθαλεν ὄλβος·

The vision endured, for we meet it again in Vergil five centuries later—with this great difference, that the Latin poet definitely makes Orpheus, the long-robed priest, its central figure.

But the Orphism which inspired the eschatology of Pindar and of Plato long failed to affect the attitude of the educated Greek towards a future state. However expressed—whether in literature or art—this attitude remains one of imperturbable resignation. The influences emanating from Attica, clothed in the matchless Attic form, permeated the whole ancient world, moulded the scepticism fashionable in the philhellene circles of Republican Rome, and everywhere opposed an obstinate resistance to the beliefs in an ultramundane existence which were to conquer in the end. Before we return to the monuments, allow me, as a contrast to Pindar, one more quotation in illustration of my meaning. It is from the elegy on the death of Bion, long attributed to Moschus, but now recognised as the work of an Italo-Greek poet of the age of Sulla.[52] The passage αἰαῖ ταὶ μα-λάχαι, familiar from Leigh Hunt's charming version,

> Alas, when mallows in the garden die,
> Green parsley, or the crisp luxuriant dill,
> They live again and flower another year;

ὀδμὰ δ' ἐρατὸν κατὰ χῶρον κίδναται
αἰεὶ—θύα μειγνύν-
των πυρὶ τηλεφανεῖ παν-
τοῖα θεῶν ἐπὶ βωμοῖς.

> But we, how great soe'er, or strong, or wise,
> When once we die, sleep in the silent earth
> A long, unending, unawakeable sleep, *

shows how completely the educated Graeco-Roman world of the first century had lost—or affected to have lost—the very conception of a life beyond the grave. While humble worshippers in Asia Minor were drawing consolation from the rites of Adonis, Cybele, and Attis, and perceiving in the yearly resurrection of the spring a parallel and a hope for their own future life, the Greek saw in that same yearly miracle only a contrast between the unchanging and eternal processes of Nature and the inevitable hour that awaits mankind at the last.

VI. THE SEPULCHRAL IMAGERY OF ASIA MINOR

(a) General Character

Fortunately for the greater happiness and consolation of mankind there were other Greek countries where belief as to an After Life was never so completely obscured as in Attica, and where it continued to find direct expression in art. The Attic stelae practically came to an end between 317-307 B.C., as a consequence

---

* αἰαῖ, ταὶ μαλάχαι μέν, ἐπὰν κατὰ κᾶπον ὄλωνται,
ἠδὲ τὰ χλωρὰ σέλινα τό τ' εὐθαλὲς οὖλον ἄνηθον
ὕστερον αὖ ζώοντι καὶ εἰς ἔτος ἄλλο φύοντι·
ἄμμες δ' οἱ μεγάλοι καὶ καρτεροί, οἱ σοφοὶ ἄνδρες,
ὁππότε πρᾶτα θάνωμες, ἀνάκοοι ἐν χθονὶ κοίλαι
εὕδομες εὖ μάλα μακρὸν ἀτέρμονα νήγρετον ὕπνον.

of the sumptuary laws passed by Demetrius of Phaleron against the excessive luxury of sepulchral monuments. After that period the use of any elaborate tomb imagery seems to have been effectively checked. For the most part the graves are now marked by simple pillars or slabs ; practically the only subject which we find carved on these later Attic gravestones being the funeral banquet, or rather, as we should call it, the 'Banquet of the Apotheosis.' The subject was of rare occurrence in the great period of Attic art, and its new frequency betokens a revival of faith in the glorified condition of the dead—a fact which it may some day be possible to explain by reference to the predominance at this time of Pythagorean Orphism.

From the close of the fourth century we have to turn to the stelae of Asia Minor for the later history of the grave-relief.   It is usually held that the Asiatic stelae derive from the Attic.   This is true of their architectural forms as a whole, but only very partially so of the subjects represented.   Rather does their elaborate symbolism derive in an unbroken line from those more primitive customs and beliefs which we have seen rejected by Attica and Athens under the influence of the Homeric poems.   A glance at the imagery of the earlier tombs and other sepulchral monuments of Asia Minor and the neighbouring islands soon makes this clear.

(b) Scenes of Apotheosis and After Life on Sarcophagi
from Cyprus and from Clazomenae.   The Chariot
of Monteleone

First we will select from the Metropolitan Museum
of New York the sarcophagus from Golgoi in Cyprus,
recently published by Professor Myres of Oxford,[53]
to whose catalogue of the Cypriote monuments in
New York we are all looking forward. The scenes
of hunting and of chariot-racing embody, as do the
reliefs of the Mycenaean tombs, the promise of noble
pastimes in a life to come ; the spirit is that of the
Pindaric description of ultramundane bliss.   The
banquet scene combines the sacramental expression
of the rewards and joys awaiting the Blest with the
notion of Apotheosis ; while the figure of Perseus
running with the head of the Gorgon is quite certainly,
to my mind, figured here with apotropaic intention,
to ward off evil spirits from the occupants of tomb
and sarcophagus.[54]   We shall find the same prophylactic character attaching to this image some eight
hundred years later on the tomb of the Secundinii at
Igel near Trèves (p. 222).   Whether we can follow
an earlier interpreter of this sarcophagus in seeing in
the Perseus a portrait of the deceased,[55] thought of
therefore as deified, I am not at present prepared to
say, though there is little doubt that in the Hellenised
East there was a tendency to regard the dead as a

PLATE XIX.

SARCOPHAGUS FROM CLAZOMENAE.
British Museum.

being of a superior order, which led soon to his Apotheosis in the form of various heroes and gods. This is a further point which distinguishes the funerary art of Asia Minor from that of Hellas.

The celebrated sarcophagi from Clazomenae in Lydia, which come well within the circle of Ionian influence,[56] exhibit, in the paintings of the interior, hunting and warlike scenes similar to those on the example from Golgoi and a number of apotropaic motives, the most striking of which is that of the young man holding a cock in each hand and with two dogs fawning upon him. Both cock and dogs render here the service of warding off evil spirits from the wayfarer to the underworld, while a degree of Apotheosis is implied by showing the young man as master of the hounds.[57] I wish we had time to discuss the wonderful friezes which decorate the interior, upper rims, and lid of the sarcophagus in the British Museum, and seem like a pictorial commentary on Pindar's visions of a Blessed After Life (plate xix.). Along the rim and on the end panels are figured the exploits which win for the dead man participation in the noble pastimes which make up the rest of the figured decoration. I must dwell one moment on the winged figures—some bearing branches—which hover above the chariots on the lid. They are the same Κῆρες[58] —Greek Angels of Death we may call them—who are figured in battle-scenes on early red-figured Attic vases, hovering above the dead and dying warriors, as in an incomparably beautiful fragment now at Palermo.[59]   The dread Κὴρ Θανάτοιο, the cruel vampire who sucked the blood of the brave, has another side to its nature ; it can also close the eyes of the hero in battle, and bear away his soul to the radiant spaces.   The Κήρ is thus a conception akin to one aspect of the Siren, with whom it appears alternately above the reclining revellers on a lovely kylix from Cyrene in the Louvre, justly interpreted as a Banquet of the Blessed—a συμπόσιον τῶν ὁσίων.[60] In the same way the scene on the sarcophagus is a joust of the Blessed, and over them, as over the revellers of the Cyrenean cup, hover the Κῆρες as ministrant spirits.

The lion, likewise, continually appears on this class of sarcophagi and on the tombs of Asia Minor, an important fact for us, since the lion is one of the most frequent of sepulchral emblems on the tombs and gravestones of Rome, and, as we shall see, on those of Roman Gaul, Britain, and the Roman provinces of Central Europe.   The presence of the lion on the tombs of Asia Minor has been explained by his connection with Cybele as protectress of graves, for Cybele in her aspect of mother-goddess of the earth's fertility is by an easy transition of thought connected with the underworld whence vegetation springs, and so with the dead, while the lion as the highest expression of the vital forces of Nature early appears as her companion.[61]   Probably several conceptions unite in the symbolism of the lion, and we shall also be able to recognise in him the emblem of the solar forces that destroy the flesh and so liberate the soul.   The transit of the dead to the upper spheres again is depicted on the magnificent bronze chariot of Monteleone, no doubt part of the furniture of a tomb, which like the sarcophagus of Golgoi is now among the treasures of the New York Metropolitan Museum.   It may be dated in the early part of the sixth century, and though found in Umbria, is certainly Ionian work.[62] On the front panel we see a gallant exploit of the dead warrior, while the reward of his prowess appears on the panel of one side, where we see him borne upwards in the winged chariot over the recumbent figure of Mother Earth (plate xv. 2(a)) ; the chariots in early times were generally winged, being a usual vehicle of the soul's transit to heaven.[63]   We have twice met with this scheme before, once on the sarcophagus of Haghia Triada, to which, however, I made only passing allusion (plate xv. 2(b)), and again on the relief from Ephesus where the Emperor Marcus Aurelius ascends heavenward in the chariot of the Sun over the recumbent Earth (plate xi.) ; in all three cases the scene is one of Apotheosis, and in all three the soul is caught up, so to speak, in a mystic chariot, like Heracles and Elijah.

(c) *Sepulchral Imagery of Lycia*

The tombs of Lycia, which very early betray in the character of their art the influence of Ionia, are specially instructive for the force of the belief in an After Life which inspire their imagery. Let us run rapidly through the splendid examples preserved in the British Museum. The Harpy Tomb is, of course, the classic example. It dates from the end of the sixth or beginning of the fifth century, when in Athens stelae of the type recording the everyday life of the deceased (p. 133) were already in vogue ; from its manifold subjects it seems to have been the burial-place of several generations of the same family. A happy reaction has set in lately against the perverted notion that saw in the carvings of its four sides mere *genre* scenes from everyday life ; they are obviously in the same line of belief and of thought as the Spartan gravestones.[64] The friezes of all four sides reveal an elaborate ritual of the grave, combined with scenes of Apotheosis and of ultramundane existence (*R.R.*, i. 470-1). The pictorial expression of the Soul's adventure is as varied here as on the sarcophagus from Haghia Triada : winged female figures, who partake both of the nature of the Harpies, or body-snatchers, and of a vehicle of Apotheosis, tenderly bear away the souls ; between them a warrior offers his armour to a god of the underworld, who is doubtless a heroised ancestor ; another of these underworld divinities receives the offering of a dove ; while on the entrance side two gracious women, mother and daughter perhaps, seated outside their own tomb, receive the offering of their living female descendants, who approach with no less stately a mien than the Athenian maidens on the frieze of the Parthenon. On the corresponding relief at the back we see a third male ancestor between two groups of women receiving, like the Spartan heroised ancestors, the offering of an egg and a cock. Outside Christian art it would be difficult to match these moving and poetic scenes. The rape of the soul by the Harpies has, in fact, a remarkable parallel on a scene carved in the portal of S. Trophime at Arles, where an angel advances from the left with a soul in his hand into the presence of Abraham, Isaac, and Jacob, who are seen seated in Paradise, each already holding two souls in his lap, in vivid illustration of the New Testament phrase, ' Abraham's bosom.' The analogy may be something more than a mere coincidence, since two other reliefs from S. Trophime offer curious analogies to two famous Greek works recently claimed as Ionian : the scene where the soul of a martyred saint as it leaves his body is lifted by bending angels into the presence of God, and that in which a great winged angel, placed frontally, weighs the souls in the scales ; both recall the so-called ' Nativity of Aphrodite ' of the Ludovisi Throne, and the 'Weighing of the Souls' of its supposed counterpart at Boston.[65]   It would be strange indeed if the central Ludovisi scene, so long associated with theories of physical birth, should in fact be connected with the spiritual rebirth ; stranger still if the Christian subjects of a mediaeval church should be the means of throwing light on the mystery still attaching to the subjects of the ' thrones,' but to discuss this interesting parallel further would take us too far afield.[66]

This Lycian sepulchral art is a rich mine of information which would repay working out in great detail.   I must be content here to give a few indications.   A beautiful and pathetic relief in the British Museum shows a funerary column, on which the apotropaic Siren stands with extended wings ; on either side sit the dead ancestors, who here, as on the Spartan reliefs, are conceived both as spirits resident within the stele and also in their human shape.[67] The relief is, moreover, one of the most exquisite compositions left us by Greek art (plate xx.), and shows what might have been accomplished by the Ionians in the way of centralised monolatric design, had not their inspiration been diverted into other channels by the influence of the Attic schools with their Homeric mythology.   Funeral scenes, on the same grand scale as on the sarcophagus from Golgoi, are also very frequent (*R.R.*, i. 469, 1, 2).   The funeral procession,

PLATE XX.

SCENE AT A TOMB.

Stele from Xanthos. British Museum.

though not unknown to Attic art, remains characteristic of Ionian, or more probably Graeco-Asiatic art,
whence it may have influenced that of early Latium
(below, p. 168). At a later date a splendid example
occurs on the long sides of the lid of the Sarcophagus
of the Mourners from Sidon (R.R., i. 406). The
Lycian tombs also frequently exhibit the motive of
the guardian lions. An impressive tomb in the British
Museum (R.R., i. 466-7), from the acropolis of Xanthos,
is cut in one block and adorned on the south side with
a lion holding the head of a bull between its paws, and
on the opposite by a lioness and her cub ; while on
the west side to the right of the door a warrior appears
in contest with a lion which faces him erect[68] (Catalogue
of Sculpture, No. 80). I have already referred to the
probable meaning of the lion as guardian of the
tomb ; the group of the lion devouring a bull or other
animal so common in Eastern and Graeco-Oriental art,
which afterwards acquires a definite mystical intention on the tombs of the Roman Empire, represents,
I believe, from the beginning the notion of a power
of light devouring the terrestrial body, since the lion
early appears as emblem of the sun.[69] Other familiar
motives are the Sirens and lions placed heraldically
on the panels of the doors on the gable ends of a
certain type of Lycian tomb (R.R., i. 469, 4).

All the sepulchral art of Lycia is strongly influenced
by Ionia, and later came under the overwhelming

influence of Attica, but even then the forms in which
belief in the After Life has found expression were never
entirely obliterated.   The superimposed friezes which
adorn in typical fashion the inner face of the walls
of the Heroon at Gjölbaschi-Trysa proclaim the belief
in a logical and sustained form (*R.R.*, i. 443-64).
Probably the tomb was destined for various members
of one family whose exploits, thrown into a succession
of legendary forms, already point to a degree of
Apotheosis.   There followed long banqueting scenes,
at which recline those who, released by death from
their earthly labours, have attained a blessed life,
while on the left of the entrance we see the act of
Apotheosis pictured, as it constantly is in Lycia, by
the ascension of the hero in a chariot.[70]   Such, of
course, is the meaning of the chariots, so far always
inadequately explained, carved on each side of the
roof of the Lycian tombs of Payava and Merehi, in
the British Museum (*R.R.*, i. 487-8),[71] wonderful
monuments which deserve closer study than has
yet been accorded to them.   The same chariots of
Apotheosis occur on the tomb of Deirmis and Aeschylus at Vienna, which stood just outside the
Heroon at Gjölbaschi.[72]   Such also is the meaning of
the chariot, whether empty or containing the statues
of Mausolus and his consort, that crowned the
Mausoleum of Halicarnassus, where, moreover, the
chariot races on one frieze of the great podium

continue the tradition of the scenes on the sarcophagi of Cyprus and of Clazomenae.

Lycian art recognised various other vehicles of the soul's ultramundane journey. The Nereids, for instance, of the slightly earlier monument from Xanthos, what are they but souls borne to another sphere by the marine monsters which we see beneath the feet of the gracious maidens ? These are the same creatures of the deep that escort the soul on countless Roman tombs. This so-called Nereid monument is of especial interest as combining in the manner of the later Roman tombs of the Rhineland the commemoration of the deeds of the dead while yet alive, with a representation of the funeral cere- monies and the imagery symbolic of the destinies of the soul—another example of the influence which Hellenised Asia was constantly to exercise on Rome. The arrangement of the figures in the pediment (*R.R.*, i. 486), it may be noted in passing, seems directly derived from that of the ancestors who face one another on each side of the pillar in the Siren tomb from Xanthos [73] (plate xx.).

(d) Chios. The Sarcophagi of Sidon. Character of Ionian Art

The whole of Graeco-Asiatic sepulchral art bears witness to similar ideas of ascension or Apotheosis, and of eternal bliss in later times also. At Chios, for

instance, in the fourth century, we find the motives
of the Clazomenae sarcophagi repeated on the marble
slab of one Metrodoros [73a] (now in Berlin), as well as a
number of tombs adorned with the figures of Sirens,
assuredly not, as the learned assert, because the dead
man had musical tastes, but as token of his soul's
survival, and also probably to guard his tomb from
evil influences.   If we pass to Hellenised Syria we
meet with the same or similar beliefs and traditions.
On the sarcophagus of the Satrap from Sidon (*R.R.*, i.
411, 2, 413), we have the banquet scene, in the sarcophagus aptly surnamed ' Lycian ' (*R.R.*, i. 409-11,
1)—since though found in the royal necropolis of
Sidon it has all the characteristics noted above in
Lycian sepulchral art—we find the apotropaic Siren,
the griffins, vehicles of the soul's transit ; the frontal
guardian lions on the sides of the lid and on the friezes
of the case, a weakened ' mythologised ' version of
the triumphal chariot of the soul.[74]   On the sarcophagus of the ' Mourners ' the scene of hunting
and the funeral pageant reappear, and on the pediments what is usually taken for a group of women in
Hades or Elysium (*R.R.*, i. 404-8).   In this context
I should like to call your attention to an exquisite
pedimental relief, to my mind undoubtedly Ionian,
formerly in a private collection at Munich, in which
its first interpreter saw the introduction of a dead
woman by Hermes to the Underworld where other

women are seen sitting and mourning in the Elysian fields (*R.R.*, i. 42).[75]   You must keep in mind the persistence of these views of a blessed future existence among the races most strongly influenced by the intellectual Ionians, that highly gifted people who, as Mr. Hogarth has reminded us, were associated with *le printemps de la Grèce*,[76] the importance of whose civilisation as superior and certainly anterior to that of Greece proper is now universally recognised. ' The rise of the Ionian civilisation,' says Professor Gilbert Murray, ' is in many ways the most wonderful phenomenon in Greek history.   Every kind of intellectual advance seems to have its origin in Ionia. The greatest works of colonisation and commerce ; the first bank, the first maps, and the first effective Greek fleets come from there.'[77]   These wonderful people are also those among whom the loftiest aspirations of mankind gained the mature expression that helped their world-wide diffusion.   Ionia was the fatherland of ' Homer,' but it was likewise the first centre of Orphism in its westward advance, and, under the banner of Orphism, two of Ionia's illustrious sons, Pythagoras of Samos and Xenophanes of Colophon, were destined, each in his different way, to be leaders of revolt against Homeric authority and Homeric theology.   We students of Rome must never forget that it was to Pythagoras, who established himself at Croton towards 530 B.C., and to the Pythagorean school, that first Southern Italy and then Rome and the Empire owed initiation into the exalted mysticism which, as we shall see, permeates much of the later Roman sepulchral imagery. I need hardly remind you that at all times of her history Rome received Greek ideas from Ionia—directly or through Magna Graecia—rather than from Greece proper.

Scenes of Apotheosis, especially of the transit in the chariot, are well known in Attic art also, but here they are limited to the cycle of mythological gods and heroes, as in the familiar case of Heracles who often appears on black-figured vases, and vases of the fine period, riding to Olympus with Athena at his side, as in the fine red-figured pelike in Munich, to quote one example out of many.* Man is not pictured as entering the courts of heaven ; if the denizens of those courts wish to come in contact with man they are brought down to him, as on the frieze of the Parthenon. It is striking how few representations in the Greek art of the fifth to the third centuries are concerned to represent another world—whether Heaven or Hell—how little the artistic imagination allowed itself to play round the unknown which by the Attic mind was simply accepted as unknowable. Polygnotos, it is true, painted a great Underworld pageant at Delphi,[78] which has left many traces in contemporary and later

* Furtwängler-Reichold, plate 109, 2.

PLATE XXI.

art, but he was a native of Thasos, and the people by whom he was commissioned to execute the picture were Cnidians, *i.e.* Graeco-Asiatics. Thasos, it may be noted, produced in an exquisite relief, now in the museum of Constantinople (*R.R.*, ii. 166, 1), one of the great masterpieces of antique sculpture, and one of the grandest conceptions of the dead in his glorified existence (plate xxi.).[79] Like the pediment of the Mourning Women and the earlier Harpy Tomb, this relief is a noble example of the sacramental function of art in giving visible form to the Soul's Adventure.

VII. GRAECO-ASIATIC STELAE OF THE HELLENISTIC PERIOD

We return, after this somewhat lengthy excursus on the earlier sepulchral art of Ionia and Lycia, to the Graeco-Asiatic stelae of the Hellenistic period.[80] Their usual shape is that of a niche or little chapel adorned with pictorial accessories, intended, it seems, to reproduce the main features of an actual cemetery. Within this sepulchral landscape the dead, who as often as not is represented by his portrait statue, is seen beside his own tomb. But since a statue is generally meant to be looked at from the front, the introduction of the portrait figure brings back the frontal pose of the dead, and tends to make the dead man, whose effigy is sometimes raised on a pedestal, once more the centre of interest. There is a corresponding tendency to suppress the survivors, or to let them appear only on a diminutive scale, so that by degrees we work back to a heroised representation of the dead. A good example of these various characteristics may be seen in the stele of Archippos in the Cook collection at Richmond (plate xvii. 2; *R.R.*, ii. 532, 1). What we observe in the sculptured stelae is borne out by epigraphical evidence, such as the celebrated testament of Epicteta of the second century B.C. in the museum of Verona, found on the island of Thera, which gives all the circumstances and regulations for the cult of a heroised family (*I.G.*, XII. iii. 330 (*Inscrr. Insul. Maris Aegei*)).[81] In addition symbols are now abundantly introduced, at times with their full significance, at others so represented as to impart to the scene the character of *genre* : a child, for example, offers to his dog the Dionysiac grapes, symbolic of resurrection ; or, on another stele, a cock, a common offering to the dead, greedily makes for the fruit which a frightened little boy tries to hold out of the bird's reach (*R.R.*, ii. 294, 3). Both dog and grapes contain a symbolic reference to the underworld, but this is softened by the motive of the picture as a whole. In Alexandria the stelae of the Hellenistic period exhibit a similar imagery.[82] It need not detain us here, as it offers no very striking variants, and dies without leaving any traces, overwhelmed, as was all Greek art in Egypt, by the persistence and strength of Egyptian traditions.

VIII. Figured Tombstones in Greek Lands outside Asia Minor and Attica

It would be a fascinating and a fruitful task to trace the sepulchral imagery of other Greek lands outside Hellas proper, and of those remoter parts of Greece where Attic influence was not all-prevailing, but a few examples must suffice. In Boeotia, rich from early days in the 'graves of the worshipped dead,' the people continued, as we learn from their rough but interesting sepulchral imagery, to be preoccupied with the life after death, and the same was the case in Macedonia. In the celebrated stele from Orchomenos (*R.R.*, ii. 373, 3), signed by the Naxian Alxenor, showing a man and his dog springing up at him, we have not so much the record that the man was a huntsman, as that the deceased is pictured here in a scheme, modified by Attic influence, which derives from that of the heroised dead as Master of the Hounds. There is at Athens another interesting Boeotian grave relief from Thebes (*R.R.*, ii. 403, 1) clearly, as far as style goes, a work in the Attic manner, but, as we shall see, if we look closely into the composition, strongly influenced by the old scheme of the heroised ancestors and their descendants. The former sit facing one another, much as on the Harpy Tomb and on the pediment of the Nereid monument in later Ionio-Lycian art (above, p. 153). In Thessaly likewise we remain within a cycle of beliefs suppressed in Attica, as on that curious stele from Saloniki, now in Constantinople (*R.R.*, ii. 169, 1), on which the heroised dead sit facing their own tombstone round which twines the soul-snake. It drinks from a cup held out by the woman, while the man holds in his left hand a long burgeoning staff, sure symbol of resurrection.

Again in Macedonia we find subjects on late stelae that remind us of Asia Minor rather than of Attica. A good example of a Macedonian tombstone is in the Devonshire collection at Chatsworth (*R.R.*, ii. 444, 5), dedicated to one Herennia Syrisca and her son. The lady, though wrapped in the graceful draperies of the third century, is seated stiffly on the left like a heroised ancestress of earlier date, on a throne-like seat, with her feet on a high footstool ; towards her advances a smaller female figure with offerings. On the opposite side, the standing figure of the son is likewise approached by a male figure much smaller than himself. A tree—symbol of re-birth or resurrection—forms an arch over the whole, and, most important of all, on either side a snake twines itself round its branches. We evidently have here, as on the Spartan reliefs, a duplication of the dead in human and in snake form. In the empty space between the heads of the personages appears the head of the underworld horse, and on a ledge to its left a tiny bird, which can scarcely be other than the soul in bird form. It is in Macedonia, likewise, that we find as late as the third century a remarkable type of sarcophagus with reclining figures on the lid unknown to classic Greece, though familiar in Etruria and Latium, and among Phoenician peoples.[83]

In conclusion, one word must be said about the sepulchral art of the Greek cities of Southern Italy. In default of actual monuments, we can learn a great deal for Tarentum and Nola and Capua from the tombs and stelae represented on vase paintings.[84] The kinship with the Asiatic examples is evident. Simple gravestones and columns and the like are indeed found, but the dominating form is that of the *naiskos*, or chapel, within which stands or sits the dead man—once more the heroised dead conceived as a being of superior order.

This survey of the sepulchral imagery of Greek lands, however incomplete, will serve to show that from the Proto-Hellenic period onward beliefs as to a future existence found expression in art, and that, although suppressed or thrown into the background of interest in Attica by the influence of the Homeric conception of the dead, which ruled in Athens from the time of the official introduction of Homer into Athens by Pisistratus at the end of the sixth century, they yet persisted in other parts of Greece. As frequently happens, the lamp of faith was kept burning among the humbler and less gifted peoples. Nor, as we

have seen, was it at any time as completely extinguished in philosophic and super-intellectual Athens
as certain scholars would have us believe, while outside Greece, in the Graeco-Asiatic countries open to
Ionian art and culture, we find from the earliest times
a rich sepulchral imagery, which, side by side with
the more primitive symbols of the ritual of the dead,
finds expression for the loftier beliefs in Apotheosis
and the definite joys of a future life. The consideration of the Graeco-Asiatic stelae had already brought
us to the very threshold of our subject and the art of
the tombstones of the Roman Empire. But here
again, we shall first have to consider in a fresh section
what were the Roman conceptions of death in pre-
Augustan times, and how far these conceptions had
succeeded in finding plastic expression.

IX. The Sepulchral Art of the Romans, from Primitive Times to the Augustan Era

(a) Prehistoric Rome and Latium

It has been said that the primitive Romans had
no sense of life after death, and made little or no effort
to pierce the gloom that envelops the state beyond
the grave ; their misty conception may be compared
to that of the Hebrew She'ol, the underworld where
dwell good and bad without distinction.[85]   To the
Romans likewise the dead were long a vague ' un-

individualised mass of spirits,' the *manes* who crowded up periodically to the opening of the *mundus*, the 'gibbering ghosts' who at fixed intervals had to be propitiated and banished from the homes that had once been theirs.[86]   The Romans had in consequence little or no native sepulchral art ; and if we except the patrician custom of keeping wax images of their ancestors in their halls,[87] it was not till the period of Greek influence that they began to evolve anything like a sepulchral imagery.

Let us turn at once to the evidence of the monuments.   In Rome itself from primitive times we have little or nothing outside the famous *Sepolcreto*, or burial-ground, discovered by Boni in 1902 in the Roman Forum near the site of the temple of the deified Faustina.[88]   The objects found in these early tombs although, artistically speaking, mean and rough, yet indicate a care for the future well-being of the dead.   At this early period they are in the nature of amulets,[89] and are placed on the dead with the intention of protecting them from malevolent influences. The cabin urns, imitated from the *capanne* or round huts of primitive Italy, show the desire to secure for the dead a permanent habitation similar to that which he enjoyed in life.

These burial customs of ancient Latium can best be studied in the great museum of the Villa Giulia, where the extensive finds from the numerous necro-

poleis in the immediate vicinity of Rome have lately
been rearranged with minute care and in chronological order.[90]   It is not a subject which I can discuss
here except in so far as to point out to students who
are looking round for ' fresh woods and pastures new,'
that there is, I believe, no branch of archaeology so
little explored and so rich in promise as this of the
burial-grounds of ancient Latium and the adjacent
Faliscan territory.   From Falerii itself you will find,
in the rooms on the first floor of the museum, an incomparable series of objects from the *tombe a pozzo*,
a fossa, and *a camera*, arranged in order of time.   The
graves in the shape of pits are the oldest ; they are
followed by those in the shape of a trench for the
reception of the coffin ; here at Falerii follows a third
series, that of the chamber tombs, which lasted, it
seems, into the period of the Roman occupation.
These tombs were hollowed out as chambers in the
rock, and here the dead were placed either on couches,
or else within the superimposed recesses cut in the
walls much as in a Christian catacomb.

All these tombs, from the earliest to the latest,
reveal a variety of objects which clearly have in view
the protection and well-being of the dead in an ultramundane existence : it is sufficient to point to the
amulet-jewellery and kindred objects, and to the
Greek vases which make their appearance from the
sixth century onward.   The stupendous finds from

the Barberini and Bernardini tombs at Palestrina, and from the Tomba Regolini-Galassi at Cervetri in Southern Etruria, only a few miles from Rome,[91] reveal on a much richer and grander scale the same care for the dead that we noted among the humbler finds of the primitive *Sepolcreto* in the Forum, and the same desire to equip his last habitation, on the magical principle so often noted, with every kind of object the permanence of which is considered essential to his well-being. It would seem, however, that these desires and conceptions are as yet limited in scope. There is no clear vision of a life *beyond* the grave, of an ultramundane existence in the true sense of the word. These tombs reveal nothing beyond the desire of keeping the dead in a state closely modelled on his earthly life ; therefore we find no rich sepulchral imagery to illustrate or symbolise the soul's supreme adventure. Neither the closing slabs, nor the walls of the tombs, nor again the urns or sarcophagi, are painted or carved as are the sides of the Haghia Triada *larnax*, for instance, with any scenes that definitely formulate a belief in a life beyond and in a possible intercourse between the living and the dead. The ornament of the different objects of furniture or of personal adornment found in these tombs has an immense iconographic interest, but its character seems to me mainly magical or apotropaic, though on this point opinions are divergent. There are scholars

who maintain that the rich symbolism of the ornaments—sphinxes, griffins, lions, chimaeras, and their
like—are used merely with a decorative intention,
and thus afford a proof of a weakened religious belief
on the part of the Latins, who, on this theory, are
content to use as mere decoration imagery which,
among the Greek and Eastern peoples from whom
it appears to be borrowed, had a distinct religious
value. I, myself, on the contrary (and I think there
must be others of the same opinion, or would be,
were the early art of Latium not so much neglected),
believe that all this decoration is part of a carefully
thought out sepulchral imagery, mainly, if not entirely,
protective in character. The question is one which
it is beyond my present scope to consider in detail.

(b) From the early Fifth Century to the End of the Republic

It is in Southern Etruria, at Veii, even nearer to
Rome than Cervetri, that we find from the beginning
or middle of the sixth century certain sepulchral
images which bring us back to the same cycle of beliefs
proclaimed on the paintings of the Cretan sarcophagus and the carvings of the Mycenaean royal
stelae. On the walls of the famous yet too rarely
visited Tomba Campana at Veii,[92] the group of a
horseman escorted by figures on foot may be inter-

preted, I think, as the progress of the dead man to
the other world; he is preceded by a man armed
with an axe presumably to cut down obstacles
in the path. It seems certain that scenes of
this character were introduced into Latium from
Etruria, which in turn had them from the Greeks of
Ionia. The journey of the dead to the underworld,
or the transit of his soul to the eternal spheres, are
especially common subjects in the Latin art of a later
date when Latium and Rome had themselves fallen
directly under the spell of Ionia. From about the
middle or end of the sixth century we begin to find
a type of funeral procession with chariots whose
steeds are sometimes winged like those of the Apotheosis chariots on the sarcophagus from Haghia Triada
and the chariot of Monteleone (plate xv. 2). It is by
no means certain that these processions, which have
survived in immense numbers,[93] always have a funerary import; but this can certainly be claimed for the
numerous pieces found in tombs. Here again, while
some argue that the return from the funeral games is
intended, and that wings are only given to distinguish
the horses of the victorious chariot, others maintain
that the scene actually represents the journey of the
dead to his home beyond this world. The analogy of
the Haghia Triada chariots seem to me to favour the
second interpretation. Here also the winged chariot
is the vehicle of Apotheosis, and the heroised or

quasi-deified dead is escorted by the members of his family. My own impression is that these processions partake of the mystic character of certain early Oriental and Greek *pompai* connected with the rites for the renewal or resurrection of the yearly vegetation. Such was the famous vegetation-ritual in ancient Babylonia, when the gods were solemnly brought in summer from the temple of Marduk in Babylon to that of Nebo in Borsippa, and taken back again in winter from Borsippa to Babylon.[94]   There are numerous parallels to this custom in Egypt and Cyrene, in India, in China, and recent scholarship goes so far as to identify the four-horse chariot of the Roman *triumphator* with the vehicle of the sun-god's progress through the skies.[95] The funeral pageantry of the Romans was from early days most elaborate in character, but it does not seem to have attained to any more striking expression in art than these unpretending little friezes till we come to a much later date.

The fragment of a wall-painting from a tomb in the neighbourhood of S. Eusebio on the Esquiline, now in the Museo dei Conservatori, is the earliest example on Roman soil of the decoration of a tomb (Helbig, 967). It dates from the third century B.C., and represents an unknown episode from Roman history. Rough as it is, it reveals Graeco-Ionian influence in its superimposed bands of decoration, an influence that may have filtered through Campania, since the technique has various points in common with South Italian vases. In the upper frieze is the remnant of a battle-scene ; in the lower two generals, unknown to history, although their names, Quintus Fabius and Marcus Fannius, are inscribed above their heads, are seen engaged in parley. This Esquiline fresco is a curious and instructive example of the early importation into Rome of a narrative method of composition which developed into the famous 'continuous style' of the Empire. The modest fragment announces already what is to be the leading characteristic of the great art of Rome—the commemoration of the *deeds* both of the people and of individuals.

It is characteristic of Roman conservatism and of Roman stubbornness in matters of art that sepulchral imagery made its way so slowly into Rome. The decoration of the *peperino* sarcophagus of L. Cornelius Scipio Barbatus, consul in 298 B.C., which was removed from the family vault of the Scipiones on the left of the Via Appia, and is now in the Vatican, is severely architectural (Helbig, 125) ; it exhibits no imagery, unless indeed the rosettes in the spaces between the triglyphs—presumably conventionalised blossoms—have the prophylactic significance which so often attaches to flowers and plants, and accounts for their introduction into the ritual and imagery of the tomb.

(c) From the End of the Republic to Augustus

Till we come to the last century of the Republic there is little funerary art in Rome. The motive which rises to most people's memory when they think of Roman tombstones is that of the dead man or the dead couple facing the spectator in a stiff frontal attitude, with the frequent addition of one or more children and other members of the family, arranged stiffly side by side. All who have been to Rome will remember the many examples still *in situ* on the Via Appia. The type is doubtless influenced by the stark wax *imagines* that stood in the hall of great Roman houses, and, though we may not go so far as to assert that the pose carries with it a reminiscence of ancestor worship, yet it shows that the Roman was primarily interested in presenting his dead to the homage of the survivors. A good illustration of this type of monument is furnished by the tombstone in the shape of a niche holding the two portraits of a man and his wife in the Capitoline Museum (*Gall.* 48ª).[96] It is usual to neglect this class of monuments, or else to criticise them severely after comparing them with the accomplished workmanship of the Attic stelae of the fifth and fourth centuries ; but the comparison is devoid of value, since the Roman craftsman, for we need call him by no grander name, is trying to express quite another idea. What he desires is not,

like the Greek, to represent beautiful scenes of parting and reunion ; his sterner purpose is to establish, by means of an almost hieratic pose, a direct
relation between the living and the dead.[97] The
same principle governs the design of the Roman
military tombstones of the provinces, which often
resemble mediaeval rather than what is usually known
as classical sculpture, and predominates in the sculptures of the monument at Adamklissi in the Dobrud-
sha, which is of course nothing but a memorial to the
soldiers who had fallen, probably in the campaign
of Crassus in 29 B.C.*[98] At times the rigid pose is
slightly modified, and the figures are made to bend
towards one another and clasp hands ; but the isolated
representation of the deceased remains characteristic
of Roman funerary portrait art as a whole. This
stiff frontal pose blended admirably with the art of the
Asia Minor stelae, one main characteristic of which,
as we have seen, was the introduction of the statue
of the deceased in a frontal attitude ; from the
fusion of these two types derive the statuary groups
within niches of the Imperial period.

The funerary statue had an important development practically unknown to great Greek art in the
recumbent figures placed upon the lids of sarcophagi,

* These tombstones, which exist in great numbers in Rome and
throughout Italy and the provinces, need collecting into a *Corpus*;
among them are to be found the best examples of the portraiture
of private individuals, as distinct from the Imperial and official portrait.

which went back to a high antiquity, and were probably introduced into Rome through the influence of
Etruscan art and custom.   We have already seen
that these figures, which are represented as reclining
at a banquet, derived ultimately from the banqueting
groups of Ionian art.   From the archaic period we
have three well-known examples in terra-cotta from
Cervetri, two in the Louvre and British Museum
respectively, and the fine group at the Villa Giulia.
The art is distinctly Ionian, and the attitude is one
accepted as symbolic of the attainment of Apotheosis.[99]

Other reclining statues, of which there are numerous
examples, are shown simply lying down, and the
scheme is very popular in both Etruscan and Roman
funerary art.   As an example I place before you the
recently discovered tombstone of a boy, now in the
Terme Museum (plate xxii.).[100]   The boy lies quietly on
his side, with eyes wide open ; nothing save the poppies
on the couch and the egg of immortality in his hand
indicates that life has left the fair young body.   The
highly bred lines of the face, the sweet curves of the
mouth, the curling tips of the hair which resembles
that of Augustus, recall the beautiful portraiture of
the children of the Julio-Claudian house.   Nowhere
outside the Latin races do we find that strong, square
structure of the head which even in extreme youth
is apparent beneath the firm elastic flesh.   The boy
might be the elder brother of the child whose portrait,

PLATE XXII.

RECUMBENT SEPULCHRAL STATUE OF A BOY.
Rome. Terme.

found at the Imperial Villa of Prima Porta, is now
in the Museo Barracco, or of that other boy, who,
masquerading as Cupid, rides his dolphin so proudly
by the side of the great Augustus from the same Villa.
On the right side are traces of a small Eros, present as
the ministering Genius of death, intended perhaps for
the boy's own Genius now parting from him, or for a
later version of the winged Ker (p. 145).   The delicate
technique reveals a Greek chisel ;   none of the innumerable reclining statues of Roman funerary art
again touched this height of pure loveliness :

> ' Lie still, and be
> For ever more a child !
> Not grudgingly
> Whom life has not defiled
> I render thee.'

From the close of the Republic onward we also find
a number of grave reliefs, which represent some
episode, generally connected with his trade, in the
life of the dead man.   The classic example is the
frieze which adorns the monument of the baker
Eurysaces outside the Porta Maggiore, along the
friezes of which run reliefs representing the various
operations of the bakery (*R.R.*, iii. 236).   Again,
on a tombstone (in the Galleria Lapidaria of the
Vatican) put up to a cutler of the name of L. Cornelius
Atimetus, we see on the one side the workshop where
the cutler grinds his knives, on the other a scene in

the front shop where a dignified customer in the toga and an obsequious assistant are seen one on each side of the counter (*R.R.*, iii. 404, 1 and 2).   It has, however, been observed, not unjustly I think, that these and similar scenes are not inspired so much by the memory of the past as by the desire to impress the future with the importance and success of the occupants of the tomb.   A recent writer has drawn up an exhaustive list of the reliefs which represent trades, and shows that the feeling which inspires them is distinctly Roman.[101]   It has little or nothing to do with the generalised view of the past life of the deceased current on Attic stelae, but a wave of belief from the Orient had to permeate this class of subject before, as in the monument of Igel, effort and toil could be conceived as the prelude to a higher and more blessed state.

The doctrines of resurrection and of immortality which began to occupy men's minds from the end of the Republic onwards, as a result of the infiltration into Rome of Oriental religions and of Pythagoreanism, both of which taught that the soul once released from its corporeal bondage could rise into ethereal realms, were soon to regenerate and transform all the old sepulchral imagery.   The new beliefs and the art they inspired overspread every region of the Empire with a rapidity which showed the greatness of the need they came to satisfy.

PLATE XXIII.

FUNERAL OF A ROMAN MILITARY OFFICIAL.
Amiternum.

In the last century of the Republic, when Rome was falling under the spell of later Greek mystical speculation, we begin to divine on the part of the Romans, as Mr. Warde-Fowler has pointed out, ' some mystical yearning to realise the condition of the loved ones gone before, and the relation of their life to that of the living.' [102]   This quickening among the Romans of a sense of the divinity of the soul has been traced back, in measure at least, to the influence of the famous Posidonius of Apamea,[103] whose teaching inspired, it is thought, Cicero's ' Dream of Scipio,' written in 54 B.C., and ten years later may have helped to soften his grief for the death of his daughter.   We can, I believe, detect a first reflex of these new beliefs as to the destiny of the soul in a curious funerary relief in the museum of Aquila (plate xxiii.).   It was found at Preturo in 1879, near the Sabine Amiternum, and had, doubtless, adorned one of the tombs which bordered the ancient *Via Caecilia*.   The relief may belong to the last years of the Republic, or even be as late as the Augustan period.   It reproduces a great funeral procession, with a love of pomp and detail which recalls the similar displays on early Dipylon vases (p. 137).   In later Greek art the scene has scarcely a parallel, and in Roman art it may be said to be unique.[104]   In the centre of the procession, on a gorgeous catafalque (*lectus funebris*), surmounted by a baldacchino em-

broidered with the crescent moon and the constella-
tions, lies the dead man ; at the head of the catafalque is placed what appears to be his helmet.
Eight bearers carry the bier, which is preceded by
groups of musicians followed by a long train of
mourners. Though this interesting relief has been
repeatedly published, little attention has been paid
to the stellated carpet of the canopy.[105]   The design
is probably looked upon as ' purely decorative,' yet
even a slight knowledge of the beliefs as to the soul's
astral destiny, which were spreading over Italy under
the influences referred to, suffices to show that this
canopy embroidered with the signs of the moon and
of the stars is simply the mantle of Heaven, the tent
of the sky, the great cosmic envelope of the universe,
the significance of which throughout the whole history
of religion and ritual has been brought forward of
late in a book as learned as it is inspiring.[106]   The idea
of the cosmic mantle is familiar to all of us from the
wonderful simile in Isaiah (xl. 22), *that stretcheth out
the heavens as a curtain, and spreadeth them out as a
tent to dwell in*.   Even more vivid is the simile in the
Psalms (civ. 2), *Who coverest thyself with light as with
a garment ; who stretchest out the heavens like a curtain*.
The conception so beautifully expressed by Isaiah and
the Psalmist is common to all ancient Eastern religions, and early penetrated into Greece and thence
to Italy.   According to an ancient Semitic legend

this ' garment of light ' calls into being by the magical action of its astral signs the whole material universe. It became an attribute of Zeus as of Jupiter Capitolinus ; it is worn on occasion by Sol, and by Solar divinities like Mithras and Attis-Mên, by Apollo and Dionysus, by Aphrodite as Urania, by the Ephesian Artemis ; as the stellated aegis of Athena it is familiar from a number of monuments ; finally it appears in Christian art as the blue, star-embroidered mantle of Our Lady and of Christ as *Kosmokrator*. Alexander adopted a great starred talismanic mantle, doubtless endowing the wearer with power over the universe. The same idea attaches to the stellated mantle worn by the Roman Emperors, from whom it passes to the rulers of the Holy Roman Empire. The mantle, in fact, is a talisman of victory, and as such acquires high spiritual significance as clothing the soul in its ascent to Heaven. It becomes, so to speak, a vehicle of Apotheosis, a meaning possibly attaching to it in the present instance.[107]

Thus the star-spangled canopy spread above the dead on the relief from Amiternum has the same symbolic value as the starry firmament painted on the vault of Mithraic caves and churches. The absence of the Sun among the heavenly bodies represented on the canopy is a significant proof of that persistent supremacy of the cult of the Moon to the exclusion of the fiercer Star which is so characteristic of popular

astral religion in hot countries where, as Cumont has
pointed out, the moon with its gentler light was looked
upon as the more beneficent of the two luminaries.
We must likewise bear in mind that within this same
cycle of ideas the Moon was looked upon as the special
abode of spirits who, if exiled awhile to our sub-lunar
sphere, would return to their original seats after a complicated ascent through the superimposed zones of
heaven, during which they gradually despoiled themselves of their earthly faculties and passions.[108]

This idea of a descent and reascent of the soul, so
common in the astral eschatology of the East, at once
puts one in mind of the noble passage in Cicero's
Somnium Scipionis, at the close of the *Republic*, now
generally thought, as previously stated (page 175),
to have been inspired by the mystical teaching of
Posidonius :

omnibus qui patriam conservaverint, adiuverint, auxe-
rint, certum esse in coelo definitum locum, ubi beati aevo
sempiterno fruantur ; nihil est enim illi principi deo, qui
omnem mundum regit, quod quidem in terris fiat, acceptius
quam concilia coetusque hominum iure sociati, quae
civitates appellantur ; harum rectores et conservatores hinc
profecti huc revertuntur.—Cic., *de Rep.*, vi. 13.

The personage on the Amiternum relief—whether
local magnate or known to a larger fame—is likewise
presented as deserving of the sempiternal beatitude ;
as ranking with Scipio and those great men of the

State who return to the heavenly seats whence they had descended for the benefit of humanity ; as participating in the astral honours accorded to Caesar in his Apotheosis, and looking down on earth *de excelso et pleno stellarum inlustri et claro quodam loco*.   The starred canopy under which the great man reclines is thus of cardinal importance as the earliest expression in Roman Western art of tho'se beliefs in an astral eschatology which received official sanction in the myth of the *sidus Julium*, of the *astrum Caesaris*, of which we have already spoken, which were to play so preponderating a rôle in the religious development of the Empire,[109] and to leave such vivid traces in its art.   The picture of the transit of the soul to the stars, brought into the service of the Imperial Apotheosis, continued to gain in power and vividness till it assumes the form given it on the celebrated ivory in the British Museum (plate xxxi.), where the Divus is borne aloft to his eternal home by the winged figures of Sleep and Death, in a scheme that might be used for the Ascension of a Christian Saint.

The relief of Amiternum, with its pompous funeral procession, smiled at by the commentators as the expression of provincial vanity, marks the intrusion into the Roman world of beliefs destined to revolutionise man's outlook on his destiny in an After Life. Henceforth it is not only Greece or Ionia that feeds the spiritual imagination of ancient Italy ; for an explanation of the new creeds we must look beyond Ionia to the Asiatic Hinterland, to those ancient Oriental civilisations where Orphism itself had had its birth, and where from the beginning of things the astral bodies were thought to hold the secret of life and death.

Tournons donc, comme la religieuse Chaldée, nos yeux vers le ciel absolu où les astres, en un inextricable chiffre, ont dressé notre acte de naissance, et tiennent greffe de nos pactes et de nos serments.*

* Paul Claudel, *La Connaissance du Temps*, p. 46.

LECTURE III

THE AFTER LIFE (*continued*)

Δὴ τότε σε πρὸς Ὄλυμπον ἄγει πυριλαμπὲς ὄχημα,
ἀμφὶ θυελλείῃσι κυκώμενον ἐν στροφάλιγξι,
λυσάμενον βροτέων ῥεθέων πολύτλητον ἀνίην
ἥξεις δ᾽αἰθερίου φάεος πατρώιον αὐλήν,
ἔνθεν ἀποπλαγχθεὶς μεροπήιον ἐς δέμας ἦλθες.

The Oracle to the Emperor Julian.

I. SYMBOLISM OF THE APOTHEOSIS OF THE SOUL. THE EAGLE AND THE WREATH

WE saw at the close of the last lecture that the belief in the soul's return to the starry spheres was already familiar to the Rome of the Late Republic, and we discovered in the relief of Amiternum a striking illustration of the doctrine. I propose now to pass from general considerations to the more detailed examination of certain of the images and symbols which now appear on the gravestones of the Empire. The belief in the soul's immortality, sanctioned as it was by the Apotheosis of the Ruler, had received fresh lustre, and it is not surprising to find that the two main symbols of the Imperial Deification—the eagle and the wreath—are also among the most popular of sepulchral images. We have seen that they were borrowed from the East, and their origin and meaning has been lately explained in the light of certain Syrian monuments. In the epoch-making paper already referred to, *L'aigle funéraire des Syriens et l'apothéose des Empereurs*,[1] Cumont, our leader here as in everything pertaining to the history of the Oriental religions, has traced back the Imperial eagle to the Eastern belief according to which the eagle, as messenger of the Sun, is entrusted by his master with the mission of bearing back to the heavens the soul that has thrown off the bondage of the body ; while the wreath, later a familiar emblem of victory, was in the same circle of beliefs symbolic of the ultimate triumph of the soul. The two emblems appear conjoined on a number of sepulchral slabs found at Hierapolis and other Syrian sites, on which the eagle is shown with outspread wings, bearing a wreath in his beak or in his talons (*op. cit.*, figs. 1 ff.). A relief carved on the face of the arch of a rock tomb at Frîkyâ, near the Syrian Apamea, offers an illuminating commentary on the meaning of this eagle and wreath motive (*ibid.*, fig. 16). Over the keystone is a bust of the dead within a laurel-wreath, immediately above which once hovered an eagle, now much broken. The motive is repeated, so to speak, in another and major key : for at one side a Victory bearing a wreath reaches out to offer it to the dead, while on the other Sol Sanctissimus looks on and seems to protect the

transit of the soul. We cannot doubt that the same
meaning attaches to a group of funerary monuments
found in the ancient Pannonia and Noricum, interesting not only for their iconography but for the vigorous
quality of their art.[2] The finest of the three is the
medallion of a centurion in the Museum of Graz,
(plate xxiv. 1 ; *R.R.*, ii. 126, 3). The officer wears the
metal cuirass adorned on the breast with the Medusa
head to avert evil influences, and girt at the waist
with the *cingulum* ; the end of the cloak or *sagum* is
visible on the left shoulder. In his left hand he holds
the sword with a pommel in the shape of an eagle's head ;
in his right is the short vine staff that marks his office ;
in the background to the left appears his shield (the
parmula). The figure, cut off below the waist, is
placed within a medallion formed by a laurel-wreath,
upon which stands a small eagle with outspread wings.
Here again we have the idea of the eagle bearing back
to the celestial spheres the soul whose victory is symbolised by the wreath. It is possible, however, that
two conceptions meet and mingle in this symbolism
when found on a soldier's grave, for the wreath was
likewise the military *corona triumphalis*, and the eagle
was the sign of the legions ; but the manner in which
the two emblems are combined is clearly influenced
by their Syrian prototypes. When the wreath adorns
the medallion of a civilian, especially if he is represented with his wife, then any military allusion is

out of the question, and the wreath can only be the crown of immortality.   At Graz and in the Museum of Klagenfurt respectively are two fine instances of medallions in the portraits of a bearded man wrapped in the toga, and his wife, placed within a laurel wreath.

The symbolism of these stelae must not cause us to overlook their artistic value.   They are master-pieces of portraiture which would long ago have attracted admiration had they adorned mediaeval Christian tombstones in a church.   Being Roman works of the second century, they have only been discussed from an antiquarian standpoint, with scarcely an allusion to their style ; yet we are far enough from the insipidity of Graeco-Roman art ; we already feel ourselves among men who in time will contribute to the great sculptures of mediaeval Europe.   And in the drawing of the faces there is a vigour of line that is worthy of Holbein.   Each of these medallions was once surmounted by a pine-cone, now broken, the symbol, as we shall presently see, of resurrection.

Examples of these wreathed medallions are common throughout the Empire, though they rarely attain such excellence.   From Rome comes the beautiful double medallion of Antistius, a Salian priest of Alba, and his wife Antistia (now in the British Museum). The character of the portraits and the fine lettering of the inscription show that the date is Augustan.   Each

PLATE XXIV.

1. TOMBSTONE OF A CENTURION. Graz.
2. TOMBSTONE OF FLAVIAN PERIOD. British Museum.

medallion is wreathed in a heavy crown of laurel ; between them lies what appears to be the staff with which the Salian priest struck his shield in the sacred dance. It is now sheathed in laurel leaves and further protected by an elaborate knot against the malign attacks of evil spirits. In each of the spandrels is a quatrefoil rosette.[3] A striking example of Flavian date, recently acquired by thè British Museum and published here for the first time,[4] shows a fine portrait of a middle-aged man within a deep circular recess heavily wreathed with laurel (plate xxiv. 2).

The oak-wreaths which appear on a small group of funerary altars are generally explained as a fashion influenced by the oaken *corona civica*, which usually adorns one face of altars dedicated to the Lares, and which was bestowed as a reward for valour.[5] Here again, as in the medallion of the centurion described above, there may be a contact of two ideas. When, for instance, the altar was set up for a magistrate or high official, the wreath may have been understood as combining in itself a double allusion to the civic worth of the dead and to his spiritual victory. On the other hand, when the altar is dedicated to the Manes (Altmann, 244), or is put up to a woman, the wreath of oak-leaves can only stand, I think, for the *corona immortalis*, though the use of the leaf of the oak may be determined by the vogue which the *corona civica* enjoyed in Augustan times, owing to its bestowal on the Emperor himself. The trailing wreath supporting an eagle with outspread wings, which so frequently adorns Roman sepulchral altars, has, of course, the same significance as the wreath and eagle. At other times the space above or below the wreath is filled by a Nereid or some fantastic escort of the soul in its voyage to the Isles of the Blest. The history of the wreath which adorns Roman monuments admirably illustrates the power of religion in bending to a high purpose symbols and emblems that have their origin in the timid outlook and puerile fears of primitive man. In the beginning it was a mere amulet, a magic device worn to protect the head against evil influences, and therefore especially needed by personages so important to the welfare of the community as kings or priests.[6] From these humble beginnings it was destined to become in time the sign of life eternal.

The wreath as emblem of immortality occurs on the impressive frieze that runs round the interior of the octagonal tomb of Diocletian in his palace of Spalato, just below the dome.[7] The frieze represents love-gods engaged in hunting-scenes and chariot-races, to symbolise the conflict between the powers of darkness and of light ; heads within medallions and masks break at intervals the continuity of the design; one, on the central space on the left as one faces the window, represents Hermes with wings, no doubt as *psycho-*

pompos or escort of the soul ; the second is the idealised portrait of Diocletian himself (plate i. 3), patron
and protector of the cults of Sol and of Mithras, who
is here imagined as borne aloft to the celestial sphere
within the crown of immortality that represents his
final Apotheosis ; a similar portrait of the Empress
on the other side balances that of the Emperor.[8]
Finally, I may note that the image of a boy carried
upward by an eagle as on a stele at Grado (*R.R.*, ii.
126, 4), generally interpreted as Ganymede, is more
probably an image of the triumphant soul borne aloft
to heaven by the eagle symbol of the soul's victory.

II. Influence of Mithraism on Sepulchral Imagery

(a) The Mithraic Legend

The influence of Mithraism in the formation of the
funerary imagery of the Empire was all-powerful.
The legend of the Persian sun-god, besides offering in
the translation of Mithras to the heavens an archetype
of the Apotheosis, was also rich in episodes capable of
interpretation as mystic parallels of the sufferings and
trials which prelude a blessed immortality. The cult
of Mithras had spread with lightning rapidity from
the moment of its introduction into Italy by the
Orientals in the army of Pompey. Its monuments
have been found in every part of the Empire, though

nowhere in greater number than along the Danube and in Germania.   Both they and the Mithraic religion have become very familiar through the great work of Franz Cumont,[9] who has also popularised his researches in a small volume which every student should read.   The majority of Mithraic reliefs are large altar-pieces that were placed above the altar at the end of the Mithraic church or chapel.   The central scene of the front face is invariably the Mithraic sacrifice : at the bidding of a higher Power Mithras slays the Sacred Bull of Ormuzd, from whose body spring the vine and corn—to be transmuted later into the wine and the bread of the holy mysteries— while his blood fertilises the earth that she may bring forth plants and animals for the service of man.   The scene is watched by two torch-bearers, the one with raised, the other with inverted, torch, emblems of heat and life, of cold and death.   The four elements also are present in symbolic form : the fire that purifies all things, and whose rôle in the Mithraic cult is pre-eminent, is figured as a lion ; water is indicated by an over-turned jar ; while the figures of the winds that appear in the spandrels of the altar-slab at once represent the element of air, and the cardinal points of the sky.   The scene thus acquires a cosmic significance, which is further heightened by the signs of the zodiac placed round the arch of the cave, while the cave itself was painted to imitate the starry vault of heaven. It is in vain that loathly reptiles sent by the Powers of Evil try to frustrate the divine purpose of the sacrifice, and attack the vital organs of the bull ; the faithful dog of Mithras keeps watch, and protects the soul of the dying beast in its ascent to heaven.

The central scene is often surrounded by a number of panels which represent various episodes of the Mithraic legend : the miraculous nativity of Mithras, for instance, in the presence of the astonished shepherds ; his victorious encounter with the Sun ; his pursuit and capture of the Bull ; and his ascension into heaven in the Sun's fiery chariot. The back of the altar-piece was likewise occasionally carved ; on the reverse of a Mithraic altar-piece at Wiesbaden, for instance, Mithras and Sol contemplate the slain victim,[10] while that of a very roughly carved example at Serajevo exhibits the rare and curious scene of the Mithraic communion, celebrated by the Mithraic adepts in memory of a Last Supper, of which, before their common ascension, Mithras and Sol partook in company with their disciples. I will not repeat here what I have said in my book on *Roman Sculpture*, of the artistic merits of many of these Mithraic altar-pieces—of the exalted expression and noble gesture of Mithras ; of the contrast which his impassioned beauty offers to the pensive attitude of his torch-bearers ; of the observation of nature revealed in the rendering of the bull's agony.[11]   The type of Mithras was, it is thought, inspired by Pergamene models ; in any case it represents the last effort of Pagan art to create the type of a divinity out of its own imaginings.   The religion that was to make the next appeal to formative art was to meet it halfway by offering to it the reality of a god incarnate.

Mithraism spread in time to every rank of society, and coalesced with cognate cults like that of the Magna Mater.   But as it was originally introduced and propagated by the army, so it remained to the last an essentially military cult, which left its traces wherever the Roman legions penetrated.   Its popularity among the soldiery is easily accounted for by its direct appeal to their naïve faith and piety.   In distant lands, on forced marches, and among the privations and discomforts of camp life, the Northern recruits under the parching heat of the Eastern sun, the Southerners and Orientals amid the unfamiliar frosts and fogs of the North, would be inspired with fresh courage by the contemplation of the wanderings and sufferings of Mithras, and gather strength from the central scene of the legend for the soldier's supreme sacrifice :

Mithras, God of the Midnight, here where the great bull dies,
Look on thy children in darkness.   Oh, take our sacrifice !
Many roads Thou hast fashioned : all of them lead to the Light,
Mithras, also a soldier, teach us to die aright !

(b) *Mithraic Symbols on Roman Tombstones*

We can watch the gradual infiltration of Mithraic symbolism into Roman sepulchral imagery from the time of Augustus onwards. It will repay us to examine one or two examples in detail, and we shall find these to be most instructive where different strata of symbolism have run together. An excellent instance of this process is afforded by the stele of one Tiberius Julius and his daughter at Walbersdorf,[12] which shows a combination of at least three types of funerary decoration. The design falls into two halves: an *aedicula* between twisted columns rests upon a carved base ; this upper part is supported upon the inscription slab, which is framed by Corinthian pilasters, and rests upon a second base with a sunk panel likewise carved in relief. Within the niche the portraits of Tiberius and his daughter are seen side by side in the isolated frontal pose characteristic of Roman sepulchral portraiture ; the relief immediately below represents an episode in the dead man's career. He is shown in the uniform of the mounted auxiliary, charging at an enemy who awaits his attack crouching behind a large shield ; behind is a second fallen enemy ; in the empty space above this figure flies the eagle of victory, significant in this case of earthly glory rather than of spiritual triumph. On the sunk panel of the lower socle two armed men thrust at one another with long spears in front of a figure of Eris ; the man on the right, who is placed frontally and raises his right hand, has been interpreted as a *lanista* or umpire. It were straining our instrument to breaking-point to read a mystic intention into either relief. At a later period battle and combat scenes might be taken to refer to the battles and perils of the soul ; but both portraiture and names show the stele to belong to the Augustan period. At so early a date such scenes are more likely to represent, in the Greek manner, episodes of the dead man's career, though the choice of subject may be influenced in a measure by the desire, which seems to have animated every true Roman, of handing down his deeds, his *res gestae*, to the admiration of posterity.

It is otherwise with the carvings above the niche, which have been admirably interpreted by Cumont. The winds on the spandrels are the same that appear on Mithraic monuments to mark their cosmic setting. The tritons blowing their horns, and facing one another on the frieze, are the mystic escort of the soul as it voyages to the Isles of the Blest ; the running lions, placed heraldically within the pediment, represent the element of fire, which, as we shall see more clearly in the monument we shall consider next, purifies the soul preparatory to its ascent.

On a small sepulchral shrine at Maros-Néméti in

Hungary, are combined a number of scenes and symbols which throw light on our subject : [13] on the inner
central wal! the family of the deceased is carved in
relief ; other personages appear on the external face
of the side walls. On each of the uprights of the
same *aedicula*, a snake gliding upwards figures, I
believe, the progress of the soul towards the celestial
regions, even as in the solar cults the snake symbolises the sinuous course of the sun across the sky.
Thus the snake, already a familiar emblem of the soul
in Greek and Roman religion and ritual, is endowed
with a new meaning. On the roof, lions devour
the Mithraic bull, characterised by the sacrificial sash,
the while they guard the pine-cone of resurrection
which crowns the monument. The frequency with
which the lion appears on the later Roman tombs,
either alone, or devouring an animal, is not sufficiently
explained by calling the lion the protector of the tomb,
or (in the case of the graves of soldiers) an emblem of
valour. When in the solar cults the image became
associated with the igneous element, it was charged
with a mystic significance, which, as we have seen,
may already have been attached to it, in some degree,
in Lycian and Ionian sepulchral art. In my opinion,
the idea which it is designed to convey is that the
purifying fire expressed by the lion must consume the
earthly tenement, represented by the bull, giver of
earthly fertility, before the liberated soul can attain

immortality.[14] At this period the motive of a lion overpowering a bull or some other animals can scarcely be otherwise explained. At times we even find a man in place of the bull. This substitution of an actual human figure for the symbolic animal makes the interpretation I propose practically certain. We must bear in mind that in the East, whence all these beliefs and cults derive, not only was fire regarded as an all-powerful purifying agent, but death by fire was looked upon as 'an apotheosis which raised the victim to the rank of the gods.'[15] I need not dwell further here on the purificatory powers appertaining to fire in Eastern belief, for the subject has been treated by Sir J. G. Frazer in a masterly passage of *Adonis*. You should consider more particularly the following quotation from Iamblichus, translated by him, since it appears to be the direct expression of the idea expressed symbolically in the group of the lion devouring or holding his prey on Roman sepulchral monuments:

'Fire,' says Iamblichus, 'destroys the material part of sacrifices, it purifies all things that are brought near it, releasing them from the bonds of matter and, in virtue of the purity of its nature, making them meet for communion with the gods. So, too, it releases us from the bondage of corruption, it likens us to the gods, it makes us meet for their friendship, and it converts our material nature into an immaterial.'—*De Mysteriis*, v. 12.

A kindred significance probably attached, as we have seen, to the Graeco-Oriental prototypes of the group.

The pine-cone appears almost as constantly on these tombstones as the cross on Christian graves. As an emblem of fertility the pine-cone was certain to acquire, under the influence of the new beliefs in an After Life, fresh value as an emblem of resurrection, since it was the fruit of the tree specially sacred to Attis,[16] the youth who from a self-inflicted death awoke to new life and to perfect union with the divinity: 'Just as Attis died and came to life every year . . . believers were to be born to a new life after death.' This cult of Attis, which came from the East with that of the Great Mother, gathered fresh force under the influence of Mithraism, and Attis—a young man in Oriental costume leaning dejectedly upon a knotted staff[17]—is not an uncommon figure on gravestones. A good example occurs on a stele from Klausenburg, now in Vienna[18]: on the front are portraits of the deceased surmounted by the apotropaic gorgon; on the left is a figure of Attis; to the right, above a dolphin, emblem of the soul or of its transit, is a female figure, probably another deceased member of the family; above her again appears an eagle bearing a wreath; and the whole is crowned by the pine-cone.

It has been suggested that the pine-cone is so

frequently used to adorn graves because of its likeness
to the grave *conus*, which is itself derived from the
omphalos-shaped tumulus or *tholos*.[19]   Further, it has
been argued that the conical stone placed over the
tumulus is simply the phallic emblem of life ; such a
stone crowned the Tomb of Tantalus in Phrygia, and
appears times without number in Etruscan and
Graeco-Roman tumuli derived from Graeco-Asiatic
models.   I imagine that this sepulchral *conus* was
never regarded as purely architectonic and ornamental,
but that it owed its popularity as a funerary emblem
to the fact that its original meaning, though modified,
was not entirely forgotten.   Nothing would be more
natural than definitely to represent the emblem of
generation by means of the cognate shape of the
fruit which from time immemorial had itself been
regarded as an instrument of fertility.   Then, again,
this primitive symbol becomes, by the purifying
influence of religion, the visible pledge of a spiritual
resurrection.

A curiously interesting and little heeded instance
of the use of the pine-cone in pre-Augustan times
occurs in a cemetery at Praeneste (Palestrina) first
excavated in 1855.[20]   It dates from a time anterior
to the Roman conquest of the town by Sulla in 82 B.C.
Each of its graves was surmounted by a square block
supporting a plinth upon which rose a cone.   The
name of the dead, with no sort of addition, is simply

PLATE XXV.

A FAMILY GROUP.
Museum of Arlon.

inscribed on base or cone. These primitive tombstones, degraded though they now are from their
function, and thrown together in a neglected heap
outside the little local museum of Palestrina, still
have the perfume of faith lingering about them ;
they proclaim by means of the naïve emblem the
belief in resurrection held by the ancient race whose
last resting-place they mark.

III. ORPHIC AND DIONYSIAC SYMBOLISM

It is among the Roman provincial tombstones of
the Imperial period that the myth of Orpheus definitely makes its appearance as a sepulchral theme.
The origins of Orphism are still wrapped in mystery,
but there seems reason to believe that, like Mithraism,
it came from the East, though it had appeared in the
West and established itself firmly both in Greece
and Italy many centuries before the Persian Sun-
god—leaving Greece untouched—had been brought to
Italy by Pompey's Oriental soldiery. Apparently
Orphism had its rise in Persia, whence it spread to
Ionia and, in the sixth century, to Attica.[21] I called
attention in the last lecture to the apparent absence of
Orphic influence on the sepulchral imagery of Attica
and Hellas in the fifth century, but in Southern Italy,
where Orphism, bringing with it the astral eschatology of the East, had become the basis of Pythagorean doctrines, we often find the myth itself, and

more especially the episode of the Descent into Hell, figured on vases. Orphism, more vividly than any other ancient creed, brings the consoling hope that the passage from this world is to a happier state ; psychic immortality is the pledge of the high promise attaching to Orphic initiation, for what else is death itself but the supreme initiation ? 'To die,' says the mystic writer whose fragment on the immortality of the Soul has been attributed to Plutarch, 'is to be initiated into the Great Mysteries.' Orpheus became the Great Mediator, the supreme witness that death is not an irrevocable fact, and it is in this aspect that his figure makes its appearance on the tombstones of the Empire. Who better than the prophet-priest who had taught the doctrine of immortality, and was pictured in later legend as the lover who descended to Hades to obtain the release of a beloved soul, could express the hopes of an After Life ? Nor can we forget that Orpheus in his double aspect of priest and lover was endeared to popular imagination by the poetry of Vergil, who in the Fourth Georgic has told in pathetic lines the quest of Orpheus for Eurydice —*dulcis coniux*,—and in the Sixth Aeneid enthrones Orpheus as impressive central figure—*longa cum veste sacerdos*—in the Elysian fields.

The monument in the market-place at Pettau, with scenes from the Orphic legend, is worth examining in detail (*R.R.*, ii. 130, 2).[22] It is a tall stele six metres high, surmounted by a mask which, like the Medusa face so often placed on graves, has the apotropaic function of warding off evil spirits ; the lion devouring the head of an animal at each corner symbolises the purifying fire which consumes the earthly dross —an interpretation as much in harmony with Orphic as with Mithraic belief. According to the former ' the Soul,' to quote a recent writer, ' in its pure state consists of fire like the divine stars from which it falls : in the impure state throughout the period of re-incarnation, its substance is infected with the baser elements and weighed down by the gross admixture of the flesh.' [23]   The flesh, therefore, must be consumed by fire, as the bull is by the lion, before the liberated soul can rise to the firmament of stars ; the notion is identical to that of baptism by fire, ' which burns all sins.' [24]

On the central frieze we see Orpheus playing to the beasts ; on the lower Orpheus has won to the very courts of death, and plays before Pluto and Proserpina.   In the pediment a female figure reclines by the side of a youth : it is Venus reunited to Adonis, whose death and resurrection, followed by his mystic reunion to the divinity, was to mark him out, like Attis, as a popular symbol of resurrection.   On the side of the monument are represented Dionysiac figures, Maenads with bunches of grapes, to symbolise the joys that await the Blessed in their eternal dwell-

ing. Were these taken literally, it might be urged
that they represented a too purely material conception of the after-joys of the Blessed ; but, by this time,
the whole cycle of Bacchic beings and attributes—
including the grape and its juice—had acquired a
purely mystic significance. Did not the vine, as
Cumont points out, spring from the back of the sacred
bull that it might afterwards give the fruit for the
wine of the mysteries ?   Dionysus himself ranks with
the most ancient and venerable nature-powers ; he
is a 'vegetation god with annual appearances and dis-
appearances,' in his earliest Thracian home 'a great
nature god of the living earth, working especially in
its vitalising warmth and juices,' [25] who, as Sabazius,
is not unfrequently identified with the Phrygian
Attis. The story of Dionysus, like other nature
myths, became in the course of time a parable of that
more mystic resurrection which is the spiritual form
of the ancient παλιγγενεσία, already an article of faith
in primitive Thrace, where, from the earliest times,
Orpheus appears closely akin to Dionysus ; it is
therefore only natural to find Dionysiac beings combined with Orphic scenes, as on the monument at
Pettau. On the right side of the beautiful stele of
Albinius Asper and his wife Restituta in the museum
of Trèves (R.R., ii. 91, 4), we see a grandly drawn
Maenad holding up a bunch of grapes, and a similar
figure doubtless adorned the lost left side. A still

PLATE XXVI.

SATYR AND MAENAD.
Museum of Arlon.

more striking instance is in the museum of Arlon (Espérandieu, 4040) : within a curtained recess stand two men and two women, probably two brothers and their respective wives ; at the sides are a dancing Bacchante clapping the castanets, and a Satyr holding up a bunch of grapes (plates xxv., xxvi.). Smaller Bacchic figures adorn the panels of the angle pilasters, and may be compared to the *putti* on the uprights of the Igel monument. At Trèves there is a good example of the group of Dionysus leaning on a Satyr, which not unfrequently crowns the tower-like monuments of the Mosel and Rhine districts.[26]

IV. THE DIOSCURI, HERACLES AND AENEAS, AS EM-
    BLEMS OF THE WANDERINGS AND TRIUMPH OF
    THE SOUL. DEATH CONCEIVED AS A SACRED
    MARRIAGE. RETROSPECT

The Dioscuri, likewise, who alternately participate in life and death, must be understood as emblems of future life. They appear on one side of a little funerary *aedicula* in the museum of Mayence,[27] for instance, while on the other is represented one of the Labours of Hercules, to remind the living of the probation which precedes reward.[28] The myth of Hercules (*vagus Hercules*), whose labours and wanderings are frequently represented, has thus come to symbolise the trials and victories of the soul ; and the same meaning must have been attached to the figure of the wandering Aeneas, so frequently found on the graves of the districts along the Danube and Rhine (*R.R.*, ii. 120, 1-2).[29] In the selection of the episode of the exiled Aeneas, bearing on his shoulders his aged father and leading his little son by the hand, the Roman provincial was, we may feel certain, proud to link what seemed to him the heroic counterpart of his own toilsome life in a distant land with the noblest legends of the origin of Rome.

The same preoccupation with life after death may be studied in a number of stelae whose decoration is drawn from a restricted group of Graeco-Roman myths reproduced as susceptible of spiritual interpretation rather than for any interest in their art-forms, which are clumsily imitated in a poor or rough technique. The story of Rhea Silvia and of Mars, which occurs, for instance, on the front face of a sarcophagus from Aquincum, now in the museum of Buda-Pest (*R.R.*, ii. 120, 4),[30] and on the west pediment of the Igel column, near Trèves, has a doubly symbolic force. The Soul awakes to a vision of the divine, even as Rhea awakes from her weary slumber to behold the immortal lover swiftly descending to comfort her, for death itself is but a sleep which leads to a blessed awakening and consolation. At the same time it seems to me certain that the story of Mars and Rhea on these reliefs may be interpreted as a Sacred Marriage, a hierogamy between the Soul and God. And the many incidents of rapes—those of Proserpina, of Ganymede, of Hylas, and of the daughters of Leucippus—and the myth of Cupid and Psyche, forecast a wedded union with the Divine Love.[31]

By the second century A.D. the sepulchral art of the Roman Empire was everywhere in possession of a rich imagery, but nowhere better than on the provincial stelae can we follow the spiritual ideals that were spreading from the East to the Western provinces of the Empire. Like that of the Christian tombs of a somewhat later date, their iconography is an illuminating commentary on the beliefs of the time. However crude their symbolism, however naïve their images or rude their art, these stelae consistently offer to the living the supreme guarantee that death is not irrevocable. Their distinctive note is the defiance of death, the assertion of life beyond the grave. We seem to read here the challenge of the apostle, ' O death, where is thy sting ? O grave, where is thy victory ? ' They forcibly bring home to us the change that had passed over the spiritual temper of mankind since the Greeks of the fifth and fourth centuries B.C., in their uncertain apprehension of things future, had been content to sink the mystery of death in the memory of life, and had adorned their stelae with scenes of meeting or farewell. They are, as it were, the visible pledge of that definite reaction from the cultured philosophy of the later Republic, which was announced in clear tones by the poetry of Vergil. The *Vitae summa brevis spem nos vetat inchoare longam* of Horace might still express in pointed phrase the fashionable scepticism of his day, and remain typical of a certain section of society far down into the Empire, as countless inscriptions testify. But the message conveyed by the humble imagery of our provincial tombstones is quite other. Here the same sense of the shortness of life bids us seek an infinite hope and fix our gaze on the illimitable stretches of the life beyond the grave. A higher hope, a nobler faith soon began to stir in all classes. Not long after the elder Pliny, at the beginning of his second book, had repudiated all belief in immortality (*Nat. Hist.*, ii. § 18 ff.), Tacitus addressed the shade of Agricola in words that seem like the distant echo of the *Dream of Scipio* :

If there be a place for the shades of the good, if, as those who know will have it, great souls are not extinguished with the body, rest in peace, and recall us thy family from our unworthy longing and the lamentations of the women, to the contemplation of thy virtues, for which it beseems us neither to mourn in private nor to lament in public.*—*Agricola*, 46.

* Si quis piorum manibus locus, si, ut sapientibus placet, non cum corpore extinguuntur magnae animae, placide quiescas, nosque, domum tuam, ab infirmo desiderio et muliebribus lamentis ad contemplationem virtutum tuarum voces, quas neque lugeri neque plangi fas est.

A few years later a wistful note is struck in the charming lines in which the Emperor Hadrian addresses his soul :

> Soul, tiny sweet and wandering,
> The body's guest and friend,
> To what strange regions dost thou tend ?
> Poor shivering naked death-pale thing,
> Now must thy wonted jestings end.[32]

But while the Imperial sage thus mused half-playfully on his soul's destiny, the soldiers of his legions and the officials of his provinces had already lifted the veil which separates the now from the hereafter. Like the higher creed of Christianity, for which they unconsciously prepared the way, the beliefs reflected on our stelae first gathered force among the poorer and humbler classes, and only penetrated by degrees to the upper strata of society.

V. Excursus on the Imagery of Tombs in Rome

I should like at this point to say something, in the nature of a parenthesis, of a class of funerary decoration, the symbolic meaning of which has been neglected of late years, and which deserves to be studied anew—the paintings, namely, and the stucco decorations of the many tombs in Rome and its neighbourhood. Besides being precious relics of ancient decorative art, they are of paramount importance for the study of the After Life beliefs of the Graeco-Roman world. Numbers of them were copied and engraved with more or less fidelity in the eighteenth century, by Piranesi among others, but owing to the general discredit attaching to Roman art during the second half of the nineteenth century, when the attention of archaeologists was concentrated on discovery in Greece, the paintings were allowed to fade often beyond recognition and the stuccoes to deteriorate. Others, again, were looted for the benefit of foreign museums and collectors, and whole tombs, which must have been of great beauty and interest, like one near the Via Flaminia and the Acqua Acetosa,[33] disappeared *sine vestigiis*. Lately, owing to the recent revival of interest in Roman art and architecture, what remains of these tombs has begun to attract attention once more, though too much still remains neglected and unrecorded.

The best known and preserved of these tombs are the two on the Via Latina, dating from the second half of the second century.[34] Both their paintings and stuccoes show the high level of excellence maintained by art in the period of the Antonines. The walls and the barrel-vault of the so-called Tomb of the Valerii, on the right of the road as we come from Rome, are entirely decorated with stucco, which was apparently left white. The decoration of the ceiling is composed of twenty-five circles, connected by a strip of moulding. Squares are placed free within each of the spaces thus formed, and each of the circular panels is adorned by some figure or group emblematic of the After Life. In the central compartment a veiled female figure rides a griffin, to symbolise the transit of the soul. The others are filled alternately by groups of Nereids riding sea-monsters, or by the rape of a nymph by a satyr, a subject which signifies, as we saw just now, the rape of the soul. The lunette of the central wall facing the entrance is decorated with an exquisite design : from a bunch of acanthus leaves spring fantastic tendrils, held down on either side by a caryatid-like figure, whose feet rest on the acanthus leaves. On her head she supports a rect-angular panel, within which dance the Seasons—the fleet Seasons that indicate the swift coming and going of all earthly life.

The so-called Tomb of the Pancratii on the opposite side of the road offers a more elaborate example of decoration in stucco and painting, and I can only touch on the principal subjects of the complicated design. On the rectangular stucco panels of the ceiling are modelled the following scenes : above the entrance, Priam before Achilles ; to the right, Ad-metus, Alcestis and Pelias. Opposite the door is the Judgment of Paris ; on the left, the admission of Heracles to Olympus, where the hero celebrates his final victory by playing the lyre in the presence of

Dionysus, Athena and Artemis ; while in the central medallion the veiled figure borne aloft by the Eagle symbolises the ascent of the Soul to its final Apotheosis. Though the two episodes from the Trojan cycle can scarcely be interpreted with reference to the other life, it is probable that like the legendary scenes depicted on the friezes of the Heroon at Gjölbaschi, they give mythical expression to traits in the character or the life of the deceased. If we knew more about the family to whom the tomb belonged we might understand why the Judgment scene that accords pre-eminence to Venus, mythical ancestress of the Julian race and tutelary goddess of Rome, was chosen to decorate the panel facing the entrance, or why it was balanced by the episode with the Ransom of Hector. The choice of this latter scene was perhaps influenced by the desire to recall in allegorical form the possession by the occupants of the tomb of the quality of mercy, which Vergil regarded as an Imperial virtue. It may be also that in the mystic language of the second century the Ransoming of Hector stands for the Ransoming of the Soul, and that the Judgment of Paris represents the choice which every mortal has to make on his entry into life. But I should not like to press the point.

I may note briefly the subjects found in a few other tombs which refer to After Life beliefs. In the central panel of the stuccoes that adorned the ceiling of the

now vanished tomb near the Acqua Acetosa were
figures of the Dioscuri with their horses, whose meaning in the sepulchral imagery of the period we have
already discussed. The funerary intention is here
emphasised by the two genii in the space above the
horses ; as on Mithraic monuments, they carry, the
one an upright, the other an inverted torch, as symbols
respectively of life and death. The panel in a niche
of the left wall contained an allegory of purification
and resurrection or re-birth ; a figure of a maiden
holding in her hand a winnowing-fan or *vannus*, a
well-known instrument and symbol of purification,
which she partly rests on a short rectangular pillar ;
inside the *vannus*, closely wrapped and veiled, we
perceive the phallic emblem of generation and life.[35]
In the once famous Tomb of the Arruntii, in the region
between the Porta Maggiore and the ' Minerva
Medica,'[36] which has now disappeared, were other
and no less interesting decorations ; the vault was
covered with stuccoes representing in the centre the
Rape of the daughters of Leucippus—like other scenes
of rape in tombs of post-Imperial date, used to symbolise the Rape of the Soul or Death as a Sacred
Marriage—while winged genii filled the diamond-
shaped panels on either side of the central medallion.
Within the panels of the border we find the griffins of
Apollo, which not only symbolise the god of light,
but are among the fantastic animals which bear away

the soul to the Empyrean.   Again, the subjects that
adorn the stuccoed ceiling of the octagonal chamber
near Tor de' Schiavi * show, in my opinion, that Piranesi
was right in identifying this structure as a tomb,[37]
though Canina and others have taken it to be part
of some *thermae*. The design is formed by intersecting
circles ; and in the interspaces float various winged
creatures, which we may interpret as usual either as
the escort of the soul, or as its means of transit to the
upper spheres ; the winged bull is in the centre ; above
him appears the winged sea-horse ; below the dolphin ;
on the right a griffin and a winged lion ; on the left
a winged boar and a winged horse.[38]

The tomb discovered under the pontificate of
Alexander VII. in a vigna belonging to S. Gregorio
on the Via Appia just outside the Servian wall, must
have offered a sort of compendium of sepulchral
decoration.[39]   In the centre was the medallion portrait of husband and wife ; at the four corners similar
portraits of their children ; in the spaces between the
central design and the wall a series of scenes which
are continued in the arch above the wall-niche, and
seem to refer to a *ver sacrum* ; while scattered over
every available space is every kind of symbolic bird
and beast.

The Tomb of the Nasonii, on the left of the Via
Flaminia as we go north from Rome, was a perfect

* On the left of the Via Praenestina Antica.

mine of sepulchral imagery ; but its beautiful decoration has been in part hacked away and taken to
foreign museums, though more remains *in situ* than
is usually supposed.[40] Here, among the numerous
scenes emblematic of the adventures of the soul in
the Underworld and After Life, were the Rape of
Persephone (now in the British Museum) ; the Rape
of Hylas by the nymphs ; and the so-called Judgment
of Solomon—really a Hades and Persephone enthroned
as judges. There are charming paintings of the
Augustan period, which retain their vivid colouring,
within the famous Pyramid of Cestius, set up towards
the close of the first century B.C. by one Caius Cestius
Epulo on the Via Ostiensis, near what is now the
Protestant cemetery ; [41] the main themes represented
are winged figures carrying wreaths and garlands.
Among the too little known wall-paintings of the
Augustan columbarium in the Villa Pamphili [42] we
see a company of the Blessed feasting in the Elysian
fields—eight persons seated in a half-circle in a green
meadow ; in the midst of them is a large dish with
eggs (as symbols of immortality), in the foreground
a jug and a cup.* The columbarium of Pomponius
Hylas, near the Porta Latina, is rich in expressive
imagery. On a frieze of the central niche we see an
episode from the legend of Orpheus (above, p. 197) ;
on another, carried out in coloured stucco, which

* Left of Via Aurelia Antica.

adorns a side-niche, the underworld story of Ocnus
and his ass.[43]   Finally, we may note as worthy of
careful study the fine stuccoes in a tomb in the Vigna
Nardi,[44] a few minutes from the Porta S. Sebastiano,
on the right of the Via Appia ; and further on, on the
same side of the road, within a vigna belonging to
the Trappists, a fine sepulchral chamber, which was
excavated, I believe, as recently as 1911.   I have
visited it twice, but cannot find that it is published.
Among its painted decorations which are still vivid,
we find the peacock, one of the most popular symbols
of resurrection.   By the church of S. Sebastiano
itself is a recently discovered tomb with fine architectural decoration.[45]   If we glance through a publication—like that of Engelmann—of ancient Roman
paintings recorded in illuminated manuscripts, we are
struck by the number which came from tombs that
have now entirely disappeared.   Another similar
collection of copies of paintings has been preserved
in the Topham volumes in the Library of Eton, and
has just been described by the Director of the British
School at Rome.[46]   Here again some of the most
valuable have disappeared along with the monuments
which they adorned.   The loss of so many tombs with
painted decoration is truly lamentable, for, besides
the undoubted beauty of much of their art, these
paintings are the key to the history of painting in the
Roman Empire, and offer, as we have seen, a com-

mentary of the first order on the beliefs of the Romans regarding the After Life. That there is a great awakening of interest is, however, plain from the attention which was immediately bestowed on the curiously interesting paintings of the Tomb of Trebius Justus, discovered three years ago on the Via Latina, though the learned seem scarcely yet agreed as to whether the subjects represented are Pagan or Christian. A fascinating theory connects the building scene of one picture with the building of the walls of Rome under Aurelian.[47]

Sepulchral monuments of stone, though less liable to destruction, have likewise not been sufficiently studied. Let me at least call your attention to the Tomb of P. Vibius Marianus, popularly known as the Tomba di Nerone, on the left of the Via Cassia as we go north.[48] On the relief facing the road the Dioscuri are represented on each side of the inscription. On either side a griffin indicates the transit of the soul, and in the field below a bull's head represents the abandoned earthly tenement.

I have said enough, I think, to show what great results might be obtained from a systematic publication of the Roman tombs, and what an irreparable loss is inflicted upon science when they are allowed to deteriorate or to disappear.[49] After this excursus among the tombs of the Eternal City we now return to our northern gravestones.

VI. Minor Symbolism of the Stelae. Scenes from Daily Life

The minor ornament of our stelae, like their main decoration, is more often than not a carefully thought-out symbolism. We have seen how pine-cone, lion and snake, already familiar on Greek tombs, acquire fresh value on these Roman provincial stelae, under the influence of Mithraism and cognate Oriental religions. The Medusa mask or Gorgoneion, perhaps the commonest ornament of the grave, whether alone or in conjunction with other symbols, retains its ancient function of warding off evil spirits.[50] The cock also may often have been placed on tombs, as in Greece, with an apotropaic intention. Ghosts are as effectively scared by crowing cocks as by ringing bells or baying hounds. The belief that evil spirits fly at cock-crow is universal :

> Ferunt vagantes daemones
> laetos tenebris noctium
> gallo canente exterritos
> sparsim timere et cedere.—*Prudentius*, i. 37.

The idea is equally familiar in our own legends and poetry. The dead sons of the wife of Usher's Well must leave her at cock-crow :

> Up then crew the red, red cock,
>   And up and crew the gray ;
> The eldest to the youngest said,
>   'Tis time we were away.[51]

Two or more fighting cocks, as on the grave of Nertus at Buda-Pest,[52] are sometimes explained as emblems of combative and watchful instincts, and they may also be prophylactic, but a deeper meaning than any of these attaches, as a rule, to their presence on later gravestones. Just as the eagle may originally have been looked upon as the *habitat* chosen by the soul of a dead monarch, so it has been pointed out that the cock might be appropriately regarded as embodying the soul of a departed warrior. It is doubtless in more than one aspect that the cock, like the Siren or the Harpy, makes his entry into sepulchral iconography. He becomes an emblem of Hermes *psychopompos*, in token of which a cock holding a caduceus in his beak is seen on the pediment of the gravestone of Mussius in Turin, on the right of the portrait bust of the older boy.[53]   But the great vogue of the cock on later Roman tombstones is due, I think, to the fact that as herald of the sun he becomes by an easy transition the herald of re-birth and resurrection.

The dolphins and marine monsters, another frequent decoration, form a mystic escort of the dead to the Islands of the Blest, and at the same time carry with them an allusion to the purifying power of water and to the part assigned to the watery element in Mithraic and solar cults. This type of sepulchral decoration arises from the belief in a place of habitation of the dead, which the Greeks placed across the river Oceanus, beyond the confines of the world. The dead man—or his soul—might be conveyed thither either by boat, or on the back of a sea-monster, a dolphin, sea-horse, or triton. The boat was one of the earliest forms of transit; it occurs in Egypt, and we saw it on the sarcophagus of Haghia Triada; it remained emblematic of the last journey down to late times, and was eventually taken over into Christian iconography. Both boat and sea-monsters are commonly found on provincial tombstones, not unfrequently in combination; on a stele in the museum of Arles, for instance, a two-oared boat, adorned on the prow with the effigy of a swan, is seen between two dolphins (*C.I.L.*, xii. 800).[54] Sometimes there may be a doubt as to whether the boat is for the dead man's use in the other world, or merely refers to his occupation in this. On a large rectangular monument at Trèves a compromise of the two ideas is effected : the cornice of the socle is carved to represent the stream of Oceanus, within which swim the soul's fantastic escort ; but at each side of the socle and upon it is placed a boat full of wine-casks (*R.R.*, ii. 90, 5).[55] These boats, which are manned by six lusty oarsmen, certainly represent the trade by which the occupants of the tomb had been enriched. Every inhabitant of the district of the Mosel seems, then as now, to have been engaged

either in the wine or in the cloth trade.   The sculpture is by no means contemptible ; the face of the
pilot of one boat, with its kindly, jovial expression,
usually explained, let me add, as the effect of liberal
draughts of excellent ‘ Moselle,’ has long been justly
admired.

Far more delightful than this somewhat ornate
monument of a pious merchant are the simple stelae
that marked the tombs of ordinary boatmen.   They
are of frequent occurrence in lands with great rivers,
where much of the traffic and commerce by water
depended upon the boatmen.   An excellent example
is in the museum of Mayence, set up by a boatman of
the Rhine, named Blussus, for himself, his wife, and
a son (*R.R.*, ii. 71, 1-2).   The portraits of the three
appear on the front face of the monument ; on the
back is carved a boat manned by two oarsmen ; the
light river craft resembles that of the Nile so closely
that we must suppose it derived from an Egyptian
model.   Below runs the inscription which records
the age of Blussus and the years of his service.[56]   A
singular charm attaches to another stele, put up, as
is recorded in the pathetic inscription, by one Marcus
Antonius Basilides, *frumentarius* of the *Legio X.
Gemina*, for the tomb of his wife and his infant son :

To the holy shade of Augustania Cassia Marcia, my
peerless wife, who lived thirty-four years eleven months
and thirteen days, and, while she fulfilled the suffering

appointed for her, met life's end in the hope of better things : and to my innocent child, Marcus Antonius Augustanius Philetus, who lived three years eight months and ten days, and whose little life a ruthless fate, not heeding the prayers of his parents, took from him.*

In the same spirit that modern Italian boatmen christen their craft *La bella Italiana* or *La bella Genovese*, Basilides has named his boat the *Felix Itala* in honour of Italy.   In the *Felix Itala* he sits, facing posterity bravely in characteristic frontal attitude, flanked by his two mates,[57] or, as Dr. Ashby suggests to me, it would be quite consistent with the spirit of the time to suppose that the three figures in the boat stand symbolically for Basilides and the wife and child he had lost.   The line between reality and allegory is at this time elusive, and it may well be that the boats carved on these tombstones carry with them an allusion to the ship in which, sooner or later, all must sail to the far-away shore.   Their simple imagery, the naïve but manly language of the inscriptions, anticipate the prayer of the English poet :

> Sunset and evening star,
>   And one clear call for me ;
> And may there be no moaning of the bar
>   When I put out to sea.

---

* Die Manibus Augustianae Cassiae Marciae coniugi incomparabili quae vixit annos xxxiiii menses xi dies xiii, quae, dum explesset fati sui laborem, meliora sibi sperans vitam functa est, et Marco Antonio

PLATE XXVII.

Two Family Repasts.
Museum of Arlon.

Scenes from everyday life are also found on the tombstones by the side of subjects which refer to the After Life ; they occur more especially as friezes on the tall pyramidal monuments of the Rhineland, the architecture of which is derived from that of Graeco-Ionian prototypes, like the Mausoleum of Halicarnassus and the Nereid Monument. A number of excellent examples may be seen in the rich museum of Trèves. From one of them comes the well-known relief with a scene in a schoolroom : a bearded Greek pedagogue, got up to resemble the traditional philosopher, sits with a pupil at each side, while a third small boy enters, satchel in hand (*R.R.*, ii. 91, 1).[58] On another we see depicted a ' Rent-day Scene,' where a number of sturdy farmers are paying in at a counter the moneys due to the ground-landlord (*R.R.*, ii. 91, 2).[59] The clerks who receive the money are dressed in a short *sagum*, while the farmers have in addition a warm hood attached to the *sagum* to draw over the head ; they carry their money-bags hanging from a broad strap, and hold a stout stick. On a third monument a frieze on the right shows the familiar Greek subject of a lady's toilet. The lady, no longer young, sits in a high wicker chair surrounded by her tiring-maids, one of whom holds up the mirror

Augustanio Phileto filio innocentissimo qui vixit annos iii menses viii dies x, cui dii, nefandi parvulo contra votum genitorum vita privaverunt ; Marcus Antonius Basilides frumentarius legionis x geminae coniugi et filio pientissimis.

to her mistress. The uncompromising realism of the
wrinkled face, the introduction of individual details,
mark the work as distinctly Roman in spirit. Balanc-
ing the scene from the life of the mistress of the
house, we see on the other side the master going out
hunting. These familiar episodes are generally exhibited—as here—on narrow friezes at the side of the
monument ; the front is more often than not occupied
by life-size portraits of the man and his wife, and the
back of the tomb is often covered with patterns of
rosettes, once brilliantly coloured. Among other
subjects of everyday life we find the family repast,
treated at times with Teutonic naïveté (cf. *R.R.*, ii.
90, 2).[60]   The scene on the relief at Mayence has
something of the solemn grandeur of Uhde's picture
of ' Saying Grace ' (' Komm', Herr Jesu, sei unser
Gast '). A delightful Family Repast occurs in the
rich collection at Arlon (plate xxvii.=Espérandieu,
4097). On the upper half of one face we see the
older members of the family sitting round a table
upon which is a trussed fowl. On the lower is the
children's dinner : three lusty infants eating out of a
soup tureen ; to the left an elder sister seems to repri-
mand them for their manners ; on the right an elder
boy plays the flute, and one of the small children
holds back a dog who has thrust his nose into the
soup. Sometimes the repast is treated purely as a
genre subject ; at others it assumes the character of

PLATE XXVIII.

2. SEPULCHRAL URN.
(Detail.) British Museum.

1. SELENE.
Relief from Argos. British Museum.

a sepulchral banquet, influenced, no doubt, on the
one hand by the Mithraic communion and the other
sacred repasts which were so characteristic a feature
of the Oriental religions ; on the other by the After
Life Banquet which from early times had been the
highest expression of Apotheosis. In these later
reliefs the two ideas probably coalesce, and the banquet partakes of the nature of a communion scene
uniting the living and the dead.

The mention of the ritual banquet leads me to say
a word concerning the vessels of various shapes which
often adorn the pediments of tombs, and which are
usually explained as conventional ornaments. The
chief of these are the patera or sacrificial platter, the
amphora, the krater or mixing-bowl, and the kantharos or chalice. Most of these already appeared
with ritual significance on Greek tombs ; and to
suppose that in centuries so charged with religious
emotion as those we have been studying, or among a
people so ' superstitious ' as the Romans, they sud-
denly lost all meaning and became purely decorative,
as most modern scholars assert, seems utterly in-
admissible. Rather do I believe that they are the
record of the mysteries deemed most holy alike by
the occupants of the tomb and their survivors. The
pair of amphorae, like the twin cruets of the mass, the
kantharos, like the Christian chalice, were emblematic
of the mystic sacrifice and communion ; but at present

the various utensils of the pagan mysteries have not been sufficiently studied. The kantharos was particularly beloved as a motive, and when foliage or flowers grow out of it, it comes within the circle of resurrection emblems. Birds often appear drinking from the top of a vase, to indicate the soul's thirst for the ' waters of life ' ; at other times the Apolline griffin guards the sacred vase. Within the pediment of the stele of the shepherd (*pecuarius*) Jucundus at Mayence we see just such a vase, with long branches growing out of it and spreading to either side.[61] There are peculiarly good examples of this class of decoration on several urns in the British Museum (*R.R.*, ii. 471, 5-7; 512, 4; 513, 8; 515, 4), one of which is reproduced here (plate xxviii. 2).

VII. The Monument at Igel. Summary and Conclusion

The splendid monument, still *in situ*, at Igel, near Trèves, with all its sculptures intact, offers us in visible form the synthesis of the beliefs which inspired the hopes of an ultramundane existence lifted far above this present world, combined with pictures of the life on earth of the occupants of the tomb. This grand family tomb was put up in the third century A.D. by the Secundinii, wealthy cloth-merchants of the country of the Treveri. From its size, and the beauty both of its architecture and sculpture, it is

PLATE XXIX.

THE IGEL MONUMENT NEAR TRÈVES.

one of the most important monuments of Roman Germania ; it now stands in solitary grandeur in the charming village of Igel, beside the line of the Roman road from Trèves to Rheims.   In antiquity it was one of many similar monuments, which may still be studied in the fine drawings and reconstructions attempted in the museum of Trèves.   Their tower-like structures with pyramidal roofs may, like the tomb of S. Rémy in Provence, be traced back to Graeco-Asiatic prototypes of the type of the Mausoleum of Halicarnassus and the Lycian tombs of Merehi and Payava (above, p. 152).   In the Gallo-Roman tomb, likewise, every available surface is covered with a profusion of carving (plate xxix.).

As far back as 1792 the Igel tomb excited the admiration of Goethe, who saw it as he travelled from Trèves to Luxemburg to join the allied armies ; he not only admired the column, but expressed a hope that it might be drawn and measured.   More than a century has elapsed and Goethe's countrymen have not as yet adequately fulfilled his wish.[62]   Both iconography and art throw a vivid light on the civilisation of this land of the Treveri with its mixed Ionian, Roman and Celtic elements.   The pleasant everyday scenes of the friezes and podium reflect the spirit in which the Romans of all lands and periods loved to record their *res gestae*, whether public or private ; the principal façade brings before us the

picture of a Gallo-Roman family ; the rest is given up
to the religious symbolism of the age, of which it is
the splendid and convincing epitome. The inscription declares the tomb to have been erected, in the
first instance, for the wife of one of the Secundinii
and the two children of the other. The survivors
are portrayed on the principal panel of the front face ;
above them are three medallions with busts of the
deceased. In the pediment, the rape of Hylas by the
water or wood nymphs—creatures of mystery and
terror like the noonday Pan—symbolises the rape
of the soul through the dread powers of death. *Ah
dolor ! ibat Hylas, ibat Enhydryasin.* And the further
allusion to the Rape as prelude of the Sacred Marriage is obvious. To the right, on the large panel of
the west face, we find two scenes from the legend of
Perseus. (*a*) The liberation of Andromeda, emblematic
of the release of the soul from its earthly chains
through divine intervention ; it is interesting to note
the novel motive of the half-figure of Athena, seen
emerging from the clouds to protect the heroic deed.
The epiphany of the goddess is represented in like
manner on the panel with the Apotheosis of Heracles.
(*b*) The scene where Perseus shows to Andromeda
the Medusa's head reflected in the water, an allusion
to the apotropaic power of the Gorgoneion to ward
off evil spirits from the tomb. In the west pediment
the story of Mars and Rhea Silvia carries, as we have

PLATE XXX.

APOTHEOSIS OF HERACLES.
Igel.

seen, the promise of awakening from the sleep of death
to a life of blessedness, with the further assurance
of wedded union with the god. These scenes are
balanced on the large panel of the east face at the
top by the scene of Thetis dipping Achilles into the
waters of Styx to make him invulnerable. The
allusion to the purificatory rite of baptism, which
was among the ideas introduced by more than one
of the Oriental religions, is evident, yet the allusion
to baptism by water is so rare that I think it must
be interpreted in this case by reference to a practice
prevalent among Teutonic and Celtic races of plung-
ing infants into cold river water immediately after
birth, partly for the purpose of purification, and
partly also because water was looked upon among
certain northern peoples as the *habitat* of beneficent
powers, under whose influence it was desirable to place
the new-born child.[63] The ritual words spoken by
the magician in the Hávamál, ' This I can make sure
when I suffuse a man-child with water : he shall not
fall when he fights in the host, no sword shall bring
him low,'[64] come very near indeed to the belief that
Achilles was made invulnerable by being dipped in
the waters of Styx. If our Treveri were among the
Celtic tribes who used these rites to purify the new-
born child and also to assure his immortality, we can
see why this special scene of the ' Baptism of Achilles '
was chosen to adorn one face of the Igel tomb. The

lower half of this panel is unfortunately undecipherable. In the pediment Luna—in Mithraic and solar monuments the inseparable companion of Sol Sanctissimus—drives her chariot, while Sol himself in his quadriga appears, as we shall immediately see, on the pediment of the adjoining face. On the rear wall of the tomb is a representation, rare at this period, of the Apotheosis of Heracles, who is shown in his chariot, mounting upwards along the path to Heaven, within the circle of the zodiac (plate xxx.). Minerva no longer rides by the hero's side, as in earlier Greek representations of the scene ; she emerges from the clouds to meet him and extends her hand to help his ascension, a motive that recalls the hand of the Biblical God stretched out to the Christian emperor on later Roman medallions of consecration. In the spandrels appear the heads of the wind-gods, emblematic of the four cardinal points that divide the sky. The winds, we must remember, were likewise looked upon as fertilising and generative powers of Nature, and moreover are peculiarly in place on a funerary monument, since the souls of the departed might become windspirits. The allusion in the images of this panel is evidently to the triumphant progress of the soul after it has, like Heracles, accomplished its cycle of earthly labours. But we are no longer in presence of a Graeco-Latin Heracles. He has acquired an Oriental character from being identified by the Greeks themselves

PLATE XXXI.

APOTHEOSIS OF A ROMAN EMPEROR.
British Museum.

with the Tyrian Melkarth, part of whose legend he absorbed into his own.   At Tyre, at one of the great festivals, this Heracles-Melkarth was burned in effigy, and Sir J. G. Frazer surmises that the festival was identical with the ' awakening of Heracles ' held in January, acutely inferring that the ceremony con-sisted in a dramatic representation of the death of the god, followed by a semblance of his resurrection :[65] so we get back by yet another path into the same cycle of resurrection emblems.   The splendid com-position of the chariot of the Apotheosis as it rushes upward amid the winds through the aether to the stars, recalls the promise of Apotheosis which that ardent mystic, the Emperor Julian, received from the oracle :

Then when thou hast put off the grievous burden of mortal limbs, the fiery car shall bear thee through the midst of the eddying whirlwinds to Olympus ; and thou shalt come into that ancestral home of heavenly light, whence thou didst wander to enter the body of man.— Eunapius, *Hist.*, fr. 26.

And even more vividly does it bring to mind the chariot of fire and the horses of fire which parted disciple and master asunder, and Elijah ascending ' by a whirlwind into heaven ' (2 Kings ii. 11).   The chariot as vehicle of Apotheosis appears again in the striking scene of an ivory leaf in the British Museum with the deification of Constantius Chlorus, the father of Constantine (plate xxxi.).[66]   The motive

has a long history, from the chariot borne through the
flaming aether on the sarcophagus of Haghia Triada
down to the time when it passes into Christian art in
scenes with the ascension of Elijah ; but nowhere does
it convey a more impressive sense of spiritual triumph
than here on the monument of Igel.

Two monuments have lately come to my notice
which offer interesting parallels to these notable scenes
of triumph and ascension through the cosmic universe
to the spheres.   The first is a sarcophagus of late
second-century date long in the Palazzo Barberini
in Rome, but so far unpublished (plate xxxii.).   In the
centre we have what at first sight seems an ordinary
Roman medallion group (*imago clipeata*), but the
medallion is itself merely a *corona triumphalis* decked
out with the signs of the zodiac, so that the transit
here again is through the celestial spheres.   The
medallion is held by two of the four Seasons arranged
on either side of the medallion, to mark the swift
alternations of time, while below it is a busy vintaging scene with the love-gods piling up the luscious
grapes—emblem, as so often in Christian art, of the
vintaging of the souls.[67]

The next is a much humbler monument, a little
stele lately found at Carnuntum, which tells with
even more vivid force the same story as the more
lavish imagery of the Roman sarcophagus.   On the
upper part of the stele within the *corona triumphalis* is

PLATE XXXII.

APOTHEOSIS ON A SARCOPHAGUS IN THE PALAZZO BARBERINI.

an eagle with outspread wings ; the winds occupy the four spandrels ; the image of Sol crowns the pediment, within which are two dolphins.[68] So here again we are confronted with the triumphant faith in the attainment, after purificatory rites, of a life of blessedness at harmony with the cosmic universe.

To return to the Igel monument : in the frieze above the Apotheosis of Heracles a genius bridles two griffins, sacred to Apollo and other solar gods, a subject peculiarly appropriate here, just below the pediment in which the 'Giver of Life,' Sol Sanctissimus himself, appears in his quadriga in a time-honoured scheme which recalls that of the Elean phalera (plate v. 2). The crown of the monument is a capital adorned with four heads framed by the intertwining coils of four snake-footed figures ; on the analogy of a fragment at Trèves, I take it that these heads represent the Seasons, the anguipedes being symbolic of the earth. This capital supports four half-figures holding up the terrestrial sphere which has the oviform shape given to it in the Orphic cosmogony : in these figures I incline to recognise the same divisions of the day and night that appear on the capitals of the 'giant' columns. Finally, above earth and the material universe, the eagle soars upward to the stars bearing with him Ganymede, symbol of the liberated soul.

The picturesque scenes from daily life that enliven the rest of the surface need no comment here. Study, however, the supper scene of the central face ; no Dutch master could have conceived it in a spirit more naturalistic, and the same applies to the scenes at either end. On the right we are introduced to the kitchen where the servants are cooking or polishing the dishes ; on the left other servants are occupied in the wine-cellar. A frieze of the podium shows big wagons laden with goods. Evidently the commerce of the Secundinii spread to distant parts, for on one panel we see their wagons crossing a mighty range of mountains, perhaps intended for the Alps. On another frieze again is a river scene ; the boats are piled with bales of cloth, and are rowed by sturdy oarsmen. The meaning of the dolphins and other creatures of the deep on the upper and lower friezes of the podium is clear from what has already been said of other representations. Thus, the imagery is taken from the same cycle as that of the sepulchral stelae, but is treated with greater freedom and mastery of expression. The beauty of the design comes, indeed, as a surprise to those who think of Roman provincial art as decadent or worse. The exquisite *putti*, for instance, that adorn the uprights on all four sides would not be unworthy of a master of the Tuscan Quattrocento.

I am aware that in stating this I am running counter to general opinion. It is the fashion to condemn the art of the Igel monument. May the ex-

planation attempted above of its iconography at least
dispel the charge of ignorant vulgarity brought against
the Secundinii by a recent writer.[69] They may have
shown themselves a little over-emphatic and over-
elaborate, a little too anxious to surpass their neigh-
bours alike in the expression of their piety and in the
record of their commerce. But the eagle, which to
those who overlook the Ganymede represents only the
vulgar ambition of a *négociant propriétaire* to appropriate to himself ' the emblem of military force and
of armed victory,' shows at least that the Secundinii
believed in a world beyond, where they too might be
liberated from their earthly cares. In these reliefs
the wish for personal fame, perhaps also for individual
survival, seems satisfied by those simple scenes which
record the successful earthly career of the deceased.
The carved panels and the statuary that adorns the
more important parts of the edifice seem rather to
proclaim joy in the soul's release from the shackling
forces of the flesh and of personality. The σῶμα σῆμα
doctrine seems here to have attained its apogee.
We are already within measurable distance of the
faith that inspires the New Mysticism :

Ici commence la pleine mer, ici commence l'admirable
aventure, la seule qui soit égale à la curiosité humaine, la
seule qui s'élève aussi haut que son plus haut désir.

We have travelled far from the primitive tombstones set up with magical intention to entrap the

ghost.   The dead man no longer lives in an obscure, uncertain region, propitiated by acts of adoration born of fear.   Magic had sought to imprison the soul ; religion had effected her liberation and sent her soaring above the earth into the radiant spaces of heaven. A new era was to bring with it a still higher revelation of the soul's exalted destiny, but we have reached the goal of our present studies, and it is well to close them upon the vision of what Rome, by holding to spiritual ideals all but repudiated by classic Greece, contributed towards the emancipation of mankind from the haunting fear of death.

NOTES

PRINCIPAL ABBREVIATIONS

A.J.A. : *American Journal of Archaeology.*

Aphaia : Furtwängler, *Aegina das Heiligthum der Aphaia.*

Arch. Anz. : *Archäologischer Anzeiger* (appears at end of *Jahrbuch*).

Ath. Mitt. : *Athenische Mitteilungen.*

B.C.H. : *Bulletin de Correspondance Hellénique.*

B.S.R. : *Papers of the British School at Rome.*

B.Z. : *Byzantinische Zeitschrift.*

C.I.L. : *Corpus Inscriptionum Latinarum.*

E.R.E. : Hastings' *Encyclopaedia of Religion and Ethics.*

Espérandieu : E. Espérandieu, *Bas-Reliefs de la Gaule Romaine.*

Helbig : W. Helbig, *Führer durch die Oeffentlichen Sammlungen Klassischer Altertümer in Rom*, 3rd ed., 1912, 1913, 2 vols.

Jahrb. : *Jahrbuch des K. Deutschen archäologischen Instituts.*

J.H.S. : *Journal of Hellenic Studies.*

J.R.S. : *Journal of Roman Studies.*

R.A. : *Revue Archéologique.*

R.H.R. : *Revue de l'Histoire des Religions.*

R.M. : *Roemische Mitteilungen.*

R.R. : Reinach, *Répertoire des Reliefs Grecs et Romains*, 3 vols.

NOTES

INTRODUCTORY ADDRESS

[1] Strzygowski's theories up to the year 1907 are summed up in the Introduction to my *Roman Sculpture*, pp. 12 ff. with references. In the intervening seven years his activity has been unremitting. His most important recent work is possibly *Amida* (Heidelberg, 1910), written in collaboration with Professor von Berchem and Miss Gertrude Bell. In it he discusses afresh the Oriental origin of all mediaeval European art. The preface is of special importance, as affording the author's review of his own work since 1885, in which he shows how his studies took him from Italy to Constantinople and Asia Minor, and thence to Persia and the further East. Strzygowski's recent attacks are mainly directed against the school represented by Professor Heisenberg, who look upon Byzantium as the direct heir of Greece, and more especially of Athens. See Strzygowski's last article in Supplement Band xix. (1913) of the *Römische Quartalschrift*, and his numerous articles and notices in the *Byzantinische Zeitschrift*. His views largely colour the important book of Oskar Wulff, *Altchristliche und Byzantinische Kunst* (vol. i. 1913); cf. also L. Bréhier, 'Études sur l'histoire de la Sculpture Byzantine,' in *Nouvelles Missions Scientifiques*, 1911.

[2] In the article 'Altchristliche Kunst,' contributed to vol. i. of the handbook *Die Religion in Geschichte und Gegenwart* (1908).

[3] This was the view of Wickhoff in the epoch-making monograph translated into English under the title *Roman Art* (1901). In the text of *Roman Sculpture* (1907) I showed reason for modifying this view, though the opening lines of the preface might lead to the supposition that I adhered to it.

[4] The relation of Château Gaillard to Syrian models is well known, but students will do well to read the inspiring article of M. Dieulafoy

in *Mémoires de l'Institut de France*, 1898 (vol. 36), pp. 325-86, 'Le Château Gaillard et l'architecture militaire au XIIIme Siècle,' a masterly handling of the question of the debt of Western Europe to Eastern art in the Middle Ages.

[5] *Palace and Mosque of Ukhaidir*, by G. Lowthian Bell, 1914. See also the following passages, pp. 72 ff., 110, 128, on the debt of Eastern to Roman architecture.

[6] E. March-Phillips, *The Works of Man*, pp. 131 ff. This high-handed abuse of Rome seems 'opportune and refreshing' to the anonymous reviewer in *Journal of Hellenic Studies*, 1912 (xxii.), p. 202. A similar alternately violent and 'saucy' style of writing spoils a far more important book, *Art*, by Clive Bell (1914). Mr. Bell certainly puts his finger on the weak spot of Greek art from the Parthenon downward and in Hellenistic and Roman times, but he fails to see that what he so justly and eloquently praises in Byzantinism (see *Art*, pp. 121 ff.) begins in the early Empire; is, in fact, the 'ascending line' which, as Riegl first perceived, makes its appearance in Rome by the side of decadent Hellenism.

[7] *A Wandering Scholar in the Levant*, 1896, p. 163.

[8] W. R. Lethaby in *Proceedings of the Society of Antiquaries of London*, 1912 (xxiv.), p. 293; cf. Strzygowski in *Byzantinische Zeitschrift*, 1913 (xxii.), p. 624.

[9] Cf. Professor Gilbert Murray, *Four Stages of Greek Religion*, p. 108: 'Rome herself was a Polis as well as an Empire. And Professor Haverfield has pointed out that a City has more chance of taking in the whole world to its freedoms and privileges than a Nation has of making men of alien birth its compatriots.' Cf. also the brilliant appreciation of the Roman Empire and of its policy by Professor Lake, *The Stewardship of Faith*, pp. 8 ff.

[10] R. W. Livingstone, *The Greek Genius and its Meaning to us*, 1912, p. 101.

[11] Cf. T. R. Glover, *Conflict of Religions*, pp. 28 ff.: 'No Roman poet had a more gentle, sympathetic love of Nature; none ever entered so deeply and so tenderly into the sorrows of men.' For Vergil's religious feeling and its exalted character see also Ferdinand Postma, *De numine divino quid senserit Virgilius*, Amsterdam, 1914.

[12] See Wickhoff, *Roman Art*, p. 45.

[13] Mr. J. W. Mackail, in his article 'Virgil and Roman Studies' in *J.R.S.*, 1913 (iii.), pp. 1 ff., brings out with his usual vivid touch this aspect of the poet. See especially p. 2 : 'So, too, with Virgil. Admiration of his poetical genius is only heightened by the fuller knowledge we are gaining of him as the voice and interpreter of the Latin civilisation in all its aspects. We no longer study him as mere literature ; or rather literature, with him, as with others, has grown into a new meaning. It is not a picture drawn and coloured on the flat, but an organic solid, attached everywhere to a three-dimensional world. At every point Virgil's work throws light on Roman studies, and has light thrown on it by them. The beautiful pattern, with which we have long been familiar, becomes stereoscopic ; the polished reflecting surface becomes translucent. We see deep into its structure, and have always the hope of seeing deeper ; we can trace layers of growth ; here and there we can watch the poetry coming into existence. And as we do so, point after point in the poetry kindles into new meaning, because it is seen in organic relation to an actual world.'

[14] J. W. Mackail, *Latin Literature*, p. 99.

[15] Gilbert Murray, *Rise of the Greek Epic*, 2nd ed., pp. 113 ff.

[16] See, for instance, Mr. Warde-Fowler, *Rome*, p. 7 ; and even Professor Haverfield, *Romanization of Roman Britain*, 2nd ed., p. 9.

LECTURE I

[1] The so-called 'law of frontality' was first put forward by the Danish sculptor Julius Lange in his epoch-making book, *Darstellung des Menschen in der älteren griechischen Kunst* (German ed. with a preface by A. Furtwängler, and a summary of the views in French, Strassburg, 1899). But what Lange christens 'frontality' involves a great deal beside the frontal pose. Accordingly E. Loewy, in his *Rendering of Nature in Early Greek Art* (English tr. by J. S. Fothergill, London, 1908), substituted the term *unifaciality* for frontality. For a useful *résumé* of Lange's and Loewy's views see P. Gardner, *Principles of Greek Art* (ed. 1914), ch. vii.

[2] Strictly speaking, the frontal pose of primitive art is restricted to statues in the round, while in relief the difficulty of drawing or carving figures and, above all, faces on a background, led to the adoption of the profile view. But the profile poses are stiff, and the figures in

relief are subject to the law of parallelism which flows from that of frontality, and deprives them of any real mobility.

³ Alessandro della Seta, *Art and Religion*, London, 1914. His earlier monograph, *La Genesi dello Scorcio nell' arte Graeca*, 1907, should be read by those interested in the technical processes by which the Greeks liberated themselves from the yoke of frontality (for which della Seta substitutes the expression *parallelism*) by the discovery of foreshortening, which enabled them to interrelate the various actions in a scene.

⁴ A. L. Frothingham in *American Journal of Archaeology*, 1912 (xvi.), pp. 368 ff. ; 1913 (xvii.), pp. 487 ff. ('Who built the Arch of Constantine ? ').

⁵ E. Strong, *Roman Sculpture*, pp. 328 ff. A good description of the reliefs of the arch, and of their relation to those in the contemporary arch of Galerius at Saloniki, by O. Wulff, *Altchristliche Kunst*, pp. 160 ff.

⁶ A. J. B. Wace in *B.S.R.*, iv. pp. 270 ff., pls. xxxv., xxxvi. (plate iii. by permission after his pl. xxvi.). But I see no reason for thinking that the figures of the north and south sides do not belong to the same period. The differences of technique are not greater than can be accounted for by the employment of more than one sculptor.

⁷ Alois Riegl, *Die Spätrömische Kunstindustrie in Oesterreich-Ungarn*, Vienna, 1901.

⁸ For both S. Trophime and Chartres see P. de Lasteyrie's monograph in *Monuments Piot*, 1902 (viii.), 'Étude sur la Sculpture Française au Moyen Age'; plate iv. is after his plate iii., 'Tympan de la Porte Centrale de la Façade Royale.'

⁹ *Maiestas Christi*—the name given to the scheme which shows the Christ as here enthroned within the mandorla. According to Strzygowski and Lethaby the type of the *Maiestas Christi* is of Egyptian origin. The mandorla 'encloses the figure of the infant Christ in his mother's arms in the Gospels of Etchmiadzin and in frescoes at Bawît' (Dalton, *Byzantine Art and Archaeology*, 1911, p. 683 and references).

¹⁰ I find myself paraphrasing here a sentence from Winston Churchill's novel, *Inside the Cup*, p. 62. The passage in which the American writer describes what the effect would be upon the Christian conception of the Christ were a natural instead of a

NOTES

239

supernatural birth attributed to Him, almost exactly expresses what
happens when the image of the divinity, instead of being shown
independent of any relation to other figures or objects, is made to
participate in a common action: 'If we attribute to our Lord a
natural birth, we come at once to the dilemma of having to admit
that He was merely an individual human person—in an unsurpassed
relationship with God, it is true, but still a human person. That
doctrine makes Christ historical, some one to go back to, instead of
the independent pre-existent Son of God and mankind.'

[11] The sculptures were discovered in the spring of 1910, south of the
town of Corfu, near the convent of Garitza, during excavations begun
by the Archaeological Society of Athens and continued by the
German Emperor. The relief is very flat; the style is non-Attic and
recalls Sicilian (Selinos) rather than Greek sculpture. Published
Praktika, 1911; cf. *Arch. Anz.*, 1911, p. 135; 1912, p. 247; 1913,
p. 106; P. Gardner, *Principles of Greek Art* (1914), p. 122.
Several architectural fragments of the temple were also found, as
well as a long altar adorned with a frieze of metopes and triglyphs
that stood in front of the temple. The pedimental fragments are now
in the local museum at Corfu. For the reconstruction of the pediment
see Sir Arthur Evans in *J.H.S.*, 1912, p. 286, fig. 2 (*Addenda*).

[12] On the apotropaic character of the Gorgon, and on the probable
derivation of the whole group with its flanking lions from a Hittite
model, see Ed. Meyer, *Reich und Kultur der Chetiter*, 1914, p. 113,
with note and fig. 83. Sir Arthur Evans (*loc. cit.*), on the other hand,
inclines to derive the type from Cretan art.

[13] Della Seta, figs. 67, 68.

[14] Loewy, *Rendering of Nature*, fig. 19.

[15] The most important discussion of Greek pedimental construction
is Furtwängler's in *Aegina das Heiligtum der Aphaia*, pp. 316-41.
Cf. my paper in *Journal of the Brit. and Amer. Society of Rome*, 1910,
iv. p. 395.

[16] A. B. Cook, *Zeus*, 1914, pp. 293 ff. and notes, explains the partiality
of early Greek sculpture for fish-tailed and snaky monsters to fill up the
angles of pediments, by supposing that they were originally used to
guard the apotropaic solar symbol which was so frequently placed
in the centre of pediments, or above the gable as acroterion. See the
examples given by Mr. Cook, figs. 212-18. For the Acropolis pediments see G. Dickins, *Catalogue of the Acropolis Museum*, 1912,
Nos. 35 ff.

[17] Furtwängler, *Aphaia*, fig. 254.

[18] Furtwängler, *Aphaia*, plates 104, 105 (for the general effect of the two compositions).

[19] Furtwängler, *Aphaia*, figs. 259-61.

[20] It is important to study the correct reconstruction which brings the Peirithoos and the Theseus close to the Apollo. Although both figures move away from the centre and from the god, the lines are so arranged as to link centre and lateral groups together. For the two Olympia pediments, see *Aphaia*, figs. 262-3.

[21] Furtwängler, *Aphaia*, figs. 265-7.

[22] *Four Stages of Greek Religion*, p. 90.

[23] Both are self-involved compositions. The Hermes is lost in sensuous dreams, and the Demeter in her grief. Neither statue is conceived in relation to the spectator.

[24] *Principles*, p. 118.

[25] To Greek archaeologists, and indeed to many others, those statements will appear pure heresies. Dr. Deissmann, for instance, who shows a deep feeling for art, says of the Eleusis relief that it is 'the most deeply religious work of ancient sculpture' which he has ever seen (*Light from the Ancient East*, p. 286).

[26] Furtwängler-Reichold, *Griechische Vasenmalerei*, i. pl. 36.

[27] We might judge differently of the principles which govern Greek composition if we knew more of the art of Asia Minor. For instance, the pedimental sculptures of the so-called Monument of the Nereids from Xanthos (Brit. Mus.), clumsy though they are in certain respects, show a finer sense of centripetal construction than most of the pediments found in Greece. The reason for this is the nature of the subject. The dead of the central group—a man and his wife with their children—are still imagined as beings of a superior order, as enjoying a state something between the human and the divine. Hence the tendency, not altogether neutralised by the obvious Attic influences, of placing the images of the dead in an attitude suggestive of them as recipients of homage. The poses are not frontal, it is true, but the lines flow towards the centre, focus the attention at that point, and lead one to look there for the dominant motive of the composition.

[28] Diodorus Siculus, xviii. 26, 27.

[29] According to a recent theory the *lustratio exercitus* represented is presumably that performed in B.C. 115 by an ancestor of Domitius (see Sieveking in the Austrian Archaeological *Jahreshefte*, 1910, xiii. pp. 95 ff. ; 'das sogenannte Altar des Cn. Domitius Ahenobarbus'). If that is the case, the instance is almost unique, for the Romans had no historical art in our modern sense, *i.e.*, as I have already pointed out in *Roman Sculpture*, p. 38, they hand down their present deeds, their *res gestae*, for the admiration of the future, but rarely search the past for those of their ancestors.

[30] I had discussed the problem of the introduction of the crowd into Roman relief, *Roman Sculpture*, pp. 46 ff. Della Seta (*op. cit.*, p. 278) says further : 'The problem had not yet been propounded in the case of the altar of Cn. Domitius Ahenobarbus, for the figures, though placed singly facing the spectator, do not form a compact mass, but are distinctly separated from one another against the background. This had already been indicated . . . on the Ara Pacis . . . for some of the figures of the *cortège*, who, instead of moving like the rest, seem to have stopped, as if to be better in view of the spectator.'

[31] See my *Roman Sculpture*, p. 57, and the remark quoted from Riegl.

[32] 'L'aigle funéraire des Syriens et l'Apothéose des Empereurs,' in *Revue de l'histoire des Religions*, 1910 (lxii.), pp. 119-64.

[33] For the Imperial Apotheosis and cognate cults see art. 'Apothéose' by Gaston Boissier in Saglio's *Dict.*, and also the chapter in his *Religion Romaine d'Auguste aux Antonins* (pp. 122-208) ; W. Drexler's art. 'Kaiserkultus' in Roscher ; arts. 'Apotheose' by H. von Gaertringen, and 'Consecratio' by G. Wissowa, both in Pauly-Wissowa ; art. 'Deification' by E. Bevan, in Hastings' *Encyclopaedia of Religion and Ethics* ; Kornemann, *Zur Geschichte der Antiken Herrscherkulte*, in *Klio*, 1901 (i.), pp. 51-146 (§ 3, 'Die römische Staatskulte der Kaiserzeit,' etc.) ; L. Purser's art. in Smith's *Dict. of Ant.* (a competent *résumé* of facts and theories) ; Marquardt, *Staatsverwaltung*, iii. pp. 91 ff. ; pp. 463 ff., pp. 275 ff. (*consecratio*) ; V. Gardthausen, *Augustus und seine Zeit*, i. pp. 466 ff. ; J. Toutain, ch. iii. of *Les Cultes païens dans l'Empire Romain* ; C. Pascal, *Credenze d'Oltretombe*, ch. xxv. E. Beurlier's *Le Culte Impérial* (1881) is still the most complete work on the subject. The entire documentary evidence for the Imperial Deification between the years 48 B.C. and 14 A.D. has lately been brought together in chronological order by Hubert Heinen in *Klio*, 1911 (xi.), pp. 129 ff. ('Zur Begründung des römischen Kaiserkultes'). Paul Wendland's *Hellenistische-römische*

Kultur, 1912 (sections 'Kaiserkult,' 'Sinn der Apotheose,' and the preceding sections on the temper of the Augustan age), contains the most illuminating pages that have yet been written on the Augustan period, its aspirations and cults.   See also Warde-Fowler, *Roman Ideas of Deity* (Lecture v., 'Deification of Caesar'—the preceding chapter on the 'Idea of the Man-God'); and O. Gruppe, *Griechische Mythologie und Religionsgeschichte*, ii. pp. 1503 ff.   Professor Ad. Deissmann's estimate of the antagonism of the early Christians to the Deification of the Caesars should likewise be read (*Light from the Ancient East*, 1910, pp. 344 ff.).

34 For Caesar's policy and desires in the direction of Apotheosis see Kornemann, *op. cit.*, p. 95 ; Teney Frank, *Roman Imperialism*, p. 342. Mr. Warde-Fowler, *Roman Ideas of Deity*, p. 113, seems to consider Caesar to have been indifferent to the idea of his own Deification.

35 The idea of the King-God developing as it did out of that of the Man-God, long proved equally repugnant to writers of the most divergent opinions—all of them apt, till lately, to stigmatise the cult of the ruler as gross idolatry or degrading servility, or else to sneer at it in the spirit of Seneca's spiteful satire on the Deification of Claudius. Christian writers naturally inherited the antipathy to the Imperial cult felt by the early Christians, who in this were probably also influenced by the monotheism of the Jews (see Ad. Deissmann, *loc. cit.*), while writers of a freethinking stamp condemned it along with every other form of ritual.   Of late years, however, a growing knowledge of the religious and political spirit which gave rise to the cult has issued in a saner view.   'Time,' says Professor Wight Duff, in a fine page on Augustan Imperialism, 'placed Augustus among the greater public divinities, and Caesar-worship attained a universality which prepared a way for the ultimate predominance of Christianity' (*Literary History of Rome*, p. 525).   Mr. Warde-Fowler, who owns that Emperor-worship, as equivalent to 'worship of a man,' was at one time abhorrent to him, handles the subject with sympathy and tolerance, and goes so far as to admit that 'its contribution to the idea of deity was wholesome rather than the contrary' (*Roman Ideas of Deity*, pp. 123 ff.).   Dr. Farnell (art. 'Greek Religion' in *E.R.E.*) says, in alluding to the deification of great men generally, that 'for better, for worse, it was a momentous fact belonging to the higher history of European religion ; for it familiarised the Graeco-Roman world with the idea of the incarnation of the Man-God.'   Professor G. Murray likewise, while condemning with characteristic vehemence the 'worship of the Man-God with its diseased atmosphere of megalomania and blood-lust,' in his discussion of Hellenistic deification points to the

inspiring character of the 'potential divinity of man' (*Four Stages of Greek Religion*, pp. 82, 139). Finally, two American historians, Professor Scott Fergusson in his *Greek Imperialism* (1913) and Professor Teney Frank in his *Roman Imperialism* (1914), show a far-seeing appreciation of the aims and motives which were at the root of both Hellenistic and Roman Apotheosis. The Hellenistic cult of the ruler is treated by J. Kaerst in an Appendix to vol. ii. pt. i. (1909) of *Das Hellenistische Zeitalter*, p. 374.

[36] For the derivation of the Imperial Apotheosis from the Hellenistic cult of the ruler, and for the influence upon the Imperial cult of the form of monarchy introduced by Alexander, see J. Kaerst, *Studien zur Entwickelung und theoretischen Begründung der Monarchie im Altertum*, 1898, ch. v. pp. 80-102 ('das römische Kaisertum'); p. 90 for the Augustan Apotheosis.

[37] See Seneca, *Epist.*, 108, 34.

[38] Cicero, letter to Atticus, xii. 36.

[39] At the end of the *De Republica*.

[40] Plutarch, *Vita Flaminini*, ch. xvi.

[41] *Anthologia Palatina*, ix. 402 (epigram attributed to the Emperor Hadrian).

[42] Letter to Atticus, v. 21. Cf. the passage in the famous letter to his brother Quintus (*ad Quint. fratr.*, i. 1. 26) written ten years earlier.

[43] Cicero, *Verres*, ii. 21, § 52 and *passim*.

[44] *C.I.G.*, 2927, 2369, etc.; Boissier, *Religion Romaine*, i. p. 121.

[45] On the *triumphator*, see Eisler, *Weltenmantel und Himmelzelt*, p. 40 ; cf. J. G. Frazer, *Early History of the Kingship*, 1906, pp. 198 ff.

[46] On the chariot of the *triumphator*=the chariot of Sol, see p. 168.

[47] J. M. Cornford, in *From Religion to Philosophy*, p. 162.

[48] Cumont, *L'aigle funéraire*, p. 157.

[49] Furtwängler, *Antike Gemmen*, iii. p. 324, fig. 168.

[50] Indian sardonyx, worked in very low relief, as a rule in three layers and sometimes five. The most general view is that it com-

memorated the departure of Germanicus in A.D. 17 on the Parthian expedition.   The figure facing Tiberius is explained as Germanicus between his mother Antonia (for whom the figure appears too young ; it is more probably an allegory) and his wife Vipsania Agrippina with the boy Caligula.   The group on the right is interpreted as Drusus Minor, son of Tiberius, with his wife Drusilla.   Of the deified princes to either side of Augustus, the one riding the winged horse is probably Marcellus, the other Drusus Major.   Tiberius holds the augural staff to indicate that the campaign is entered upon under his *auspicia* (Stuart-Jones, *Companion,* p. 426 ; Strong, *Roman Sculpture*, pp. 89 ff.).

[51] Cumont, *op. cit.*, p. 152.

[52] Some editions prefer to read *bibet* ; but does the present *bibit* really strike a false note, as maintained by Mr. Warde-Fowler (*Roman Ideas of Deity*, pp. 128, 152, etc.) ?

[53] J. Kaerst (*Studien*, p. 88) seems, however, to date the worship of the living Emperor from Augustus, and to consider that Augustus was actually worshipped under the name of different gods (cf. Gardthausen, *Augustus*, i. p. 885 and ii. pp. 517 ff.).

[54] Temple of Ancyra, *C.I.G.*, 4039.   Temples at Pergamon and Nicomedia, Dio Cassius, 51, 20.   For the *ara* in Lyons, see *C.I.L.*, xiii. p. 227.   On the cult of Roma and Augustus, see Kornemann, *op. cit.*, p. 99, and the numerous examples given by Marquardt, *Staatsverwaltung*, iii. p. 464, note 4.   On the cult of Rome before the Empire, see Warde-Fowler, *op. cit.*, pp. 129 ff.   The oldest instances seem to be at Smyrna as far back as 195 B.C. (*Porcio consule*, Tac., *Ann.*, iv. 56).

[55] On this episode, see the comments of Warde-Fowler, *Roman Ideas of Deity* (1914), p. 87.

[56] Arabian sardonyx.   The scene is generally referred to the Pannonian triumph of Tiberius in A.D. 12, when, before ascending the Capitol, he alighted from his car to do homage to Augustus.   To the right of the car stands Germanicus, the adopted son of Tiberius, who shared in the glory of the Pannonian exploit. (Suetonius, *Tiberius*, 20 ; Gardthausen, *Augustus*, i. p. 1228 ; Stuart-Jones, *Companion*, p. 424 ; Strong, *Roman Sculpture*, pp. 88 ff.)

[57] The frequent use of this emblem is clear evidence of the astrological leanings of the Emperor, who, like Tiberius, was versed in the occult sciences.   The Capricorn appears on the reverse of the gold coins of Augustus inscribed *signis receptis* ; see Gabrici, ' Numismatica di Agusto,' in Milani's *Studi e Materiali*, ii. p. 151, fig. 1.

[58] *Roman Sculpture*, plates xxvii., xxviii. ; *R.R.*, 1. 93-96.

[59] Warde-Fowler, *op. cit.*, p. 143.

[60] See on all this P. Wendland, *op. cit.*, pp. 142 ff.

[61] See Wight Duff, *Literary History of Rome*, pp. 524 ff.

[62] *E.g.* Warde-Fowler, *op. cit.*, p. 136, asserts that in Rome 'worship had not . . . the advantage of being combined with a genuine feeling for the plastic arts.' On what evidence does the same writer tell us of the sculptures of the Ara Pacis and the corslet of the Prima Porta Augustus, that these would not 'have been religiously impressive for the beholders, as well as interesting to the sculptor and his employer' (*op. cit.*, p. 138)?

[63] A curious example of the influence of the stiff Roman grave portraiture on Imperial art may be seen in the large cameo let into a book now in the Library at Trèves (Furtwängler, *Antike Gemmen*, iii. p. 323, fig. 167), showing an Emperor of the first century—possibly Claudius—and his family, facing frontally and tightly packed side by side as on a tombstone of the Via Appia.

[64] In the archaic period the pediment was left open, but figures or groups adorned its upper cornice. An interesting series of figures of warriors now scattered between Berlin and Copenhagen survives from an early temple at Cervetri. It is interesting to note that the central warrior, who stood over the apex, is placed with the torso turned frontally, though his legs appear in profile in order doubtless to unite him, partially at least, with the rest of the composition. For the figures, see Arndt, *Glyptothek Ny Carlsberg*, plate 171 ; and Wiegand, 'Terres Cuites Architecturales d'Italie' (in Arndt's text).

[65] The terra-cottas from the Faliscan temples are in the museum of the Villa Giulia. See my article in *Journal of Roman Studies*, 1915, v.

[66] L. Milani, *Museo Archeologico di Firenze*, 1912, plate c.

[67] Better seen in *Roman Sculpture*, plate xliii. (after Petersen's *Ara Pacis*), where the modern pieces of the sides are omitted.

[68] *Roman Sculpture*, plate x., fragment on right.

[69] W. Amelung, *Führer durch die Antiken in Florenz*, No. 99 ; Alinari photo, 1163.

[70] *Burlington Magazine*, June, 1914.

246   APOTHEOSIS AND AFTER LIFE

[71] Lucan's exhortation to Nero to fix his seat hereafter in the precise middle of the sky, assuring him that otherwise he will upset the equilibrium of the heavens (*de Bello Civili*, i. 45 ff.), reads now like fulsome flattery, but as a fact it probably reflects current belief as to the place assigned to the deified Emperor in the cosmic system. Likewise when Gaius and Nero were adored in the East as the New Sun, or when Nero is said to have introduced the radiate crown, derived through Hellenistic monarchs from Eastern sun-worship, they were but developing the religious policy of Augustus, who, if not yet exactly identified with the Sun, was, as Wendland (*op. cit.*, p. 147) points out, considered as endowed with parallel power (see what has been said above of the scene of Apotheosis on the Vatican altar of the Lares); Horace, *Odes*, iv. 5, 5 : *Lucem redde tuae, dux bone, patriae*, etc. ; cf. i. 12, 46. Cumont, in commenting on the passage of Lucan cited above, and on the similar praises bestowed by Statius on Domitian, denies that they are mere flatteries : ' Non ; les rites et les représentations de l'apothéose prouvent que les louanges des poètes expriment très exactement les croyances du culte Impérial. *C'est moins de leur part de l'adulation que de l'adoration* (*L'aigle funéraire*, p. 156).

[72] Eckhel, *D.N.*, vi. 278.

[73] The identification is, I believe, due to Mr. H. Stuart-Jones ; for the relief, see his *Companion*, plate l. It was published by E. Michon in *Monuments et Mémoires*, 1909 (xvii.), plate xvii.

[74] *Roman Sculpture*, plate lxiii.

[75] Domascewski in the Austrian *Jahreshefte*, 1899 (ii.), pp. 173 ff. See my *Roman Sculpture*, pp. 214 ff. For monotheism and Jupiter in Vergil, see F. Postma, p. 153 of the monograph cited, n. 11.

[76] *Roman Sculpture*, plate lxxi. 2. On coins, Sabina, and likewise Faustina, are represented borne upward by the eagle or by the peacock, against a stellated mantle which represents the starry firmament, and also perhaps carries with it the notion of a vehicle of Apotheosis (see Lecture II., p. 177). The two types of coins are shown on plate ix. 2.

[77] *Roman Sculpture*, plate lxxiii. and p. 216.

[78] The identification of the winged figure as the Aion is due to L. Deubner, *Röm. Mitth.*, 1912 (xxvii.). The Aion carries in his hand the orb or globe encircled by the zodiac, and with the snake as symbol of Eternity.

[79] *Roman Sculpture*, plate lxxxix.

[80] Cf. F. Cumont, *L'aigle funéraire*, p. 155.

[81] This important document has been published by Kornemann, *Klio*, 1907 (vii.), pp. 278 ff. (Papyrus Gissensis 20); the opening lines are specially interesting in the present context.

ἅρματι λευκοπώλῳ ἄρτι Τραιαν[ῶι]
συνανατείλας ἥκω σοι, ὦ δῆμ[ε],
οὐκ ἄγνωστος Φοῖβος Θεὸς ἄνα-
κτα καινὸν Ἀδριανὸν ἀγγέλλ[ων]
ὦι πάντα δοῦλα[δὶ] ἀρετὴν κ[αὶ]
πατρὸς τύχην θεοῦ χαίροντες.

As Kornemann (p. 280) suggests, it is evident that Apollo has mounted to heaven with Trajan on the Sun chariot, and then himself announces Hadrian's accession to the throne. The idea is the same as on the Vatican altar with the Apotheosis of Caesar.

[82] *Roman Sculpture*, plate xciv. and p. 308; the identification is Studniczka's. The same stone guarded by the Imperial eagle appears enthroned in solitary splendour on a chariot guided by a star as solar emblem on the reverse of coins of Elagabalus (Cohen, iv. p. 240).

[83] Riegl, *Spätrömische Kunstindustrie*, p. 81, with illustration; Thédenat, *le Forum Romain*, pp. 262 ff.; Huelsen, *The Roman Forum*, 2nd ed., pp. 98 ff. It is also illustrated by von Sybel, *Christliche Antike*, ii. fig. 20. For the interpretation of the relief as a sacrifice in honour of Mithras, see Frothingham in *A.J.A.*, 1914, pp. 146 ff.

[84] See Cumont, *Mysteries of Mithras*, pp. 209 ff.

[85] Reproduced by Koepp, *Die Römer in Deutschland*, 2nd ed., 1912, p. 141, fig. 112.

[86] Venturi, *Storia dell' Arte Italiana*, i. p. 54.

[87] *Roman Sculpture*, pp. 151 ff. and plate xlv. I now find a further confirmation for the Domitianic date from the affinities of style between these reliefs and the friezes of Domitian's *Forum of Minerva*; it is a point I discuss in my new book on *Art in the Roman Empire*. Huelsen's idea (*Roman Forum*, 2nd ed., p. 104), that these reliefs were once introduced into the balustrade of the rostra, now seems to me untenable. Dr. Carter has shown that the background is continuous from one relief to the other, and this fact, together with the arrangement of the animals on the front face—

placed as if moving towards one another and towards the same point—tends to show that they were simply placed on each side of the entrance to some sacred enclosure (*A.J.A.*, 1910, xiv. pp. 310 ff.). I should like to suggest tentatively that this was the space surrounding the equestrian statue of Domitian near to the site of which the reliefs were found. The mutilation of the head of the Emperor is one point in favour of this view ; and the background of notable buildings seems in the spirit of Statius, *Silvae*, i. pp. 22 ff. (for Carter's view see *op. cit.*, p. 317).

[88] O. Wulff, *Altchristliche und Byzantinische Kunst*, i. pp. 160 ff.

[89] This is a characteristic of later Roman architecture which has been often dwelt upon. See H. Stuart-Jones in *Quarterly Review* for January 1905, pp. 136 ff.

[90] For this class of sarcophagi, see Garrucci, vol. v., plate 339 ; example in Verona, *ibid.*, plate 333, 1 ; von Sybel, ii. p. 155 ; Kraus, *Geschichte der Christlichen Kunst*, i. p. 112.

[91] On the other hand, to represent all Christian art, and much Christian literature and ritual as a mere development and transformation of the antique, is an old view which many are now combating (cf. p. 10 of my Preface to Della Seta's *Religion and Art*). Rather must we admit with von Sybel (*Christliche Antike*, i. pp. 10, 181, and often), that within the sphere of the later antique were two independent developments, the heathen and the Christian ; but there were points of contact as in the present instance.

[92] See the criticism of S. Reinach in *Revue Archéologique*, 1907, ii. p. 184 n. This leaf of a diptych or book cover is variously assigned to Theodosius and to Constantine, and the balance of opinion seems, on the whole, in favour of the first attribution. See O. M. Dalton, *op. cit.*, p. 199 and note 1. I incline to retain Strzygowski's view that the ivory represents Constantine (cf. *Roman Sculpture*, p. 345 and plate cv.), though he does not, it seems, necessarily think the date Constantinian (*B.Z.*, 1913, p. 281).

[93] Ch. Diehl, *Manuel d'art Byzantin*, fig. 307; Dalton, *Byzantine Art and Archaeology*, p. 224 and fig. 138 ; Vöge, *Berlin Catalogue*, i. No. 7.

[94] *Ibid.*, fig. 308 ; Dalton, p. 227 and fig. 139 ; Molinier, *Ivoires*, p. 197.

[95] Kubitschek, *Ausgewählte Römische Medaillons in Wien*, 1909, plate xxi., from which plate xiii. 1 is reproduced.

[96] Reproduced here from a photograph kindly sent to me by M. Naville. The disc was found in the Arve, near Geneva, in 1721. No. 4 of the list given by Strzygowski in the article cited note 103. For the style see F. de Mély in *Monuments Piot*, 1900, vii. p. 74.

[97] The long series of ivory diptychs affords splendid examples of the new principles of frontal composition, and should be carefully studied. The fine plates of Molinier's great work make the task easy, and von Sybel in his *Christliche Antike*, ii. pp. 232 ff., has given a valuable classification based on the dated examples. I may rapidly mention here a few of the more remarkable pieces in the hope of attracting students to these exquisite little monuments of later Imperial art which are so consistently neglected by classical archaeologists and left to enrich the repertory of early Christian art. I have already mentioned the diptych of the consul Probus with the figure of the Emperor Honorius. The one leaf of the diptych of Felix of the year 428 in the Cabinet des Médailles shows the consul standing frontally between the looped-up curtains of a baldachino with the sceptre in his left hand and his right upon his breast (von Sybel, ii. p. 432 and fig. 67). The diptych of the young consul Orestes of the year 530 in the Victoria and Albert Museum is a good example of the later style of ornate diptych (O. M. Dalton, *op. cit.*, fig. 120). The consul is seated on an elaborate chair between the figures of Roma and Constantinople; in his right hand is the *mappa*, the napkin to be thrown as a signal for the commencement of the games: in the open space below are servants with sacks of money for distributing the consular largesse. In the spaces above the inscriptions are medallion portraits of the reigning Emperor and Empress. A lovely ivory at Monza (*R.R.*, iii. 62) shows on its left-hand leaf the portrait group of a Roman lady and her young son, and on the opposite leaf the portrait of her husband in the military accoutrement which betokens a soldier of rank (Dalton, *op. cit.*, p. 194 ; Molinier, *Ivoires*, plate ii.). The personages have been called Stilicho, Serena and their son Eucherius, and Galla Placidia, Valentinian and Theodosius II., but none of these identifications are in the least certain. (Cf. Delbrueck, 'Porträts Byzantinischer Kaiserinnen,' in *Röm. Mitth.*, 1913 (xxviii.), p. 335.) The massive composition of a diptych at Halberstadt suggests monumental sculpture rather than the delicate technique of ivory : in the centre stands a consul with a high official on either side of him ; on an upper frieze the Emperor and his son are seen enthroned between Roma and Constantinople, each with the solar nimbus ; this group of four, who are shown seated with their feet on a bench, is flanked by an Imperial guardsman at either side (*R.R.*, ii. 65 ; von Sybel, ii. fig. 68 ;

Dalton, fig. 118, consular group only). Good examples of diptychs are given by Venturi, *Storia dell' arte Italiana*, vol. i.; a number are reproduced under various Museums in Reinach's *Répertoire*; see also art. 'Diptychon' in Saglio's *Dict.*, and Hans Graeven's monograph 'Heidnische Diptychen' in *Röm. Mitth.*, 1913 (xxviii.).

[98] I see absolutely no reason for following Mr. Wace in dating these reliefs in the epoch of Constantine (*J.H.S.*, 1909, p. 64). On the contrary, the adoption of the symmetric full-face position for all the personages of the Imperial group points decisively, I think, to a later date, and generally the style is later than that of the Diocletianic reliefs on either the arch of Constantine or the arch of Galerius at Saloniki. See O. Wulff, *op. cit.*, p. 166; from Wulff's plate the composition seems to me more impressive than I had supposed.

[99] Dalton, p. 569 and fig. 356; see p. 10, No. 5, of the article by Strzygowski and Pokrowski cited in note 103.

[100] These discs are illustrated by O. Dalton, *Byzantine Art and Archaeology*, figs. 57-62, 358.

[101] *Archaeologia*, 1879 (45), plate xix. A fine example of the frontal chariot occurs on a fragment of silk preserved at Cluny (Diehl, p. 259, fig. 133).

[102] Dalton, fig. 34, who dates the relief at about the eleventh century. I should like to note here, in view of making it better known, the Ascension of Alexander in a cage drawn by griffins which appears in one of a series of fourteenth-century Burgundian tapestries with the story of Alexander and Bucephalus, in the possession of Prince Doria (Alinari photos, 29737-29742).

[103] Plate i. 1, after the fine coloured plate given by Strzygowski and Pokrowski, 'der Silberschild aus Kertsch,' in *Matériaux pour servir à l'Archéologie Russe*, 1892 (with a list of the nine extant silver discs of this class). See also O. M. Dalton, *Byzantine Art and Archaeology*, p. 569; Ch. Diehl, *Manuel*, p. 290, fig. 150. A good example of the *Adventus Augusti*, the Emperor returning or arriving as *triumphator*, familiar from many coins and reliefs, is in the Terme Museum (Paribeni, *Guida*, No. 103). A similar composition (but with the figure of the officer omitted) to that of the Kertsch disc occurs on a gold medallion of Justinian stolen from the Bibliothèque Nationale in 1831, but of which a cast exists in the British Museum. See Diehl, *op. cit.*, p. 292; *Cat. of Byzantine Coins in B.M.*, vol. i., frontispiece; Strzygowski and Pokrowski, p. 34; the medallion is illustrated here from a cast kindly supplied by Mr. G. F. Hill (plate i. 2).

[104] He wears the pearl diadem with jewelled clasp, as we see it in the statue of Barletta now claimed as a portrait of Valentinian, and the pendant pearl-drops. His tunic is embroidered with the *clavi*.

III

LECTURE II

Bibliography.—The literature which deals with the different aspects of ancient beliefs in the After Life is immense, and it is doubtless only very partial justice that I have been able to do to it in the bibliography upon which these lectures are constructed. Works that throw light on special points will be mentioned in connection with these, but a few general considerations may be of assistance to students.

(1) *General.*—The books dealing with the magical origins of art and of the gravestone and with sepulchral imagery are legion. The early chapters of S. Reinach's *Orpheus* will be found invaluable. See also Hubert and Mauss's article 'Magia' in Saglio's *Dictionary*. Della Seta in his *Religion and Art* deals comprehensively with the subject, not only as regards the sepulchral art of Greece and Rome, but that of all the ancient races. It will be seen in the sequel that I take a less exalted view than his of the art of Attica, of its mythological tendencies and spiritual values. This is said that students who read his book, as I earnestly recommend them to do, may not be confused afterwards by my remarks.

(2) *Greek.*—For the sepulchral monuments of the Greek period nothing has yet been written to surpass in value and interest Furtwängler's masterly introduction to his description of the Sabouroff Collection (Adolf Furtwängler, *La Collection Sabouroff*, Berlin, 1886). Here students will find an exhaustive discussion of the meaning and origin of the gravestone as ἕδος of the soul ; of the cult of the dead and the cult of the hero to which it gives rise ; of the bearing of both upon the development of the later ritual of the gods. In this preface, written nearly thirty-six years ago, Furtwängler put forward ideas on which researchers in that line have worked ever since. At the same time his theory, based on Fustel de Coulanges' *La Cité Antique*, ch. i., that 'among the Greeks as elsewhere the cult of the souls contains a very primitive fund of beliefs anterior to any adoration of the gods,' possibly requires modifying, or should at least be held in suspense. The question is debatable ; for a lucid and recent *résumé* of opinions see R. Dussaud, *Introduction à l'Histoire des Religions*, 1914, pp.

197-214. Conze's *Attische Grabreliefs* (3 vols., Berlin, 1893-1906) forms the indispensable basis for all study of Attic sepulchral art.

A selection of Greek sepulchral monuments is conveniently grouped together in Professor Percy Gardner's *Sculptured Tombs of Hellas*, which has the one drawback, however, that it was written as far back as 1896, and that much has been discovered since. M. Collignon's *Statues Funéraires de la Grèce*, though the title leads us to suppose it restricted to statuary, fortunately contains much also about sepulchral reliefs. For Greek ideas as to death Rohde's great book *Psyche*, now in its fourth edition (1909), and Gruppe's *Griechische Mythologie u. Religionsgeschichte*, must be continually consulted, and read through by those who have the time ; also Gruppe's various articles in Roscher's *Lexikon*, as well as in Bursian's *Jahresbericht*.

(3) *Roman.*—For Roman monuments there exists as yet no comprehensive history or handbook. Altmann's *Die römischen Grabaltäre der Kaiserzeit* deals with the important class of grave altars ; C. Robert's huge Corpus of antique sarcophagi (*Die antiken Sarkophagreliefs*, 3 vols. ; still in continuation) must be continually referred to for Roman art ; but I am mainly concerned with *stelae*, and only refer incidentally to altars or sarcophagi. A. de Marchi, *Culto Privato de' Romani*, two volumes full of curious information for the cult of the dead ; V. Macchioro's ' Il Simbolismo nelle figurazioni sepolcrali Romane' in *Società Reale di Napoli, Memorie della Reale Accademia di Archeologia*, vol. i. (1911) ; the pages dealing with the cult of the dead in Warde-Fowler's *Religious Experience of the Roman People*, and F. Cumont's *Les Idées du Paganisme Romain sur la Vie Future*, 1910, are of the first importance. So are the following : (1) For Roman tombstones with scenes from trades : H. Gummerus, 'Darstellungen aus dem Handwerk auf römischen Grab und Votivsteinen,' in *Arch. Jahrbuch* (1913), pp. 63-126. (2) For the tombstones in the provinces (*a*) Br. Schröder, 'Studien zu den Grabmälern der Römischen Kaiserzeit'; (*b*) R. Weynand, 'Form und Dekoration der römischen Grabsteine des Rheinlandes'—these two in *Bonner Jahrbücher* for 1902 ; (*c*) A. Furtwängler, ' Das Tropaion von Adamklissi und Provinzialrömische Kunst,' in *Abhandlungen der K. Kaiserlichen Akademie der Wissenschaften*, 1903, with full references to previous literature on the subject. The articles ' Funus' by Ed. Cuq and ' Sepulcrum' by E. Cahen in Saglio's *Dictionary* are admirable compilations of the Greek and Roman material. Cumont's *Religions Orientales dans le Paganisme Romain*, his smaller book on Mithras (both translated into English, the first with a suggestive introduction by Professor Grant Showerman), and his *Astrology and Religion among the Greeks and Romans*,

should likewise be consulted for the After Life beliefs of the ancient world.

[1] A distinction should be drawn between ghost and *revenant*; or rather, if the *revenant* = 'ghost,' then 'spirit' should be reserved for the excarnate soul. The fear of the ghost is a subject that has been treated many times, see especially J. G. Frazer, *The Belief in Immortality and the Worship of the Dead*, 1913 (full of curious information from all parts of the world); J. C. Lawson, *Modern Greek Folklore and Ancient Greek Religion* (1910), deals fully with fear of the ghost in ancient and in modern Greece. For the 'mischievous freedom of the ghosts,' see Warde-Fowler, *Religious Experience*, p. 85. The literature on the subject is almost interminable. Gruppe, *op. cit.*, ii. pp. 75 ff., is a valuable introduction. For the salutary effects of the fear of the ghost in historic Greece, see Farnell, *Higher Aspects of Greek Religion* (1912), pp. 88 ff.; cf. *ibid.*, p. 54.

[2] The gesture is often seen on sarcophagi—for instance, on a sarcophagus at Ostia (Castello) with the Death of Meleager (Vaglieri, *Guida*, p. 149, No. 4). The soul can leave the body through the mouth (Crusius, *Untersuchungen zu Herondas*, pp. 53 ff.), as on the fragment of an early Attic vase to which I shall return later (p. 145), where it is received by a Ker or winged daemon.

[3] See A. J. Evans, 'Tree and Pillar Worship,' *J.H.S.*, 1901, p. 119. On the tombstone as ἔδος or seat of the soul, see also Weicker, *Seelenvogel*, p. 9; Furtwängler, *Coll. Sabouroff*, Preface. For theories concerning the origin of the sepulchral stele, see also Deonna, *L'archéologie, sa valeur, ses méthodes*, i. p. 208.

[4] See J. G. Frazer, *Spirits of the Corn and the Wild*, Preface, p. vi : 'This refusal of the savage to recognise in death a final cessation of the vital progress, this unquestioning faith in the unbroken continuity of all life, is a fact that has not yet received the attention which it seems to merit from enquirers into the constitution of the human mind as well as into the history of religion'; and Furtwängler, *Coll. Sabouroff*, *loc. cit.* 'La question de savoir s'il y a ou non une existence après la mort n'a été soulevée que par la philosophie des peuples civilisés. L'ancienne croyance, commune à tous les peuples, même aux plus grossiers, ne connaît que l'être au delà du tombeau ; elle sait que la mort n'est pas anéanti, qu'il continue à vivre sous telle ou telle forme à l'état d'âme et qu'il conserve comme génie une puissance qui n'est enfermée dans aucune limite visible, ce qui lui permet d'exercer son influence sur les vivants.'

[5] So great was the fear of a return of the dead that sometimes, in the case of inhumation, to make matters doubly sure, the corpse was huddled together and tied up : examples of this practice occur in almost every Italian prehistoric museum, from the early cemeteries of Italy, in what is called the *cadavero ranicchiato* ; few anthropologists believe now in the once captivating theory that the huddled-up pose was intended to imitate the human foetus, and that the body was thus placed in expectation of re-birth.   Belief in the necessity of destroying beyond recall what we dread and consequently hate, underlies not only a whole series of beliefs and superstitions connected with the dead, but also a number of practices, such as the burning of witches and the *auto-da-fé*, which, springing from what were conceived by primitive man as necessities, afterwards, when their original intention had been forgotten, survive as apparently senseless and cruel practices.   In addition to the fear of the *revenant*, we have, in studying the origin of burial customs, to reckon with the belief which makes its appearance very early, that unless the body be entirely destroyed the dead cannot find their rest.   Hence perhaps originates the custom of cremation and other attempts, such as despoiling the dead body of its flesh and leaving the bones painted red, which has been observed in certain Neolithic burial caves of North Italy ; the obvious breaking of the bones in other cases, *e.g.* the *cadavero ranicchiato* already alluded to, to do away finally with the flesh.   Cf. J. C. Lawson, *Modern Greek Folklore* (especially pp. 412 ff.), and Warde-Fowler, *Religious Experience of the Roman People*, p. 91.

[6] Found in 1903 by the Italian excavators about two miles from Phaistos, in a tomb of a type otherwise unknown in Crete, but familiar in Lycia, *i.e.* a walled square chamber with a door (cf. the Harpy Tomb), R. Paribeni, *Monumenti Antichi dei Lincei*, 1908 (xix.), pp. 1-86 (plate xv. 1, 2 (*b*) after his plates).   See also F. von Duhn, 'der Sarkophag aus Hagia Triada,' in *Archiv für Religionswissenschaft*, xii. (1909), pp. 161-85 ; Karo, *ibid.*, vii. (1904), p. 130, n. 1. ; Lagrange, *La Crête Ancienne* (Paris, 1908), pp. 61-67, whose theories are discussed and disputed by A. J. Reinach, *R.A.*, xii. (1908), ii. pp. 278-88 ; E. Petersen, 'Der Kretische Bildersarg,' in *Jahrb.*, 1909, p. 162 ; R. Dussaud, *Les Civilisations Pre-Helléniques dans le bassin de la Mer Egée*, 2nd ed., 1914, pp. 402 ff., J. E. Harrison, *Themis*, 1912, pp. 158 ff. ; A. J. Reinach, art. 'Themis,' in *Rev. Hist. Rel.*, 1914, lxix. 3, p. 342. The sarcophagus which is in the Museum of Candia is dated at about 1400-1200 B.C. (see C. H. H. Hawes, *Crete the Forerunner of Greece*, pp. 86 ff.).   It is a small chest or λάρναξ of a type commonly found in Crete, see A. J. Evans, *Prehistoric Tombs of Knossos*, 1906, pp. 9 ff. :

'They are narrow and short, but apparently the body was laid in them with the knees drawn up' (cf. the *cadavero ranicchiato* above, note 5). For the symbolism of the cult scene on the sarcophagus, as also for the symbolic shape given to certain Minoan tombs, see A. J. Evans in *Archaeologia*, 1914, pp. 54 ff.

[7] This interpretation of the scene follows in the main Petersen, *op. cit.*

[8] Professor Boni's own report is, I believe, not yet published. For the *mundus patet*, see Warde-Fowler, *Roman Festivals*, pp. 211 ff. ; the same in *J.R.S.*, 1912, i. p. 25, and J. E. Harrison in *Essays and Studies presented to William Ridgeway*, 1913, pp. 143 ff.

[9] Furtwängler, Pref. *Coll. Sabouroff*: 'On a attribué aussi à l'âme la connaissance de l'avenir et recherché les moyens de l'interroger sur cet avenir.'

[10] First and last stanzas of a poem by Edmond Holmes, in *The Quest*, vol. ii. (No 4, July 1911) pp. 762 f.

[11] *Berlin Cat. Sc.*, 883 ; Deonna, *Les Apollons Archaïques*, p. 17 ; L. Curtius, *Antike Herme*, p. 18, figs. 12-14 ; cf. Pfuhl in *Jahrb.*, 1905 (xx.), p. 79.

[12] For Tamuli and the Sicilian tombs of the giants cf. Pinza in *Monumenti Artichi, Lincei*, xi. 1 (1901), and see *Addenda*.

[13] Lechat, *Sculpture Attique avant Phidias*, p. 251 ; cf. Deonna, *op. cit.*, p. 17.

[14] Collignon, *Statues Funéraires*, pp. 16 ff.

[15] Deonna, *op. cit.*, p. 34 and references.

[16] On the κοῦρος = the 'initiate youth,' see Gilbert Murray, *Four Stages of Greek Religion*, pp. 42 ff. G. Lippold, *Griechische Porträt-statuen*, 1912, takes a different view ; while admitting (pp. 13-15) the overwhelming number of sepulchral statues of κοῦροι, he seems to consider that all these were actually for the graves of young men, and that old men were commemorated by draped statues, in support of which he also quotes Tyrtaeus. The difficulty lies, as Lippold himself admits, in the almost total absence of draped male statues in the early archaic period.

[17] On the short side with the winged chariot, cf. below, note 63. For the soul-bird, see the exhaustive monograph by E. Weicker, *Seelenvogel*, 1902.

[18] The influence of modes of burial upon eschatological beliefs has been well put by von Sybel, *Christliche Antike*, vol. ii. pp. 38 ff., 'Jenseitsgedanken des Altertums.' It would seem as if the belief in the resurrection of the flesh and the belief in the immortality of the soul, which, though not mutually exclusive, represent radically different conceptions of ultramundane survival, spring respectively from the rite of inhumation which keeps in view a possible or even an ascertained activity of the dead under ground, and from cremation which by effectively destroying the body leaves the soul free to ascend or reascend into the upper air.   Mr. Lawson (*op. cit.*, p. 489) remarks of funeral methods in ancient and modern Greece 'that a preference for cremation, considered as a means to the single religious end (*i.e.* the destruction of the body), has been manifested'; and although in his opinion inhumation equally aimed at destruction, there is no doubt that it left a loophole for the introduction of the doctrine of a resurrected body.   Probably cremation is in measure responsible for the Orphic assertion that the body is the prison of the soul (σῶμα σῆμα).

[19] For the red colour as representing the aether, see Deubner, *Röm. Mitth.*, 1912 (xxvii.), pp. 11 ff.

[20] The various modes of conveyance to heaven are enumerated by A. Dietrich, *Eine Mithras Liturgie*, pp. 179 ff.

[21] Cf. V. Macchioro, *Simbolismo*, p. 124.

[22] This idea was held by E. P. Biardot among others, *Terres Cuites grecques funèbres dans leur rapport avec les mystères de Bacchus*, Paris, 1872, who, however, after the fashion of the time, went on a false track of mythological interpretation in his desire to see in every object some allusion to Dionysiac mysteries.

[23] For the Mycenaean stelae from the shaftgraves, see literature cited by E. v. Mercklin : *Rennwagen bei den Griechen*, pp. 7 ff. ; S. Reinach, *R.R.*, ii. p. 316, 6 ; p. 317, 2 ; Perrot, vi. pp. 762 ff. ; Drerup, *Omero*, pp. 31, 205 ; P. Gardner, *Sculptured Tombs of Hellas*, figs. 18, 19, 20.

[24] *Tree and Pillar Cult, loc. cit.*

[25] The best that has yet been said on these Spartan reliefs is by Furtwängler, *Coll. Sabouroff* (text to plate i., example in Berlin).   See also M. N. Tod and A. J. B. Wace, *Catalogue of the Sparta Museum*, pp. 102 ff., with references to recent literature ; P. Gardner, *Sculptured Tombs*, plate ii., pp. 76 ff. ; Collignon, *Statues Funéraires*, pp. 71 ff. Students are likewise recommended to read the earlier articles on

these stelae by Milchöfer in *Arch. Zeit.*, 1881, p. 294, and in the earlier volumes of the *Athenische Mittheilungen*; also Furtwängler, *Ath. Mitth.*, 1882, vii. pp. 160 ff. For the 'banquet of the dead,' see Deneken, art. 'Heros,' in Roscher's *Lexikon*; and W. H. D. Rouse, *Greek Votive Offerings*, pp. 3-36.

[26] The snake is the dead man's 'spirit in another form,' as P. Gardner puts it, *op. cit.*, p. 82 ; it is what Professor Gilbert Murray calls the 'old superhuman snake, who reappears so ubiquitously throughout Greece, the regular symbol of the underworld powers, especially the hero or dead ancestor' (*Four Stages*, p. 33).

[27] Furtwängler, *Coll. Sabouroff*, text to plate i., where see references to earlier literature, has pointed out that the cock, like the dog, was held in Persian beliefs to ward off evil spirits. The cock, moreover, is said to have been introduced from Persia ; but this, as the Spartan stelae, which cannot from their style be later than the seventh century, show, must have been earlier than is generally supposed (Furtwängler). For the apotropaic function of the cock, see Conze, *Attische Grabreliefs*, i. p. 10. The beautiful frieze of cocks and hens from a monument at Xanthos (*Brit. Mus. Sculpt. Cat.*, 82) is certainly apotropaic, it being consistent with archaic custom to surround a monument, whether temple or tomb, with a band of protective influences. For the symbolism of animals see art. 'Animals' by N. W. Thomas in *E.R.E.* ; O. Keller's *Thiere des Altertums*, 1887-1912 (2 vols.) ; and Gruppe, *op. cit.*, pp. 792 ff. Below, note 57, and Lecture III. note 50.

[28] The offering of eggs to the dead has a magical intention, since, as Dr. Nilsson has pointed out ('Das Ei im Totenkult der Alten,' in *Arch. für Religions wissenschaft*, 1908 (xi.), pp. 544 ff.), the egg is an apparently inanimate and inert substance which contains within itself a potent principle of life, and that which has a special vital power must perforce awake or enhance the vital powers of those to whom it is offered. See also A. Dietrich, *Mutter Erde*, p. 103.

[29] The pomegranate is likewise held by the enthroned female figure ; for its meaning on the Spartan reliefs, see Furtwängler, *Coll. Sabouroff*, i., text to plate i. ; Milchöfer in *Ath. Mitth.*, ii. pp. 464, 469, etc. The pomegranate would be thought to contain in its myriad seeds the principle of life, and, like the egg, became an easily understood instrument of re-birth. It possibly appears in this sense on the garments of the priests in *Exodus*, xxviii. : 'And upon the skirts of it thou shalt make pomegranates of blue, and of purple, and of scarlet.' Cf. E. Benzinger in the *Jewish Cyclopaedia*, art. 'Pomegranates,' who remarks that throughout the East the pomegranate is the

general symbol of luxuriant fertility and life; see, however, the various explanations of these pomegranates given by Flinders Petrie in Hastings' *Dictionary of the Bible* (art. 'Bell'), i. p. 269, and *ibid.*, art. 'Art' ('lotus and bud in the shape of pomegranates, misnamed in Palestine "bell and pomegranate"'); Eisler, *Weltenmantel*, p. 25.

[30] The interesting relief in Lansdowne House (*R.R.*, ii. 519, 3), so quaintly interpreted as 'Homer meditating on the Iliad,' comes within the same category. It represents the dead man seated leaning on a staff; under his seat, in the place often occupied by a dog, appears the griffin as vehicle of the soul; opposite him is a tree stem around which twines the snake-soul; on the top a bird and branching foliage—all emblems of survival and resurrection. The real provenance is unknown. The same influences pervade the stele, said to come from Saloniki, in Constantinople, where the dead couple seated are faced by the snake which feeds from a cup held by the woman, while the man holds in his hand a burgeoning staff (Mendel, *Catalogue*, No. 91).

[31] J. A. K. Thomson, *Studies in the Odyssey*, Oxford, 1914, p. 93: 'For the Homeric religion the world of the dead hardly exists any more than it did for the religion of Israel.' The comparison does not seem altogether exact (see below, note 85).

[32] The Homeric conception of death, and its subsequent influence on the Greek mind and on Greek art, have been admirably summed up by von Sybel in the Introduction to his *Christliche Antike*, from which my own summary in the text is largely paraphrased. Cf. also Della Seta, *Religion and Art*, pp. 179 ff. ('the funerary conception in Homer'), and Carlo Pascal, *Le Credenze d'Oltre Tomba*, I. ch. xii. ('L'oltre tomba Omerico').

[33] Stele of *Xanthippos*, from the monastery of Asomatos, near Athens; generally interpreted as the stele of a shoemaker, unless indeed it is a votive offering to Asclepios for the cure of a bad foot (*Brit. Mus. Sculpt. Cat.*, 628). The bird held by the girl is the symbol of the soul.

[34] Style of the Pheidian period.

[35] *Actors, e.g.* the Attic stele at Lyme Park (*R.R.*, ii. p. 520, 3; first published by me in *J.H.S.*, 1903, plate xiii.).

[36] Cf. Della Seta, *Religion and Art*, p. 229. This is true, on the whole; yet occasionally on an archaic stele (*e.g.* Villa Albani, of a mother and her children = *R.R.*, iii. 153; Helbig, No. 805) the interest is as equally distributed between the dead and the living as

on the stele of Hegeso. For an example in which the dead is almost forgotten in the crowd of sorrowing relatives, see *R.R.*, ii. pp. 402, 403, etc. Furtwängler's view, *Coll. Sabouroff*, Pref., that all the persons represented on these stelae are either already dead or thought of as dead, is, I think, untenable.

[37] See Della Seta, *op. cit.*, pp. 227-31.

[38] Pp. 84, 184, and *passim*. Gardner's views largely represent those of the scholars cited in note 25, who first interpreted the Spartan reliefs.

[39] Plate xvii. 1, after Conze, *Attische Grabreliefs*, pl. i. (see text for references to the older literature). A new drawing by Gilliéron shows that only one horseman is depicted on the socle, not two as formerly surmised (Loeschcke, *Arch. Anz.*, 1913, p. 64, who explains the picture as that of the 'heroised dead'). The dead man is frequently represented as rider, *e.g.* on the socle of the stele No. 73 in *Coll. Barracco* ; the action of galloping suggests the further notion of racing or riding as a noble pastime ; for the discarded notion of a scene of mortal racing see *Ath. Mitth.*, iv. pp. 44, 291.

[40] The socle in the archaic period seems to have been not unfrequently reserved for symbolic scenes or objects ; see, among others, the archaic Ionian stele from the island of Symi in the Museum of Constantinople, G. Mendel, *Cat.*, 14, where the boar on the socle is assuredly introduced as a prophylaxis ; cf. Loeschcke in *Jahrb.*, 1887 (ii.), p. 223 ; and the Barracco stele mentioned in note 39.

[41] For the meaning of both dog and horse in Greek sepulchral imagery see Furtwängler, *Ath. Mitth.*, vii. 163, and his introduction to *Coll. Sabouroff*, p. 26 ; and cf. the articles of Milchöfer and Loeschcke, quoted in note 25. P. Gardner (*J.H.S.*, v. 131) suggested that a *mortal* horse and dog were intended in these reliefs, but this view is untenable. For the underworld dog see Erwin Rodhe, *Psyche*, ed. 4, ii. p. 83 (dog of Hekate) ; i. p. 242, etc. ; Gruppe, *op. cit.*, pp. 803 ff. For the dog on the Chrysapha reliefs, Tod and Wace, *op. cit.*, No. 10 ; see below, note 56. On the stele of Eutamia the guardian dog may likewise be intended to convey an allusion to the lady's name. L. Malten's exhaustive article 'das Pferd im Totenglauben' in *Arch. Jahrbuch*, xxix. (pub. Jan. 30, 1915) only reaches me as I revise these notes for press. Malten treats most fully of the horse as ἕδος of the soul and in the ritual of the dead, of the dead as horseman, and also discusses the dog, the bird in its many forms, etc., in relation to the same cycle of beliefs. Malten postulates more definitely than has been done so far, that dog, horse, snake, so often

accumulated on grave reliefs as underworld symbols, are originally *habitats* or forms in which the soul appears (*Erscheinungsformen*).

[42] Numerous examples in Gardner, *op. cit.*, who, however, does not go beyond seeing in these birds votive offerings or gifts. For the birds = souls which the dead hold in their hand on archaic grave reliefs, especially in Cyprus, see Weicker, p. 26, note 5, who admits the duality of representation 'as human being and as soul.'

[43] The lion, to whom we shall often have occasion to return, occurs at a very early date in Phrygia as guardian of the tomb, P. Gardner, *Sculptured Tombs*, fig. 25, pp. 64 ff., and Sir William Ramsay in *J.H.S.*, 1888, 1889, and 1890. A good instance in Greece, at Corfu, from the tomb of Arniadas (Gardner, p. 200) ; the classic examples are the lion of Cnidus in the British Museum, which was set up on the tall pyramidal structure on the promontory to commemorate the victory of Conon in B.C. 394 (Gardner, pp. 225 ff., fig. 77), and the celebrated lion of Chaeronea still *in situ*. For other examples see Gardner, pp. 130 ff.; Collignon, *Statues Funéraires*, figs. 147-53. The three first all in Athens ; of these, fig. 148 is especially interesting as showing the Graeco-Oriental motive of a lion holding between his paws the head of an animal which he has overcome (see p. 151). At a later date aetiological stories (Lais, Leaina, etc.) were invented to account for the lions on certain tombs, when their apotropaic and other more primitive functions had been forgotten. For the lion and its meanings and mythology, see, further, Gruppe, *Handbuch*, p. 380. The basis for all study of the symbolism of the lion on graves remains Usener's *de carmine quodam Phocaico* (in his *Kleine Schriften*, iii. 18). See below, note 69.

[44] The splendid stele of Dionysus of Kollytes, surmounted by a bull, in the Athenian Ceramicus, is present to every one's mind, Collignon, fig. 154, also fig. 155 and fig. 156 (bull in British Museum).

[45] See A. Brückner and E. Pernice, 'Ein Attischer Friedhof' in *Ath. Mitth.*, xviii. pp. 73-191, and the more recent work of Frederick Poulsen, *Die Dipylongräber und die Dipylon Vasen*, Leipzig, 1905 ; for the vase placed *on* the actual grave, *ibid.*, p. 19.

[46] Saglio, *sub. voc. funus*, fig. 3342.

[47] Plate xviii. after Fairbanks, *White-figured Lekythoi in the Museum of Boston*, plate vi. As a class they can best be studied in E. Pottier's 'Lécythes blancs attiques' (in *Mélanges des Écoles Françaises d'Athènes et de Rome*), whose classification is important to the

student of sepulchral ritual. Without seeking for examples outside P. Gardner's ch. ii. ('Worship of the Dead'), I should like to show briefly how closely the scenes on the lekythoi reflect the same beliefs as to the other life that we note in connection with the most primitive grave monuments. For instance, there can be no doubt, to my mind, that in fig. 8 (lekythos from Eretria) the bunch of grapes which a lady hands to a boy at her feet is symbolic of immortality. What Professor Gardner calls a 'curious convention,' *i.e.* the introduction of the actual dead into the scenes, is simply a proof of the belief that the dead is immanent in his own stele (fig. 9). When the dead are represented as playing the lyre, it is probably in allusion to their ultra-mundane pastimes (*R.R.*, ii. 373, 4, at Athens, but it is noteworthy that the stele comes from Acarnania, *i.e.* is non-Attic). Most significant of all is fig. 11, from a red-figured vase in the British Museum (*Cat. Vases*, iv. plate 4), where the pathetic central figure standing on the grave is well explained by Gardner as the dead 'herself in spiritual presence.' As a rule, the scenes of the cult of the tomb are confined to *lekythoi*. Besides the one mentioned in the text, specially beautiful examples are Fairbanks, pp. 203 and 283, in Athens and Paris respectively. On the whole question of votive offerings at graves see Furtwängler in *Coll. Sabouroff*, ii. pp. 16 ff.

48 See R. W. Livingstone, *The Greek Genius and its Meaning to us*, p. 86.

49 I use the words 'gave a new turn . . .' advisedly—as it is impossible to look upon Plato as anything but a mystic by temperament, though his acceptance of the mystical faith of Pythagorean Orphism may have been a later development in him. Neither Orpheus nor the Orphic beliefs find any direct expression in Attic sepulchral art, though Orpheus with his lute appeared, as a purely mythological figure, in the Nekuia of Polygnotus at Delphi (Paus. x. 30, 3, and cf. ix. 30, 3).

The allusions to the Orphism of Plato on p. 141 and the first part of this note were written before I had become fully aware of the debated question whether Plato was initiated into the Orphic doctrines by Socrates—on this supposition himself an Orphic—or after his master's death, and independently of the teaching of Socrates. (See F. M. Cornford, *From Religion to Philosophy*, §§ 126-9, who in § 129, 'Plato's Conversion to Pythagoreanism,' seems to state the problem very clearly ; A. E. Taylor, *Varia Socratica*, 1911, *passim* ; J. Burnet, *Greek Philosophy from Thales to Plato*, 1914, pp. 151 ff.) Pisistratus is credited with the introduction into Attica, alike of Homer and of Orpheus ; (for Orpheus see Gruppe, *Handbuch*, p. 1034 ; Roscher,

iii. 1196 and 1132 ; Burnet, *op. cit.*, p. 32); of the two religious currents, therefore, which are generally held to be antagonistic and irreconcilable. But their existence side by side, though Homer long kept the upper hand, may account in measure for the persistence of resurrection and After Life symbolism noted on certain Attic stelae. Presumably the Orphism so often scoffed at by Plato (e.g. *Rep.*, p. 363, C, etc.) is a popular form of Orphism full of naïve superstition, while the Orphism for which, as some now have it, Socrates was put to death (see A. E. Taylor, *op. cit.*, pp. 30 ff. ; J. Burnet, pp. 180 ff.) must have represented a reformed faith introduced by the Pythagoreans of Magna Grecia (cf. Adam, *Religious Teachers of Greece*, p. 191). All hese are questions of vital importance for our sepulchral imagery.

[50] See Lecture III. p. 197.

[51] For the sentiment cp. also Pindar's second Olympian ode, 57 ff., 131 ff., and especially the passage beginning ἔνθα μακάρων νάσος ὠκεανίδες. See J. Adam, *Religious Teachers* (Lecture vi., ' Pindar ').

[52] Wilamowitz, *Bucolici Graeci*, p. 94. Cf. Christ, *Griechische Literaturgeschichte*, ii. 1, 151, for the authorship.

[53] *Antike Denkmäler*, iii. plates v.-vi.

[54] C. M. Kaufmann, *Jenseitshoffnungen*, pp. 11 ff.

[55] Colonna Ceccaldi, *Monuments Antiques de Chypre*, 1882, p. 71.

[56] *Antike Denkmäler*, 1889, i. plates xliv.-xlvi. for the specimens in Berlin, Vienna, and Smyrna, and the London fragment mentioned below in note 57; for the example in Constantinople see *Mon. dell'Inst.* xi. plate liv.; S. Reinach, *Rev. des Études Grecques*, 1895, p. 161, enumerates as many as eighteen of these sarcophagi scattered among various museums. A complete list of examples known up to 1901 in A. Joubin, *de Clazomeniis Sarcophagis*. For the splendid example in the British Museum see A. S. Murray, *Terracotta Sarcophagi Greek and Etruscan in the British Museum*, 1898, plates i.-vii.; for examples recently acquired by Berlin, *Ant. Denkmäler*, ii. plates xxv.-xxvii. and plate xxviii. My plate xix. is after Murray, *op. cit.* pl. iii. (detail of interior).

[57] The young man with the two dogs occurs on a fragment in the British Museum ; see *Ant. Denkm.*, i. 46, 3. For its interpretation see Furtwängler in *Arch. Anz.* (1889), p. 147, who shows that the youth between two dogs, signifying that he is their master, is in a sense a symbol of Apotheosis. Furtwängler also recalls here that in Persian belief dog and cock protect the soul from evil spirits on its way to the underworld, cf. Loeschcke, 'Aus der Unterwelt' in *Dorpater Programm*,

1888, and the criticism of his views by O. Immisch in Roscher, art. 'Kerberos,' pp. 1127 ff. I abide by the view expressed in the text that the cocks are ἀποτροπαῖα. Cf. Lecture III. p. 214. For this function of the cock see especially Gruppe, *op. cit.*, ii. pp. 794 ff.

[58] See the epoch-making article 'Ker,' by Otto Crusius, in Roscher, ii. pp. 1150 ff., and Weicker, *Seelenvogel* (1902), pp. 2-7, who discusses the origin and nature of Keres, Erinyai, Sirens, etc., and shows their cognate characters, and how the Ker, for example, from being a daemon of the vampire class that sucks from the dead the blood which is the principle of life, and so draws out his soul, can also be identified with the soul (cf. O. Crusius, *loc. cit.*, who conjectures that the soul was thought to take on wings at the moment of separation from the body). In this way the Ker, as Weicker points out, sheds its character of death daemon to put on that of 'angel of death.'

[59] Published by P. Hartwig, *Journal of Hellenic Studies*, 1891, xii. p. 340.

[60] *Bull. Corresp. Hellénique*, 1893, p. 238, fig. 6 ; Weicker, *op. cit.*, fig. 9, pp. 14 ff., who gives the interpretation followed above.

[61] See above note 43 ; and below, note 69.

[62] The Chariot of Monteleone, first published by Furtwängler in Arndt Bruckmann, *Denkmäler*, pl. 586-587 = (his *Kleine Schriften*, ii. pp. 314 ff., pl. xxx.-xxxii.) Plate xv. 2 (*a*) from a recent photograph.

[63] So also in Roman times ; cf. the winged chariot that bears the deified Caesar on the Vatican altar, above, p. 67.

[64] E. Loewy in *Mélanges Perrot*, 1903 ('Zum Harpyien Monument'), pp. 223-225, shows that the pre-eminent position accorded to the women of the family on the principal face of the monument points to the matriarchal customs of Lycia where the leading position of women, spoken of by Herodotus (i. 173) is borne out by the inscriptions. Milchöfer had likewise regarded the scenes of the Harpy Tomb as homage or worship rendered to the heroised dead (*Ath. Mitth.*, 1879, iv. p. 168 ; *Arch. Zeit.*, 1881, xxxix. p. 53). Gardner, *Sculpt. Tombs*, p. 72, regards the little kneeling female figure below the Harpy on the west side to be that of the donor or dedicator of the tomb. Winged figures similar to those of the Harpy Tomb occur on the archaic fragments from Ephesus (*Brit. Mus. Sculpt. Cat.*, p. 37, Nos. 36-45), cf. Weicker, *op. cit.*, p. 126, and note 1.

[65] We are here confronted with a fresh proof of the close connection, so often pointed out, between the inhabitants of Southern Gaul and the Ionians. Marseilles had been colonised by the Phocaeans, and other towns of the *littoral* may well have been of Ionian origin. The resemblance between the 'Nativity of Aphrodite' and the relief of a martyrdom at S. Trophime is noted by Dom Leclerq in the admirable article 'Anges' in the *Dictionnaire d'Archéologie Chrétienne*. Dom Leclerq likewise quotes the scene of the weighing of the souls by the angels, but could not at the date of his article have known of the Boston Throne.

[66] The parallelism between the stooping angels and the stooping nymphs is as remarkable as that between the *nude* kneeling souls in the trays of the one balance, and the *nude* standing souls of the other. On the other hand, the cloth held in front of the 'Aphrodite' may have the same significance as that in which in Christian art the angels receive and *clothe* the spirits as they pass to another world ; cf. the ivory in the British Museum with the martyrdom of S. Menas, above whom hovers an angel spreading out his mantle to wrap about the newborn soul of the saint (*Cat. Early Christian Antiq.*, No. 297, and plate iv.). It is in the same order of ideas that on the relief of the Death of Our Lady in S. Maria in Trastevere (above the tomb of Cardinal d'Alençon), the soul in the form of a swaddled babe is held up by S. John.

[67] Weicker, *Seelenvogel*, p. 96, fig. 25.

[68] The art types of this tomb are discussed by Fr. Poulsen (*der Orient und die frühgriechische Kunst*, 1912, pp. 150 ff., figs. 179-80), who consider that they belong to the Phoenicio-Cypriote cycle. See Poulsen, *ibid.*, figs. 182, 183, for a fragment of relief from Isinda in Lycia, now in Constantinople, with men, horses, and dogs moving to the right. It resembles in style the Lycian processional reliefs in the British Museum.

[69] On the lion in Asia Minor, see Cumont, *Oriental Religions*, p. 224, note 2, and references. A. B. Cook, *Zeus*, p. 238 : 'Greeks and Romans alike, therein agreeing with the Egyptians and the nations of the nearer East, looked upon the lion as an animal full of inward fire and essentially akin to the sun.' Both bull and lion, from their tawny or reddish colour, were early connected with the idea of fire (Gruppe, *op. cit.*, ii. pp. 797 ff.) ; the sacrifice of bulls to the Sun (= Fire) was of extreme antiquity, and, as Gruppe points out, at the back of this ritual we doubtless have the conception of Fire or Sun reabsorbing the particles (bulls) once detached from it. As the lion

represents fire, the meaning of the lion devouring the bull is evident. But the bull, as we shall see (Lecture III. p. 194), is something more than the divine fiery particles to be reabsorbed ; it also represents, I take it, at least on the tombs, the earthly tenement within which the particles are imprisoned ; hence the bull must be devoured before the particles can be liberated. I propose shortly to deal with the imagery of the group of lion and bull at greater length than is possible here.

[70] O. Benndorf, *Das Heroon von Gjölbaschi-Trysa*, Vienna, 1889. I may briefly indicate those of the scenes that bear most immediately on the present subjects :—(*a*) Over the entrance, outside : four heads of winged lions, and between them in the centre the mask of the Medusa, all apotropaic ; beneath each pair of lions the heroised couple facing. (*b*) Over the door, inside : the row of dwarf-like figures is again apotropaic ; the dancing figures on each side are emblematic of After Life joys, like the Bacchic figure on Roman tombstones (pp. 199 ff.). (*c*) On the left of the doorway the chariot of the Apotheosis (B. plate xxii.) here combined with the episode of Bellerophon and the Chimaera. Behind the group of Apotheosis is a long banquet scene with the Blessed reclining, etc. Cf. Koepp, *Jahrb.*, 1907, p. 70, and H. Thiersch, *ibid.*, p. 265, for the reinterpretation of certain subjects at Gjölbaschi which show the continued predominance of women in Lycia (cf. note 64 on Harpy Tomb).

[71] *Brit. Mus. Sculpt. Cat.*, 950. *Tomb of Payava*. On each side of the arched roof a chariot drawn by four galloping horses. Not the horses but the chariot itself is winged. The two huge heads of lions looking out frontally on either side are, of course, prophylactic ; the hunting scenes of the frieze carry the usual reference to After Life pastimes ; the reliefs at either end comprise in the two upper panels guardian sphinxes, and in the lower panels portraits of the heroised dead. The reliefs on the chamber of the tomb which resembles a sarcophagus in house form, represent on one long side a combat scene, probably an exploit in the life of the deceased ; on the second long side a judgment scene, unexplained. On one short side two armed warriors leaning on their spears stand side by side ; on the other, a venerable draped man places a crown on the head of a nude youth.

British Museum Scupt. Cat., 951. On the *tomb of Merehi* we have on each side of the roof the chariot of the Apotheosis, and in place of the apotropaic lions of the tomb of Payava, a chimaera on the one side, and a panther on the other, used with similar intent to ward off evil spirits. On the friezes along the crest of the roof—(*a*) Combat scenes ; (b) a judgment scene, the figure of an old draped man placing a crown on a nude youth ; (c) the banquet of the Blessed. The chariot group, which, of course, can be no other than the chariot of the Apotheosis, occurs frequently in Lycia. The most important parallels are on the reliefs with the Apotheosis from Gjölbaschi already noted.

[72] Benndorf, *Heroon*, plates i., ii. of text, and plate xxxii. of atlas ; tomb with apotropaic lion and banquet of Apotheosis. Cf. the reliefs from the facade of a tomb at Tlos in valley of the Xanthos, cast in British Museum, No. 260 = R.R., ii. 112, 5 ; in the centre of each panel of door apotropaic heads ; on relief to left Bellerophon as emblem of victory and Apotheosis (though I am not unmindful of Pindar, *Pythian*, ii. 39). Another sarcophagus from Gjölbaschi is in Constantinople (Mendel, *Cat.*, 110). The representation is not so 'enigmatic' as the commentators make out. Along the crest are represented the joys of the After Life (?) ; on each side of the lid, within a panel, is the chariot of the Apotheosis. In the smaller lower panel, a lion passant with head turned apotropaically to the front ; the lion has his paw on the head of a bull—already, I believe, to indicate the consummation of the earthly body ; at each side two huge apotropaic gorgon heads in high relief ; apotropaic also are the heads of animals that projected from the shorter ends, and the mask projecting from the long frame of the roof. Within each of the oval panels of the short ends appear the dolphins as vehicle of the soul's transit. On the panels of the chest protective garlands hang between *boukrania*. This Lycian tomb is as well guarded against the attacks of evil spirits as any primitive Latin temple with its coronal of protective gorgoneia and other emblems in terra-cotta, see my article in *J.R.S.*, 1915, v. p. 164.

[73] I cannot help reminding students in connection with the Mausoleum and the Nereid monument, which each show statues placed in the inter-spaces of the columns, that the famous Niobids of Florence probably represent a similar decoration from one of the large temple tombs which became increasingly fashionable in Greek Asia Minor ; cf. Collignon, *Statues Funéraires*, p. 264.

[73a] For the grave reliefs from Chios, and the stele of Metrodoros, see Studinczka in *Ath. Mitth.*, 1888 (xiii.), pp. 192 ff. On the imagery of the Siren, see the first part of Weicker's *Seelenvogel*. The Siren appears first as a *habitat* of the Soul and then becomes a Mourner.

[74] Mendel, *Cat.*, 63. The contest scenes (Centaurs, death of Kaineus, etc.) are, as Mendel points out, borrowed from Attic motives,

but I imagine they are used with symbolic content. The sculptor is certainly under the spell of Pheidian influence, and almost hypnotised by its suggestion, so that he has transformed into somewhat meaningless scenes the bold sepulchral imagery of the Lycian tombs.

[75] Furtwängler in *Abhandlungen der K. Bayerischen Akademie der Wissenschaften*, xxii. (1902), pp. 99-105, *Das Heiligtum der Aphaia*, fig. 268 ; Collignon, *Statues Funéraires*, fig. 56. The relief, said to have been found in Rome, was, when I first knew it, in the possession of Dr. Hommel in Munich. Furtwängler pronounced it Attic ; it seems to me decidedly Ionian. For the motive of Hermes placing his hand on the shoulder of the woman to introduce her to the underworld Furtwängler compares the Ildefonso group in Madrid, which is also probably sepulchral. The motive of the mourners sitting in the Elysian fields seems borrowed from the *Nekuia* of Polygnotus.

[76] D. G. Hogarth, *Ionia and the East*, p. 7.

[77] G. Murray, *Rise of the Greek Epic*, 2nd ed., p. 276.

[78] For an attempted reconstruction, see C. Robert, 16 *Winckelm. progr.*, 1892, and cf. Schoene in *Arch. Jahrb.*, 1893, viii. 213.

[79] *Revue de l'Art* for 1910, i. pp. 404 ff., and *Jahrb.*, 1913, p. 309 and plate xxvi., from which plate xxi. is taken.

[80] These reliefs have been exhaustively studied by E. Pfuhl in *Jahrbuch.*, 1905, pp. 47 ff. and pp. 123 ff. (see also *op. cit.*, 1907, pp. 113 ff.), with analysis of the many symbolic objects represented upon them (sirens, chests or λάρνακες, baskets, altars, tables, double horn of abundance with fruits ; cf. British Museum 704 = *R.R.*, ii. 503, 1) ; three fine examples of these stelae are in the Cook Collection at Richmond (*R.R.*, ii. 532, 1, 3, 4), and the Ashmolean at Oxford is specially rich in examples from Smyrna. Collignon, *Statues Funéraires*, pp. 270 ff.

[81] For the testament of Epikteta see Benndorf, *Heroon*, pp. 45 ff. The shrine appears to have been to the Muses and to the heroised family of Epikteta, *i.e.* she founded a hero cult for her husband Phoinix and two dead sons Andragoras and Kratesilochos, into which Epikteta was herself admitted. The articles of the dedication, consisting of the testament of Epikteta, and the statutes of the confraternity which she established for the administration of the cult, were engraved on eight columns on a great marble podium which was set up on the site and carried the statues of the foundress and her dead.

[82] The Alexandrian stelae have been described by E. Pfuhl in *Ath. Mitth.*, 1901, xx. pp. 258-304.

[83] W. Altmann, *Architektur und Ornamentik der Antiken Sarcophage*, pp. 31 ff., with references ; cf. M. Collignon, *Statues Funéraires*, pp. 347 ff.

[84] See Rudolph Pagenstecher, *Unteritalische Grabdenkmaeler*, 1912.

[85] On the Hebrew She'ol see C. F. Burney, *Israel's Hope of Immortality*, pp. 7 ff. and *passim* ; also Dr. R. H. Charles, *Religious Development between the Old and New Testament*, 1914 (ch. iv. 'A Blessed Future Life '). It is usual to compare the Hebrew She'ol to the Greek or rather the Homeric conception of existence after death (Burney, p. 14), but the resemblance to the Roman view seems to me much closer. She'ol and the Roman *Manes* alike represent a stage where the dead were neither differentiated nor individualised. The Homeric conception, on the other hand, seems rather the outcome of a feeling of discouragement and helplessness on the part of a people who had tried to lift the veil and solve the supreme mystery, and failed in the attempt. The *Nekuia* of the XI. Odyssey represents a falling-away from substantial and positive beliefs to a negative state of mind which looks upon the dead as strengthless and powerless, the mere shadows of their former selves. Yet these strengthless dead are in possession of their human faculties and mindful of their life on earth, a fact which differentiates them by a whole world of thought and experience from the dim underworld of She'ol. It would seem as if the action of memory in framing any conception of the dead were not sufficiently taken into account. The living perforce tend to think of the dead in the terms of this life, and to imagine them very like what they were on earth. This process by which the other world becomes peopled with highly individualised images issued in the 'unlimited individualism' with which Dr. Charles reproaches the Greek doctrine of immortality. Different religions or different phases of the same religion may tend to check or to promote this action of the memory, and our stelae afford interesting indication of the fluctuations of belief with regard to a future state. In Greece a definite picture of a future existence is first attempted ; then, under Attic influence, the vision is lost sight of, and in its place we get a mythological or historic view of the dead, though outside Attica the belief in a future state was never completely suppressed, and reasserted itself in later antiquity. In Rome, on the other hand, in the beginning, everything seems obscured by a magic mist, but when once under the influence of the later Greek mysticism belief as to a future state had definitely emerged, it was never again lost sight of.

[86] For the Roman view of death, and the cult of the dead, see, especially, J. B. Carter, in *E.R.E.*, under 'Ancestor-worship—Roman'; G. Wissowa, *Religion und Kultus der Römer*, 2nd ed., 1912, pp. 232 ff. ; Warde-Fowler, *Religious Experience*, pp. 84 ff. and *passim* ; Cyril Bailey, *Religion of Ancient Rome*, pp. 49 ff.

[87] Saglio's *Dictionary*, art. 'Imago,' by Ed. Courbaud, pp. 409 ff., and art. 'Imagines Maiorum,' by H. Meyer in Pauly. In the exclusively patrician right of the *ius imaginum*, which points to so different a conception of the dead from that of the mass of the people of Rome, we may perhaps see the trace of beliefs introduced by a conquering race.

[88] See Hülsen, *Roman Forum*, trans. Carter, 2nd ed., 1909, pp. 222-229, for an account of the *Sepolcreto*.

[89] On early jewelry as amulets see Deubner in *E.R.E.* ('Charms and Amulets').

[90] Now well described by Dr. Weege in Helbig's *Führer*, vol. ii. pp. 312-355. In speaking of the Villa Giulia, however, we must not forget the excellently arranged collection in the Museo Kircheriano, with finds from the necropoleis of Latin sites (Castel Gandolfo, Albano, etc.).

[91] *Tomba Barberini* in Museo di Villa Giulia, Helbig, ii. No. 1766 ; and see the excellent article by Della Seta in *Bolletino d'Arte*, 1909, iii. pp. 161 ff. *Tomba Bernardini* in Museo Kircheriano, see Helbig, ii. pp. 259-271. *Tomba Regolini-Galassi* in Museo Gregoriano of Vatican, Helbig, i. pp. 352, 387, and the new book (1914) by B. Nogara and A. Pinza, *La Tomba Regolini Galassi e gli altri materiali cocvi del Museo Gregoriano-Etrusco*.

[92] Della Seta, fig. 133 and p. 250, puts this more tentatively.

[93] A number of these friezes are mentioned by Mrs. van Buren in her article on terra-cottas, *J.R.S.*, 1915, v. ; see also Giuseppe Moretti in *Ausonia*, 1912, vi. pp. 147 ff.

[94] See C. Fries, 'Studien zur Odyssee,' in *Mittheilungen der Vorderasiatischen Gesellschaft*, 1910, pp. 4 ff.

[95] C. Fries, *op. cit.*, p. 19. This is the passage which I had in mind in describing the Roman *triumphator* on p. 64. With regard to the triumphal chariot, Fries remarks that chariot and horses were the attributes of the Sun, and recalls H. Winckler's theory that their number *four* possibly represented the four Seasons.

[96] *Catalogue of the Museo Capitolino*, by members of the British School at Rome, p. 122, Galleria, No. 48a ('Sepulchral Monuments of the Rupilii').

[97] Della Seta, *Religion and Art*, p. 231, gives a different reason for the reappearance of the frontal figure in Hellenistic and Roman times, and thinks that it was consciously adopted as affording more scope for the reproduction of individual expression.

[98] Furtwängler in his discussion of the Adamklissi monument has well shown the importance of this class of sculpture as representing an old Italian strain, but he believed that this art was limited to the provinces and to those cities where the Roman legionaries had set up the tombs of their comrades. In point of fact this military or provincial sculpture, as Furtwängler called it, is simply the art of the Roman tombstone as we find it in Rome itself from the last century of the Republic onward.

[99] Collignon, *Statues Funéraires*, pp. 346-78, 'Figures couchées.' See my article on the terra-cottas in the Museo di Villa Giulia, *J.R.S.*, 1915, v. p. 161, for the group on a sarcophagus from Cervetri.

[100] The statue was found in 1911, behind the Abbey of Tre Fontane, and published by Ghislanzoni, *Notizie Scavi*, 1912, p. 38. For a similar sarcophagus lid, with a boy reclining on a bed, from Torre Nuova, see Rizzo, *Notizie Scavi*, 1905, p. 408. It is a lifelike portrait of the second century (incised pupils) ; the boy, with his chubby round face and short nose, has none of the aristocratic beauty of our little Augustan prince, though here again the excellence of the workmanship suggests that the portrait is that of a boy of illustrious parentage.

[101] Gummerus in *Arch. Jahrbuch*, 1913, pp. 63-126.

[102] Warde-Fowler, *Religious Experience of the Roman People* ; the chapter on 'Mysticism' is of capital importance.

[103] For the influence of Posidonius see Warde-Fowler, *The Religious Experience of the Roman People*, p. 382 : 'The person really responsible for the tendency to this kind of mysticism was undoubtedly the great Posidonius, philosopher, historian, traveller, who more than any other man dominated the Roman world of thought in the first half of the last century B.C., and whose writings, now surviving in a few fragments only, lie at the back of nearly all the serious Roman literature of his own and indeed of the following age.' Cumont, *Oriental Religions*, p. 164 : 'The works of that erudite and religious writer influenced the development of the entire Roman

theology more than anything else.' Again, the influence of Posidonius not improbably filtered to Vergil, and helped him to remould the old traditional conception of an underworld.

[104] I ought perhaps to say 'unique' as a funeral procession. I do not forget the elaborate funeral rites depicted on the tomb of the Haterii (*R.R.*, iii. 285, 286).

[105] For the literature see my article in *J.R.S.*, 1915, v. pp. 153-156.

[106] Robert Eisler, *Weltenmantel und Himmelzelt*, 2 vols., Munich, 1911.

[107] The starred mantle is seen floating behind the deified Empresses Sabina and Faustina, who, on the coins struck in honour of their Deification, appear mounting to Heaven—the one on the peacock, the other on the eagle (plate ix. 2, from casts kindly given to me by Mr. G. F. Hill).

[108] See F. Cumont, 'Les idées du paganisme romain sur la vie future' in *Bibliothèque de Vulgarization du Musée Guimet*, 1910 (xxxiv.), and the same writer's *Théologie Solaire du Paganisme*, p. 3.

[109] These ideas were by no means limited to the official circles of benefactors of the State. Cicero, when planning a tomb for Tullia, wished to avoid the appearance of a mausoleum, so that nothing might detract from the idea of her 'Apotheosis': 'Fanum fieri uolo, neque hoc mihi erui potest. Sepulcri similitudinem effugere non tam propter poenam legis studeo quam ut quam maxime adsequar ἀποθέωσιν' (*ad Att.*, xii. 361) ; *i.e.*, in other words, Cicero did not wish for the ordinary type of tomb, but for a shrine which might proclaim the idea of Tullia's admission among the gods.

IV

LECTURE III

[1] Before the eagle became messenger of the Sun he may have been regarded as ἔδος of the soul, more especially of the souls of departed monarchs. What more natural than to suppose that the majestic and solitary bird with its piercing vision and grandiose swoop was chosen as his *habitat* by the soul of the departed sovereign? The eagle's long flight till he becomes a mere speck and then disappears in the upper regions of the air might well suggest the flight of a royal soul

to the stars. In time it was only natural to modify this cruder conception of the eagle as the actual soul into that of the messenger that carries the soul back to a Divine Master. At a later date, the eagle would pass, like the whole doctrine of Apotheosis, into the service of lesser personages also.

[2] I have discussed these medallions in *J.R.S.*, 1911, i. pp. 16 ff., where see references. See also the Catalogue of the *Mostra Archeologica nelle Terme di Diocleziano*, pp. 52, 60, 61.

[3] See my article on Antistius and Antistia in *J.R.S.*, 1915, v. pp. 147-152.

[4] By the great kindness of Mr. Arthur H. Smith. The medallion was acquired in 1914, with a number of other objects formerly in the collection of General Montresor of Denne Hill, near Dover, in Kent, and is said to have been brought to England from Rome in the middle of the eighteenth century.

[5] These altars can be conveniently studied in Altmann, *Römische Grabaltäre der Kaiserzeit*, 1905.

[6] Frazer, *Adonis, Attis and Osiris*, p. 419.

[7] M. Franz Cumont drew my attention to this instance of Apotheosis. The meaning of the Spalato frieze has been overlooked.

[8] Niemann, *der Palast Diokletians in Spalato*, 1910, plate iv., also fig. vi. 1, p. 115.

[9] Students who have no time for Cumont's large work are referred to his smaller *Mithras* (Eng. ed. 1912), from which I have mainly drawn my short account of the Mithraic cults and monuments. ' The mysteries exerted a powerful influence in fostering some of the most exalted aspirations of the human soul : the desire for immortality and the expectation of final justice. The hopes of life beyond the tomb which this religion instilled in its votaries were one of the secrets of its power in these troublesome times when solicitude for life to come disturbed all minds ' (*Mithras*, p. 148). See also H. Stuart-Jones in *Quarterly Review*, 1914.

[10] This piece which comes from Heddernheim is of great importance for its imagery (see the references in Reinach). The cap on a pole between Sol and Mithras has been correctly explained by Eisler as the ἀστερωτὸς πῖλος—the emblem of the sky or the cosmos. The animals pictured as rushing upward, on the surface of the monument above the cave, are conceived as springing from the blood of the slain bull.

[11] *Roman Sculpture*, pp. 309-312 (plate xcv. for the fine stele from Osterburken).

[12] Published *Oesterr. Jahreshefte*, 1909, xii. fig. 114 (Hofmann) ; and *Beiblatt*, p. 213, for Cumont's interpretation of the reliefs above the niche ; cf. also his *Astrology and Religion*, pp. 192 ff.

[13] *J.R.S.*, i. p. 19 and references.

[14] See above, p. 151, and notes 43, 69 to Lecture II. The lion motive is very common, but I may mention here two striking examples : A stele at Mayence (Weynand, 124) with the apotropaic Medusa in the pediment ; beneath, a crouching lion on each side of a pine cone. Another from Auinale in Algeria (R. Cagnat in *Strena Hellbigiana*) shows a husband and wife and two children, and above two lions guarding the sacred banquet. Cumont, *Textes et Monuments*, ii. p. 527, inclines to recognise these groups as Mithraic (though see *ibid.*, p. 440). The lion and bull motive was, as we have seen, very ancient, and was current in Asia Minor, etc., long before the introduction of Mithraism from Persia ; but it seems reasonable to suppose that its extraordinary vogue on later Roman tombstones was due to the popular Mithraic cult where the lion had so prominent a rôle.

[15] Frazer, *Adonis, Attis, Osiris* (3rd ed., 1907), p. 146.

[16] For Attis see Hepding, *Attis und seine Mythen*, 1903 ; Cumont in Pauly-Wissowa, *s.v.* Attis.

[17] Cumont, *Oriental Religions*, p. 59.

[18] *J.R.S.*, i. p. 17, note 3.

[19] For the connection between omphalos and tholos see Rohde, *Psyche*, 4th ed., i. p. 132; against it, Diels in *Miscellanea Salinas* (1907), p. 14. For the pine cone over graves see Pfuhl in *Jahrb.*, 1905, pp. 88 ff. In the relief at Munich, of a peasant driving his cow to market, the pine cone over the gate of the Priapic Sanctuary must be placed there as emblem of generation. At the same time it cannot be asserted that all cones and conical emblems necessarily derive from the pine cone or the phallus, cf. G. F. Hill in *Church Quarterly Review*, 1908 (lxvi.), p. 131. For the phallos on graves see examples cited by Gruppe, ii. p. 266, note 2.

[20] *C.I.L.*, xiv. 3046-3310 ; and *Ephemeris Epigraphica*, ix. pp. 449 ff., Nos. 79-871. The material is a local calcareous stone. In a few cases, always of women's tombs, the cones are replaced by statues, in one or two by pillars. A reconstruction of this ancient cemetery would form an admirable college thesis.

S

[21] The Persian origin of Orpheus seems now fairly established by R. Eisler in *Weltenmantel u. Himmelzelt*. This book contains an *exposé* of Orphic doctrine, its origins and its ends. The same author's four papers on 'Orpheus the Fisher,' in the *Quest*, vols. i. and ii., 1909 and 1910, are full of curious information and theory which bear on the eschatology of Orphism, and therefore indirectly on late Roman sepulchral imagery. The literature that has gathered round Orpheus of late years is immense, and the subject daily gains in attraction ; but the book that shall bring together all the evidence, monumental and literary, and also draw conclusions therefrom—somewhat on the plan of Cumont's great work on Mithras—is still lacking. I myself hope to make an insignificant contribution to the subject by a list of all Roman sepulchral monuments representing Orpheus or affected by Orphic beliefs. In the present lectures I have had perforce to content myself with giving the barest indications. All study of Orphism must necessarily be based on the monumental work of two German scholars, E. Rohde in *Psyche*, and Gruppe in his *Religionsgeschichte* and in the exhaustive article 'Orpheus' contributed by him to Roscher's *Lexikon* ; for the Orphic hymns see Dieterich, *Hymni Orphici* ; the latest discussion of the Orphic tablets is by Delatte in the *Musée Belge* for 1912, where references to previous literature are given ; the various papers on Orpheus by S. Reinach in *Mythes, Cultes et Religions*, and his paper on Orphic eschatology in *Strena Helbigiana* should likewise be consulted. In England a good deal of interesting work, based in a measure on foreign research, has lately been done. See especially an eloquent and lucid *résumé* in James Adam, *Religious Teachers of Greece*, p. 92 (Lecture v., 'Orphic Religious Ideas'), and F. M. Cornford's paper on Orphism and the Pythagorean Schools in *From Religion to Philosophy*, p. 160 onwards (especially Section vi., 'The Mystical Tradition'). The *Asiatic Dionysos*, by G. W. M. Davis, suffers from the author's failure to cite original authorities—not even Eisler being mentioned for the Persian derivation of Orphism. Recently Orpheus and Orphism have been brought into fresh prominence by the researches of the St. Andrews school— and notably of Mr. A. E. Taylor—into the sources of Platonic or, according to these scholars, Socratic mysticism and eschatology. In his *Varia Socratica* (Oxford, 1911), p. 268, Taylor has the following striking passage : 'Behind Socrates . . . we dimly discern the half-obliterated features of Pythagoras of Samos, and behind Pythagoras we can only just descry the mists which enclose whatever may be hidden under the name of Orpheus. And behind Orpheus, for us at least, there is only the impenetrable night.' If the rôle played by Orphism, in what the world will doubtless continue to call the

Platonic philosophy, is as great as the St. Andrews school claims, the religion of Orpheus is likely to prove the greatest known to the ancient world, and we shall not be surprised to find the reflection of its eschatology on the tombstones of the late Roman or Graeco-Roman period. That its rôle in the religions of the later Empire was very important we must all be convinced—though not enough has been done towards defining it and correlating it to kindred cults. Of these the principal was Mithraism, which, owing to Cumont's brilliant series of books, has perhaps held the field too exclusively of late years.

[22] *Mostra Archeologica Cat.*, p. 56; *J.R.S.*, i. p. 18.

[23] F. M. Cornford, *From Religion to Philosophy*, p. 197.

[24] Bousset, *Hauptprobleme der Gnosis*, p. 294.

[25] Farnell, *Cults of the Greek States*, pp. 101 ff.; on Orpheus and Dionysus see further Gruppe in Roscher, iii. pp. 1110 ff. On the connection of Attis and Dionysus see Cumont, *Oriental Religions*, p. 48; on the Thracian Dionysus see especially the monograph of Foucart, 'Le Culte de Dionysos en Attique,' in *Mém. de l'Acad. des Inscrr.*, 1904 (xxxvii.), pt. 2, pp. 1 ff.; and Gruppe in Roscher, iii. p. 1084 f.

[26] See the excellent reconstructions of these tombs in E. Krüger's *Kurzer Führer durch das Provinzialmuseum in Trier*, 1911.

[27] *J.R.S.*, i. p. 22; Koepp, *Römer in Deutschland*, 2nd ed., fig. 133. The Dioscuri are favourite figures on sepulchral reliefs, as is natural from the fact that their cult is developed out of that of the heroised dead (Furtwängler in *Coll. Sabouroff*, and in Roscher), and that they never lost their connection with the underworld; a good instance is *R.R.*, ii. 129, 2—on the lower half the Dioscuri with their horses; above the bust of Sol or Mithras within a wreath between two genii. In an age of syncretism they seem to get confused with the mysterious Thracian riders, who are beings of similar origin, since one of the commonest forms in which the dead were conceived was as horsemen. The Thracian horsemen appear on certain stelae at Sofia (G. Kazarno in *Archiv. für Religionswiss.*, 1912 (xv.), Nos. 4 and 8), where the riders stand on each side of a female divinity trampling over a fallen figure—in symbol of victory over the powers of evil rather than over any mortal foe. The sanctity of the scene is emphasised by the woman on the left with her hand to her lips (*favete linguis*). The Dioscuri appear carved on the funeral chariot of a relief of Constantinian date in British Museum (*R.R.*, ii. 509, 1). The connection of the Dioscuri with the purifying forces of fire (Gruppe, ii. p. 727) also accounts in measure for their popularity as emblems on graves.

[28] Koepp, fig. 134. Appositely enough, the labour is the chaining of Cerberus. On the front of the aedicula between two hangings appear the deified figure of the deceased—a woman—with a libation cup in her hand and the peacock at her feet.

[29] *Aeneas: J.R.S.*, i. p. 18, note 3. It is remarkable that on the other face of the Intercisa stele we have the subject of Bellerophon, the old Lycian symbol of Apotheosis.

[30] Rhea Silvia, *Mostra Archeologica Cat.*, p. 69.

[31] On the sacred marriage of the soul, cf. Gruppe, ii. p. 865 ; C. Pascal, *Credenze*, i. pp. 99 ff.; also Lawson, *Modern Greek Folklore*, pp. 547 ff., on the conception of death as a ἱερὸς γάμος.

[32] The translation of these lines has baffled Prior, Pope, Byron, Merivale, and Christina Rossetti. To all these versions I prefer the one given in the text kindly done for me by Mr. Hugh Dorrell, a student of our school. There seems no reason to doubt, as some have done, the genuineness of the lines or their attribution to Hadrian, cf. Deissmann, *Light from the Ancient East*, p. 293.

[33] J. H. Cabott, *Stucchi figurati esistenti in un antico sepolcro fuori delle mura di Roma*, 1795.

[34] The best publication is still that of Petersen in *Annali dell' Istituto Archeol.*, 1860, p. 384 ; 1861, p. 190. For certain details of the stucco decorations see Ronscewski, *Gewölbeschmuck*, plates xvii., xviii., xx., and fig. 17, p. 30 ; fig. 20, p. 34.

[35] See the plates in Cabott (above, note 33).

[36] *C.I.L.*, vi. p. 3418, and references.

[37] *Antichità di Roma*, ii. plate xxx. Cf. Ashby in *B.S.R.*, i. pp. 156 ff. : 'Stuccoes from the ceiling of a tomb octagonal above, circular below, near Tor de' Schiavi.'

[38] Ronczewski, *Gewölbeschmuck*, plate xxiii.; Piranesi, ii. plate xxxiii.

[39] Ashby in *B.S.R.*, vii. pp. 19, 20, 34 ; cf. Amelung in *Atti della Reale Accademia Pontefìcia* for 1910, pp. 203 ff.

[40] P. S. Bartoli, *Picturae antiquae cryptarum Romanorum et Sepulcri Nasioniorum*. The pictures in the British Museum appear to have been purchased from George Richmond, R.A., in 1885; see my article in *B.S.R.*, 1915, vii. p. 316, note 3.

[41] Pyramid of Cestius: Piranesi, *Antichità*, iii. plate xlviii.; cf. Nardini, *Roma Antica*, iv. plate i.

[42] Von Sybel, *Christliche Antike*, i. p. 187 ; E. Samter in *Röm. Mitth.* 1893 (viii.), p. 134 ; Nilsson, *Archiv. für Religionswiss.*, p. 543.

[43] Ashby and Newton in *B.S.R.*, and my notes, *ibid.*, pp. 469 ff.

[44] Vigna Nardi, *Studi Romani*, i. pp. 355 ff. (Fornari).

[45] Tomb near S. Sebastiano.

[46] See *B.S.R.*, 1914 (vii.), pp. 1-62 and plates i.-xxiv.

[47] Discovered in 1911, and published, with elaborate commentary, by O. Marucchi in *Bulletino di Archeologia Cristiana*, 1911, pp. 201 ff. ; cf. Delbrueck in *Arch. Anz.*, 1912, pp. 293 ff., figs. 12, 13, 14.

[48] Photo Moscioni ; Piranesi, *Antichità*, iii. plate xiv. ; Canina, iv. plate 277.

[49] I cannot help recalling here the many beautiful tombs at Pozzuoli, the ancient Puteoli, near Naples, which, like so many of the Roman tombs, have been allowed to perish miserably and to disappear. Even when the tomb still exists, the subjects represented have become undecipherable. Fortunately a number were engraved by Paoli in his *Antiquitates Puteolanae* ; see especially plates xxxii., xxxiv. Here also were to be seen the familiar winged figures, friezes of sea monsters, the rape of the soul, and the sacred marriage typified by Rhea Sylvia. See also Charles Dubois, *Pozzuoles Antiques, Tombeaux*, pp. 349-355. For the fine painted decorations of tombs in Naples see *Monumenti Antichi*, 1898 (viii.).

[50] For the cock on tombs see note 27 to Lecture II. The lines from Prudentius are quoted from Weicker, *Ath. Mitth.*, xxx. p. 301. The symbolism of the cock persists into Christian times. On a fragmen of tissue (sixth century imitation of a Coptic model) from the treasury of the Sancta Sanctorum, now in the Library of the Vatican (see P. Lauer in *Monuments Piot*, 1906 (xv.), plate xvii.), we see the cock wearing the nimbus as herald of resurrection (?) within a *corona triumphalis* (?). M. Lauer appositely recalls the two 'cocks facing' on a tissue of the thirteenth century, explained by Madame Isabelle Errera (*Collection d'anciennes étoffes*, p. 10, No. 16) as symbols of the sun. In Japan the cock is likewise held to symbolise the sun. Possibly no emblem combines more meanings into itself. A good instance of the apotropaic cock, with further allusion, it may be, to resurrection and to this bird's connection with the sun, occurs on the stele of Antiphanes at Athens (star or sun ? in background). Perrot et Chipiez, *Histoire de l'Art antique*, viii. p. 661, fig. 339.

[51] *English and Scottish Popular Ballads*, ed. Child and Kittredge, p. 168.

[52] *Mostra*, p. 65 ; *J.R.S.*, i. p. 19 ; *C.I.L.*, iii. 10,514.

[53] Stele of Mussius, *C.I.L.*, vi. 22763.

[54] Bruno Schröder in *Bonner Jahrbücher*, 1902, p. 67 and note 3.

[55] Hettner, *Illustrierte Führer durch das Provinzialmuseum in Trier*, 12[a], 12[b], 12[c] (pp. 13 ff.); Koepp, *Römer in Deutschland*, 2nd ed., fig. 98 and p. 161.

[56] Blussus, Koepp, figs. 138, 139 ; inscr. *C.I.L.*, xiii. 7067.

[57] *J.R.S.*, i. p. 14 ; *Mostra*, p. 59. The interesting inscription is now probably published in the last *Bericht des Vereins Carnuntum*, which I have not seen.

[58] See also Koepp, *Römer in Deutschland*, 2nd ed., fig. 96 and p. 161.

[59] Koepp, *op. cit.*, fig. 97.

[60] Cf. Koepp, *op. cit.*, fig. 94.

[61] The naïve shepherding scene which adorns the base of this stele, and the quaint epitaph which turns from verse to prose in the writer's evident despair of mastering the metre, are also worthy of attention. The stele is given by Koepp, fig. 140 and p. 158 ; inscr. *C.I.L.*, xiii. 7070. For a similar stele, of a *suarius*, see *Notizie Scavi*, 1898, p. 479 and fig. 3. On the upper part appears the inscription ; on the lower the *suarius*, wearing a *tunica succincta*, drives seven pigs to graze.

[62] The only German publication of the whole monument seems to be that by C. Osterwald of the year 1829 (with preface by Goethe). The best reproductions remain those by Laborde in the *Monuments de France*.

[63] See E. Mogk's ' Baptism ' in *E.R.E.* For its significance in Mithraism and the later Gnostic sects see Bousset, *Hauptprobleme der Gnosis*, ch. vii. (baptism 'originally a magical rite for freeing the soul from evil influence,' *ibid.*, p. 294).

[64] *Havámál*, v. 158, quoted by E. Mogk, art. ' Baptism—Teutonic,' p. 140 in *E.R.E.*

[65] J. G. Frazer, *Adonis, Attis, Osiris*, 2nd ed., p. 85.

[66] Every detail of the curious scene has now been made clear by Hans Graeven, *Röm. Mitt.*, 1913 (xxviii.), pp. 271 ff. and plate vii. The figure in the funeral chariot drawn by elephants is the Emperor, or rather his *imago*; the youthful figure in the chariot above the *rogus* is Sol, with the appropriate arching drapery above his head; above again, the Emperor is seen carried from the *rogus* to heaven by the twin brothers Sleep and Death, and is received by five divinities (?) who emerge from the clouds at his approach. Graeven has further shown it to be more than probable that the deified Emperor is Constantius Chlorus.

[67] Matz-Duhn, *Antike Bildwerke in Rom*, 1881, ii. p. 301, No. 3016.

[68] This stele has been pointed out to me by M. Cumont; it is probably published by now in the last *Bericht des Vereins Carnuntum*, which I have not seen.

[69] See Camille Jullian in his small book *Gallia*, p. 204; cf. *J.R.S.*, i. pp. 14 ff. It is satisfactory to note that the beauty and importance of the sepulchral art of the land of the Treveri, and its influence over later cathedral and other sculpture, is beginning to be acknowledged; cf. H. Thiersch, *An den Rändern des Römischen Reiches*, 1911, pp. 128 ff. See also the recent discussion of several of these monuments (especially from Arlon) by F. Cumont, 'Comment la Belgique fut romanisée,' in *Annales de la Société Royale d'Archéologie de Bruxelles*, 1914, pp. 82 ff.

ADDENDA

P. 7. *'Domus Flavia'* of Palatine.—Dr. Ashby points out to me that, in view of the great interest now attaching to the Palatine and its palaces, it may be well to add that even if (as I think probable) Vespasian and Titus are responsible for the plan of the *Domus Flavia,* they themselves apparently lived in the old *Domus Tiberiana,* which was simply refaced on the side of the Forum (west), while Domitian seems wholly responsible for the great palace connected with the name of his dynasty, and left untouched from his time till Septimius Severus and Julia Domna added to it on the south. Whether Domitian worked on plans already approved by his father and brother, and the exact share of Rabirius in the plan, are questions that cannot be yet completely cleared up.

P. 40. For the sculptures from Corfu see also Martin L. d'Ooge in *Art and Archaeology,* 1915, vol. i. pp. 153-158, with excellent illustrations. Plate vi. is after his figs. 1, 2.

P. 101. *The Art-type of the Christ.*—Since writing the above, it has become evident to me that the iconography of Christ, especially that of the early beardless type, brings us by another road into the same cycle of ideas as those developed in my lecture. It is the merit of H. Dütschke to have called attention to the resemblance between the type of the youthful beardless Christ and the portraiture of Alexander (*Ravennatische Studien,* 1909, pp. 104 ff., a book I regret not having read earlier). The kinship between the two which seems undeniable, will cease to surprise us when we remember the beliefs and hopes of an apocalyptic-messianic character that centred about Alexander looked upon as the 'Prince of Peace' who was to return and unite all mankind under his rule in a brotherhood of love. Thus Alexander was offered to the imagination of the ancient world as a divine
280

being at once differing from the gods of the Graeco-Roman Pantheon, and in a sense exalted above them to a monotheistic position. What wonder that his portraiture, idealised into a type, should influence the plastic conception of the Christian God for whom his followers would naturally avoid borrowing the features of any of the abhorred Pagan deities. In the matter of the actual central figure, then, as well as in the pose and place of that figure, we find the idea of the Monarch-God influencing the artistic formulas of the new religion. I may add here as an instance of the influence exerted by the Alexander idea upon ancient religious imagery, the frequency with which the Roman Emperors (Augustus, Nero, Caracalla, Gallienus, and others) were represented in the pose of Alexander, or with features actually assimilating to his. These 'Alexandroid' images of Emperors, long thought to reflect the madness of the one or the impudent audacity of the other, were in absolute conformity with the beliefs of the Roman world and implied the attainment of Apotheosis, expressed in this case by identifying the deified monarch with the Monarch-God *par excellence*. In another order of beliefs, Commodus is portrayed as Heracles, as in the well-known bust of the Conservatori, in sign of Apotheosis through identification with Heracles. It is a striking thought of Dütschke, and one which throws considerable sidelight on the subject of Apotheosis, that the bearded type of our Lord first appeared in the scenes of His earthly career, while the youthful beardless type was reserved, in the beginning at any rate, for the glorified Christ (*Ravennatische Studien*, pp. 120 ff.).

P. 111. *The 'Paradiso' of Tintoretto.*—I have often been questioned as to this final illustration of my thesis. It was chosen not in the least because I personally feel any extraordinary admiration for this colossal work, but because so well-balanced and well-constructed a grouping of myriad figures around a central motive would, I believe, have been impossible in Greek art, or in any art previous to the introduction of the centralised principle of composition which first *appeared to stay* in the art of the Roman Empire.

P. 114. *Sepulchral Imagery.*—In this connection my cordial thanks are due to Professor Haverfield and the Editors of the *Journal of Roman Studies* for allowing me to quote freely from articles contributed by me to vol. i. and vol. v. of the *Journal* (especially i., 'The

Exhibition illustrative of the Provinces of the Roman Empire, at the Baths of Diocletian' ; and v., 'The Decorated Screen on a Relief from Amiternum.' See above, pp. 177-180.

P. 122. *Pillars at Tamuli in Sardinia.*—I am indebted to Dr. Ashby for calling my attention to these.

P. 129. *The Spartan Reliefs.*—In addition to the literature quoted in the notes, see also Erich Küster, *Die Schlange in der Griechischen Kunst und Religion,* Giessen, 1913, pp. 76 ff. I regret that this excellent monograph was not known to me before. It is the most comprehensive treatise that has yet appeared on the beliefs attaching to the snake in Greece, on the cult of the hero and the sepulchral iconography pertaining thereto (see especially p. 78 for the egg and the cock ; p. 75 and p. 82 for the pomegranate). I also note with interest that Küster dismisses the old mythological explanation of the Magoula basis (*R.R.*, ii. 362), marked by the snakes on the narrow sides as the stele of a 'hero,' and rightly surmises that the scenes of the two principal faces refer to events now unknown in the life of the occupant of the tomb.

P. 141. *Vergil and Orpheus.* — See on this important point Dütschke, *op. cit.,* p. 185.

P. 154. *The Sirens as token of the Soul's Survival.*—The Sirens, as later the Muses which so often appear on Roman sarcophagi, are possibly placed on the tomb to ensure to the dead participation in the 'minstrelsy' which Pindar reckons among the joys that await the Blessed (above, p. 140). In the case of the Roman sarcophagi of the second century A.D. with figures of Muses, Dütschke (*Ravennatische Studien,* 1909, p. 185) shows the absurdity of continuing to explain the presence of the Muses by reference to the learned or musical attainments of the dead.

P. 197. *Orphic Symbolism.*—See also Dütschke, *op. cit.,* pp. 179 ff., pp. 185 ff. I would ask those who think I go too far in attributing mystic or symbolic meanings to the imagery of the Roman tombs to read Dütschke's learned and eloquent pages. I deeply regret that his book was not known to me when I prepared or revised the lectures.

Pp. 201, 207. *The Dioscuri in Sepulchral Imagery.*—For the original connection of the Dioscuri with the underworld see now Küster, *op. cit.*, pp. 77 ff.

P. |213 and p. 277, note 47. *Tomb of Trebius Justus.*—These interesting paintings, unique of their kind, are rapidly becoming celebrated ; see O. Wulff, *Altchristliche Kunst*, 1914, i. p. 69 and fig. 71 ; C. M. Kaufmann, *Handbuch der Christlichen Archäologie*, 1913, pp. 427 ff. and figs. 164, 165.

P. 215. *Marine monsters as mystic escort of the dead.*—Cf. Dütschke, *op. cit.*, p. 181.

P. 222 and plate xxviii. Owing to an error due to the present difficulties of postal communication, the relief of Selene in the British Museum (Cat. 2166) has been substituted on plate xxviii. 1 for a sepulchral relief of the same type as the one reproduced on plate xxviii. 2. The monument is votive, and therefore does not fall within the category of sepulchral reliefs described in the text ; it has, moreover, been published by M. Delatte in the *Musée Belge*, 1913, pp. 321-337. Yet in view of its charm and interest I let it stand here. The background with the seven planets and the crescent moon recalls the stellated canopy of the relief at Amiternum (above, p. 177), while the frame adorned with the signs of the Zodiac is very familiar in Mithraic altar-pieces (above, p. 188) and in the whole religious and sepulchral imagery of the period (above, p. 226 ; p. 228).

The sepulchral relief from the urn of Cossutia Prima, plate xxviii. 2 (*R.R.*, ii. 671, 5 = *Brit. Mus. Cat. Sc.* 2364), exhibits an interesting imagery (pine-tree, eagle, snake, and eagle holding in his beak the butterfly as symbol of the soul ; on the front face, Eros driving a quadriga, and on the pilasters vine branches springing from vases, in addition to a rich and delicate ornamentation which points to the Flavian period).

P. 224. *Ah dolor! ibat Hylas, ibat Enhydryasin.*—Propertius, I. xx. 22. (*Corpus Poetarum Latinorum*, ed. J. P. Postgate.)

Pp. 278, 279, notes 57 and 68. I regret that these and certain other notes must remain incomplete. But I, in common with many others in Rome this year, labour under the great disadvantage of having no adequately equipped archaeological library, now that we are cut off by political circumstances from the great library on the Monte Tarpeo, for so many years the hospitable centre of our studies. No city perhaps is so rich as Rome in libraries and in books bearing on art and archaeology, but much has to be done in the way of co-ordination—a work, I may note, which has been undertaken by Commendatore C. Ricci in the library which he has begun to organise in connection with the Ministry of Fine Arts. Meanwhile the difficulties of hunting up and finding books are great ; and even in preparing notes of so modest a compass as the present I was often baffled in my researches, nor could I always verify the references I had taken down in England. I am once more reminded of my debt to Miss Hutton, who with her well-known and often-tried liberality has made herself responsible for so much beside the wearisome bringing together of the illustrations.

Note to Plate II.—The Brescia medallion is now dated by C. Albizzati (*R.M.* 1914, xxix., pp. 247 ff. and fig. 3) in the second quarter of the third century A.D., by analogy with the portraiture of the period. For the women cp. Julia Domna, Julia Mamaea, Otacilia, etc. ; for the boy, Gordian III., Philippus *Junior*, etc. The proposed dating is confirmed by the lettering of the inscription.

INDEX

285

Mars, 74, 95, 97 ; on basis in temple of Neptune, 58.
Mars Ultor, temple of, 78.
MAYENCE (Mainz):
Museum : column of Jupiter,61,81 ; stele of Blussus, 217 ; stele with family repast, 220 ; sepulchral aedicula, 201.
Picture of, on lead medallion, 97.
Medallions : of Valens and Valentinian, 103 ; of Justinian, 109 ; of city of Mayence, 96.
Melkarth, 227.
Mithraic banquet,189,221 ; bull,188 ff., 193.
Mithraism, 187-197.
Mithras : wears cosmic mantle, 177 ; ascension of, 189; cults of, 113; on Diocletianic basis, 95.
Moguntiacum. See Mayence.
Monolatric principle in art, 32, 41, 98.
Monotheism, Judaic, 100; in Jupiter, 79, 86, 110 ; in Zeus, 51.
MONTELEONE, chariot of, 167.
Moon, cult of, 177, 178 ; on column of Mayence, 81.
Moselle (river), 216.
Mundus (Palatine), 120, 163.
MUNICH :
Glyptothek : sculptures from temple at Aegina, 44.
Antiquarium: pelike with Apotheosis of Heracles, 156.
Murray, Prof. Gilbert, quoted, 21, 51, 155.
Museums. See under names of different localities.
MYCENAE, tombs on Acropolis of, 128, 166.
Myres, Prof. J. L., 144.

NAPLES (Museum), vase with sacrifice to Dionysus, 54.
Nativity of Aphrodite, 37, 53, 150.
Nebo, temple of, 168.
NEMRUD DAGH, tomb of Antiochus of Commagene, on the, 87.

Neolithic peoples, 12.
Nereids, Monument of, 219.
Nero, on column of Mayence, 81.
NEW YORK : Pennsylvania station, 27 ; Grand Central station, 27.
Metropolitan Museum : chariot of Monteleone, 147 ; plate from Cyprus, 107 ; sarcophagus from Golgoi, 144.
Nola, 161.
Numen Augusti, 74.

OAK-WREATHS, 185.
Oikoumene, the, on *Gemma Augustea*, 72.
OLYMPIA, temple of Zeus at, 41, 46 ; Apollo of W. pediment, 47.
Olympian religion, character of, 50.
Orbis Romanus, 81.
' Orient or Rome,' cry of, 4.
Ormuzd, bull of, 188.
Orpheus, 198.
Orphic doctrines, 113,139,141,180,197.
Orphism. See Orphic Doctrines.

PAINTINGS of Roman tombs, 205-213.
PALESTRINA. See Praeneste.
Palestine, Flavian conquest of, 7.
Pan-Orientalists, 4.
Pantheon, 12 ; dome of, 25; the Olympian, 50, 110.
PARIS :
Cabinet des Médailles : cameo with Apotheosis of Julio-Claudian prince, 67 ; Grand Camée de France, 68 ; diptych with Christ, Romanus and Eudocia, 102; lead medallion of city of Mayence, 96 ; of Justinian (stolen), p. 250, n. 102.
Louvre : basis of Gn. Domitius Ahenobarbus, 58 ; Flavian relief with sacrificial scene, 84 ; stele of Sosinos, 133 ; portrait of Helena, 24 ; the Barberini ivory, 18, 101 ; cylix from Cyrene, 146.
Rothschild Collection : cups from Boscoreale, 73.

T

VATICAN (Rotonda) : Genius of Augustus, 70.
—— (Museo Gregoriano) : Tomba Regolini-Galassi, 165.
Temples : of Jupiter Capitolinus, 78; of Mars Ultor, 78; of Neptune, 58; Pantheon, 12, 25; of Vesta, 12.
Tombs: near Acqua Acetosa, 206; of the baker Eurysaces, 173; of 'Arruntii' and 'Pancratii' on Latin Way, 206, 207; of Nasonii, 210; of P. Vibius Marianus, 213; of Trebius Justus, 213; of Pomponius Hylas, 211; at Villa Pamphili, 211; Pyramid of Cestius, 211; near S. Gregorio, 210; near S. Sebastiano, 212; in Vigna Nardi, 212; in Vigna of Trappists, 212; of the Scipiones on Via Appia, 169.
Velabrum : Gate of Silversmiths, 92.

SABAZIUS, 200.
Salian priest, 185.
SALONIKI, arch of Galerius at, 99.
SARCOPHAGI : from Clazomenae, 145; from Golgoi, 144 ff.; from Haghia Triada, 119, 148, 165, 228; Etruscan, at Villa Giulia, 172; Phoenician, 161; of L. Cornelius Scipio Barbatus, 169.
From Sidon in Constantinople : of Alexander, 49; of the Mourners, 151; of the Satrap, 154.
Christian, at Verona, 100.
Sardis, sepulchral stone from, 122.
Scorpion, sign of the Zodiac, 72.
Secundinii, tomb of (see also Igel), 222.
Selene, on relief from Ephesus, 90; on relief from Argos, 280; on cylix in Berlin, 38, 108.
Selinos, temple at, 40.
Sepolcreto in Roman Forum, 163.

Septimius Severus, on Gate of Silversmiths, 80, 92; on Sacchetti relief, 92.
SEPULCHRAL IMAGERY :
(a) Symbolic Objects and Animals : amphorae, 221; birds, 222; blossoms, 169; boar, winged, 210; boat, 137, 216; bull, 136, 193; cock, 131, 145, 214, 215; dolphins, 229, 230; dog, 136, 145; eagle, 183, 189; egg, 131, 172, 211; foliage, 222; four elements, 188; Gorgoneion, 183, 224; grapes, 199; griffin, 151, 209, 213, 221; horse, 135; horse, winged, 69; kantharos, 221; lion, 146, 192, 193; lion and bull, 151, 192-195; Medusa head (see Gorgoneion); pine-cone, 193, 196; pomegranate, 131; rosette, 169, 185; sea monsters, 216; Seasons, 201, 228; Siren, 115, 146, 150-154; snake, 130, 193; vannus, 209; winds, 192, 226, 229; wreath, 186.
(b) Figures : Aeneas, 202; Attis, 195; Bacchic figures, 199, 210; Dioscuri, 209; Eris, 192; Ganymede, 229; genii, 209; Maenads, 199; Nereids, 186, 207; putti, 230; Orpheus, 198, 211; triton, 192, 216.
(c) Symbolic Myths : Admetus and Alcestis, 257; Hector, ransoming of, 208; Heracles, apotheosis of, 207, 226; Labours of, 201; Hylas, rape of, 224; Perseus and Andromeda, 224; Perseus with head of Gorgon, 144; Pluto and Proserpina, 199; Orpheus and Eurydice, 198; Rhea Silvia and Mars, 202, 224; Thetis and Achilles, 225.
(d) Symbolic Scenes: banquet, 126, 146; baptism, 225; chariot racing, 126; hunting, 126; Judgment scenes, 207; revelling, 126; ver sacrum, 210.
SERAJEVO, Mithraic altar-piece, 189.